THE 6 PRINCIPLES

SECOND EDITION

FOR EXEMPLARY TEACHING OF ENGLISH LEARNERS®

GRADES K–12

FOREWORD BY **JIM CUMMINS**

TESOL Writing Team
Deborah J. Short, *Lead Writer*
Wing Shuen (Alice) Lau
Helene Becker
Nancy Cloud
Andrea B. Hellman
Linda New Levine
Fatima Aldajani

Foreword by Jim Cummins

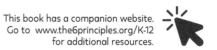

This book has a companion website.
Go to www.the6principles.org/K-12
for additional resources.

bookstore.tesol.org

TESOL International Association
1925 Ballenger Avenue, Ste 550
Alexandria, VA 22314 USA
www.tesol.org

Associate Director of Publications: Tomiko Breland
Copy Editor: Wendy Rubin
Design and Typesetting: Citrine Sky Design
Head of Education and Events: Sarah Sahr

Recommended citation:
TESOL International Association. (2024). *The 6 principles for exemplary teaching of English learners: K–12* (2nd ed.). TESOL Press.

ISBN 978-1-953745-12-5
ISBN (ebook) 978-1-953745-13-2
Library of Congress Control Number 2023950806

PURCHASE ORDERS AND
BULK PURCHASES
Discounts are available for
tax-exempt purchase orders and
bulk purchases. Please contact
publications@tesol.org for
more information.

Second edition, 2024

CONTENTS

FOREWORD

I t is a privilege to write a foreword to this immensely valuable book. The 6 Principles for exemplary teaching of English learners elaborated in these pages provide an evidence-based foundation for schools to examine their own instructional practice and work collaboratively with colleagues, parents, and policymakers to enable English learners to acquire strong social and academic language proficiency. A major strength of the book is its inclusion of the entire school community—administrators, English language teachers, content teachers, school librarians, guidance counselors, and other groups of educators—within the scope of exemplary teaching of English learners. As noted in Chapter 1, most of these education professionals have not had opportunities in their preservice education to access the knowledge base and instructional expertise necessary to work effectively with English learners. The detailed discussion in Chapter 5 of concrete ways in which these various groups of educators can apply The 6 Principles opens not just a culture of shared responsibility within the school, but also a culture of shared opportunity. As our expertise to work effectively with diverse learners expands, so too does our sense of affirmation as *educators*.

An additional strength of the book is the way in which it highlights the instructional implications of well-established research findings that are frequently overlooked in teaching English learners. For example, it is now well established that bilingualism represents a positive force in children's cognitive and academic development, particularly when literacy is developed in both languages. However, in classroom contexts where multiple languages are represented, many educators have been unsure about how to engage students' multilingual repertoires. In response to this uncertainty, the classroom vignettes and instructional suggestions throughout this book illustrate how teachers, school librarians, and other professionals can mobilize students' home languages as cognitive resources and instructional tools to enrich the learning of all students.

Another significant emphasis throughout this book is on the importance of encouraging English learners to become avid readers, ideally in both English and their L1. There is extensive research evidence regarding the impact of print access and literacy engagement on the development of students' reading comprehension skills (e.g., OECD, 2010). As noted in Chapter 2, students who read extensively "encounter more words and meet each word more frequently, which can result in a larger vocabulary and deeper word knowledge." Unfortunately, this research was largely ignored in reading policies instituted under the No Child Left Behind legislation that operated between 2002 and 2015 (Cummins, 2007).

The importance of promoting active literacy engagement is illustrated in the Programme for International Student Assessment (PISA), an international assessment initiative involving more than 70 countries and hundreds of thousands of 15-year-old students conducted by the Organisation for Economic Co-operation and Development (OECD) over the past 20 years. The PISA research has consistently shown that reading engagement is a stronger predictor of reading achievement than students' socioeconomic status (SES). Furthermore, the OECD (2010) reported that there was about a one-third overlap between the negative effects of low SES and the positive effects of reading engagement. The implication is that schools can potentially "push back" about one-third of the negative effects of socioeconomic disadvantage by ensuring that students have access to a print-rich environment and become actively engaged with literacy.

This finding assumes relevance in the present context because a large proportion of English learners come from lower-income communities with significantly less access to print in their schools and homes than is the case for students from middle-income communities (e.g., Duke, 2000). Immersion of these students in a literacy-rich environment from the day they enter school is a powerful tool in accelerating their academic catch-up trajectory. *The 6 Principles for Exemplary Teaching of English Learners: Grades K–12* suggests multiple strategies both for engaging parents as partners in this process and creating a culture of literacy engagement throughout the school.

My expectation is that this lucid and inspirational book will act as a catalyst for a process of collective pedagogical inquiry in schools across the United States and internationally. Obviously, all schools operate in broader policy contexts that enable and constrain organizational and pedagogical initiatives to varying degrees. However, within schools, educators always have choices—degrees of freedom within which we can chart directions that reflect and shape our identities as educators. This book charts the landscape in ways that enable us to embark confidently on that journey.

Jim Cummins
University of Toronto

References

Cummins, J. (2007). Pedagogies for the poor? Re-aligning reading instruction for low-income students with scientifically based reading research. *Educational Researcher, 36,* 564–572.

Duke, N. (2000). For the rich it's richer: Print experiences and environments offered to children in very low- and very high-socioeconomic status first-grade classrooms. *American Educational Research Journal, 37,* 441–478.

OECD. (2010). *PISA 2009 results: Learning to learn—Student engagement, strategies and practices (Volume III).* http://www.oecd.org/dataoecd/11/17/48852630.pdf

PREFACE

A Note on the Second Edition

The field of English language teaching uses a wide variety of terms to describe students, teachers, and their programs. In the first edition of this book, we used the term *English learner* for students identified as not yet proficient in English (according to a state-approved assessment). Since that book's publication, many organizations, including TESOL International Association, have shifted toward the use of more asset-based language. In this second edition, we use the term *multilingual learner of English*, in recognition of the full linguistic repertoire of our language learners and the assets they bring to language learning, as well as in celebration of linguistic diversity. We still use *English learner* occasionally when context requires it.

In a world where people are always on the move and the globalization of society leads us to interact regularly with a diverse group of neighbors, coworkers, shopkeepers, online friends, and even strangers, we all learn a little bit about language and culture every day. Sometimes these interactions are unexpected and delightful; sometimes they are deliberate or routine. Just as our lives touch other people, their lives touch us. Our interactions are most fruitful when they are supported by clear communication, respect, and cross-cultural understanding.

TESOL International Association (hereafter TESOL) is a community of professionals devoted to nurturing these three factors by means of its mission to advance the quality of English language teaching through professional development, research, standards, and advocacy. Our mission is particularly noteworthy because there are approximately 2.3 billion English speakers worldwide according to the British Council (Patel et al., 2023). Nearly 400 million people speak English as a home language, and nearly 2 billion speak it as an additional language. English is the most common lingua franca, with 67% of the world's population either speaking English or being exposed to it. More than half of the content on the internet (60%) is posted in English, and English is the most widely used language for international business and academic publications. For these reasons, effective English language teaching is critical.

The British Council report (Patel et al., 2023) points out that although the future of English language pedagogy and assessment is shifting with the advent of new technologies (including AI) and a decreased focus on native-like proficiency, English language teachers are and will still be needed. Teachers will continue to play a central role in language learning by providing high-quality instruction, which includes motivating learners, incorporating effective techniques, selecting appropriate materials, and more. The report does note, however, that many teachers will need additional skills, such as strategies for integrating content knowledge in English-medium instruction and applying educational technology tools.

The future of English language teaching is of prime interest to TESOL. The association of language educators has close to 11,000 members who represent 165 countries and 117 active affiliates worldwide. The educational setting has changed remarkably since TESOL's founding in 1966. What we know about teaching and learning has evolved. The global pandemic that began in 2020 has shaped the way we view instruction just as much as second language acquisition research and educational policies have over the past 50+ years. Our teachers no longer teach social conversational skills and basic reading and writing; they must plan lessons with more academic interaction among learners in class and more application of the four language domains to authentic, real-world uses. Our classroom environments are now in person, online, or hybrid. Newer technologies—from laptops and tablets to digital learning platforms to mobile apps—have become common instructional tools in many places (although a digital divide in access persists).

Throughout these years, TESOL's desire to provide the best guidance for language instruction has remained steadfast. TESOL has articulated a vision and a set of universal principles that hold the promise of exemplary education for multilingual learners of English. These principles are the natural progression of work TESOL has done over the years in numerous standards documents that describe *what* students should learn. These include pre-K–12 English language proficiency standards, standards for pre-K–12 teacher preparation programs and for short-term TEFL/TESL certificate programs, standards for teachers of adult English as a second language and English as a foreign language learners and for their programs, standards for using technology in instruction, and guidelines for developing EFL professional teaching standards. These standards represent broad statements of skills and conceptual knowledge that teachers or learners should have as the result of a course or program. The 6 Principles initiative, which was conceptualized in 2017, explains *how* a learner would gain the skills and knowledge identified in the standards and in curricula in schools around the world.

These are The 6 Principles of exemplary teaching:

1. Know your learners.

2. Create conditions for language learning.

3. Design high-quality lessons for language development.

4. Adapt lesson delivery as needed.

5. Monitor and assess student language development.

6. Engage and collaborate within a community of practice.

This book, *The 6 Principles for Exemplary Teaching of English Learners: K–12* (2nd edition), is the first in a series of TESOL books and publications that bring to life the underlying linkages among TESOL's core values, standards, and position statements and the current state of English language teaching.[1] The 6 Principles are research based and set a foundation for teachers and learners to succeed in a variety of program types. The principles are applicable for all classrooms focused on English as an additional language, and they serve educators of children and adults, dual language learners, emerging bilinguals, and multilingual students.

This K–12 volume lays out important information that teachers should know about English language development, along with The 6 Principles and practical examples of how these principles can be enacted in classrooms. Although this book primarily reflects K–12 classrooms in the United States, many of the examples and suggestions transfer easily to other types of classrooms. Additional resources, such as webinars and online courses, have been designed to help teachers

---

[1] The other 6 Principles books address exemplary English teaching for (1) adult and workforce education, (2) postsecondary academic and specific purposes, and (3) young learners around the world. Quick guides are references (1) for paraprofessional educators, (2) about remote learning, and (3) about second language acquisition.

and other educators apply these standards in their specific contexts. Many are available on TESOL's website.

Audience

Teachers of multilingual learners of English in K–12 classrooms are the primary audience for this book. These educators include the following groups:

- English language development (ELD), bilingual, and dual language teachers (subsequently, for brevity, *English language teachers*) in self-contained, cotaught, or resource classrooms
- elementary grade–level teachers and secondary content teachers
- special educators, reading teachers, and teachers of elective courses such as music, art, and technology

Some of these teachers may not view themselves as teachers of English, but they are. They provide direct instruction to students learning English as an additional language, even if their subject is third-grade math, middle school social studies, or high school biology. These teachers model proficient use of the language; they incorporate the four language skills of reading, writing, listening, and speaking in their instruction; and they expect learners to demonstrate their knowledge through these skills as well. All teachers must help develop students' academic English skills while supporting their growing knowledge base in the content areas. For learners to have access to challenging, grade-level curricula and be successful in school, teachers must understand how second language development occurs and apply that understanding to their lesson designs and assessments. They must also teach in culturally responsive ways that value the learners' languages and heritages.

Secondary audiences for the book include

- school and district administrators;
- instructional coaches;
- other school or district personnel, such as curriculum directors, guidance counselors, reading specialists, and paraeducators; and
- teacher educators and professional developers.

Administrators and coaches have a leadership role in their schools or districts and should help the teachers with whom they work understand the importance of knowing one's learners and how best to instruct them. They are also involved in creating the conditions for learning and thus need to know how to support language development while meeting curriculum goals and standards. Other personnel play additional roles in students' lives, from planning their academic schedules to supporting their social-emotional needs and well-being to designing curricula and assessments. Teacher educators and professional developers can use this book to introduce preservice teachers to The 6 Principles and help in-service teachers add to or refine their current practices.

Besides using The 6 Principles to guide instruction, school-based educators can use the book to evaluate their school or district programs. As part of school improvement efforts, this book can serve as a tool to drive reform, confirming positive aspects of existing programs and practices and identifying those that might merit change. The book is designed to generate thoughtful discussion and reflection among educators who serve multilingual learners of English.

What's New in the Second Edition

This second edition reflects our evolving knowledge about second language acquisition and pedagogy for multilingual learners of English. It also addresses some shifts in educational policies in the United States and what we have learned about supporting our learners during and after the global pandemic. We have updated the research to include recent studies that support The 6 Principles in theory and practice, incorporated new vignettes from teachers around the world, and written a new chapter to showcase the implementation of The 6 Principles in three different cases. We made several key changes throughout the book:

- **Enhanced focus on student assets, use of home language, and culturally responsive teaching.** We have added more attention to the assets students bring to school, including their funds of knowledge and their home language and literacy skills. Discussions of translanguaging and dynamic bilingualism are presented along with culturally responsive practices to help teachers tap into their learners' cultural and linguistic resources.

- **Enhanced focus on technology.** Educational technology increasingly plays a significant role in the teaching and learning process. Since the onset of the global pandemic, almost all teachers use tech tools (e.g., learning management platforms, online texts, mobile apps) to some extent with their students. We have provided explanations of how and why to use educational technology and descriptions of sample tools throughout the chapters.

- **Enhanced focus on literacy development.** We have provided more discussion on how multilingual learners of English develop and strengthen their reading and writing skills in English. Moving beyond just teaching phonics and vocabulary, we discuss how academic conversations, background building, tapping into experiential knowledge, and interaction with peers help bolster these important academic skills.

- **New focus on social-emotional learning (SEL).** SEL is a process for developing students' lifelong skills to help them build positive relationships, establish and work toward goals, enhance self-awareness, manage emotions, and make responsible decisions for personal and academic success. In this edition, we explore ways that teachers can support students' well-being and incorporate SEL practices in classroom lessons.

- **New appendix with discussion questions for book study groups.** Readers can reflect on the discussion questions for each chapter and share ideas and responses with colleagues.

We discuss chapter-specific additions in the Overview.

Overview

The book is organized in six chapters:

- **Chapter 1: A Vision for Exemplary English Language Teaching** lays out TESOL's vision for exemplary teaching of multilingual learners of English, along with the rationale for the U.S. K–12 focus of this book, and introduces The 6 Principles. In this second edition, we have expanded the discussion of the need for The 6 Principles to address societal and educational changes that have taken place since 2018.

- **Chapter 2: What Teachers Should Know About English Language Development to Plan Instruction** summarizes the main factors of second language learning as they apply to K–12 settings in the United States. This chapter also identifies what teachers should know in order to provide developmentally appropriate instruction and build on students' linguistic and cultural assets, as called for by The 6 Principles. In this edition, we give more attention to the components of language and how they correlate to the four language skills; literacy development practices; and research on asset-based language instruction, educational technology and SEL. We have included new tables that illustrate key points of the discussion.

- **Chapter 3: The 6 Principles for Exemplary Teaching of English Learners** is the cornerstone of the book, as it explains The 6 Principles in detail and grounds them in research. For each principle, we identify a broad range of K–12 instructional practices that guide teachers as they get to know their learners, set up a classroom that promotes student interaction, craft lessons that integrate language and content, modify their lesson delivery on the spot if students struggle, assess student language development, and participate in the school community of practice. In this new edition, we have added more practices to Principles 3, 5, and 6; updated and added new examples of practices for all principles; and included more vignettes and teachers' artifacts to help readers implement The 6 Principles more readily.

- **Chapter 4: Additional Roles for Teachers of Multilingual Learners of English** describes the various roles that teachers play in educational contexts outside the classroom. Teachers can function as change agents when they (a) advocate for these learners; (b) act as liaisons among families, communities, and the school system; and (c) serve as resources for other teachers and administrators on instruction, assessment, curriculum design, scheduling and programming, professional development, and other aspects of teaching and learning. We discuss additional roles that teachers have, such as coteacher and school leader, in this revised chapter.

- **Chapter 5: Establishing a Culture of Shared Responsibility** suggests ways in which school and district administrators, instructional coaches, and other specialists can apply The 6 Principles in their spheres beyond the classroom. All professionals can work together to ensure that multilingual learners of English receive quality programs and services designed to support their language development needs and foster educational success in a positive, welcoming school climate. We have updated information and added discussions for paraeducators, technology coordinators, and family liaisons.

- **Chapter 6: Implementing The 6 Principles in Different Contexts** is a new chapter in the second edition. Based in real classrooms, this chapter illustrates how teachers have applied The 6 Principles framework in several settings: an English language development class in a middle school; an online, graduate-level university foundations course for TESOL; and professional development sessions for practicing teachers. The teachers share their high-quality teaching practices to help other educators conceptualize what these principles look in action.

Moving Forward

The TESOL profession has much to offer the world in expertise in English language teaching and support for multilingualism and cross-cultural communication. *The Action Agenda for the Future of the TESOL Profession* (TESOL International Association, 2018a) calls for TESOL professionals to draw on their knowledge, experience, and expertise and be involved in the development and implementation of language policies, practices, and research at local and national levels.

The 6 Principles suite of resources complement those efforts and define the best practices for our classrooms, as well as what teachers need to know about second language learning to make informed instructional decisions and how to advocate for our students and their families. Our goal is to promote high-quality English instruction in every classroom while respecting and affirming all languages and cultures. We invite you to learn about The 6 Principles and implement them with your own classes. We also encourage you to join TESOL, if you are not yet a member, and use The 6 Principles for professional learning with your colleagues.

Acknowledgments

Educators around the world strive to implement best practices in English language development with a myriad of learners in diverse contexts. They have contributed to our understanding of second language learning and teaching. We are grateful to the educators who have shared their experiences with us through print resources and personal connections. We would also like to acknowledge Jaslyn Davies, Katryn Dougherty, Karen M. Gregory, Kathy Lobo, Julia Muething-Sallans, Gretchen Oliver, Karamjeet Singh, Christian Rafael Quevedo Lezama, Jeimi Venegas, and Michele Wilbert for letting us tell some of their stories about implementing The 6 Principles. We thank the TESOL Board of Directors and the central office staff for their ongoing support of The 6 Principles initiative. Tomiko Breland, Sarah Sahr, and Amber Crowell Kelleher deserve special recognition.

This second edition builds on the first. We are thankful that Karen Woodson, Sherry Blok, Christel Broady, and Ximena Uribe-Zarain provided assistance in the previous edition, and Jim Cummins deserves our sincere gratitude for writing the foreword. We very much appreciated the insights and productive feedback offered by the reviewers of the first book, who represented our TESOL international community and the bilingual and general education fields. We also offer our gratitude to those users of the first edition who provided reviews and feedback that helped inform this second edition. All of these individuals care about our learners and their teachers, and they have helped us write a better book.

Dedication

We dedicate this book to two friends and colleagues, Dr. Anna Uhl Chamot (1934–2017) and Dr. Emily "Cathy" Day (1942–2021), with deep appreciation for their years of service, research, writing, and teacher development on behalf of multilingual learners of English and their educators.

1 A VISION FOR EXEMPLARY ENGLISH LANGUAGE TEACHING

Ms. Tejada opened the door to see her daughter and three classmates.

"Mami, estos son mis amigos de la escuela," said Gabriela. "Ricky, Chantal, y John. Estamos trabajando en un proyecto."

"Welcome," said Ms. Tejada. "Please come in. What project are you working on?"

The young teens entered, and John turned to Gabriela's mother. "We are working on a project about Darwin's journey around the world. We have to make a map of his trip, tell why he made the journey, identify challenges and solutions, and describe different groups of people he met and different things he saw."

Ricky continued, "We have to tell about his discoveries, too."

Ms. Tejada said, "Goodness, that's a lot of work. How will you do all that?"

"Watch us, Mami," said her daughter.

The teens moved into the dining room and opened their tablets from the school. Chantal spread out a printed world map. She placed a toy boat on the southern coast of England and took a picture. Ms. Tejada saw her draw a route to the Canary Islands in red marker, place the boat there, and take another picture. Chantal did the same for the Cape Verde islands. "Où, eh, where next?" she asked John.

John said, "Remember how to Google, ah, la carte? Let me show you." He helped Chantal find a web page with the route of Darwin's ship.

To her mother, Gabriela said, "Chantal es de Haití. Ella es nueva y está aprendiendo inglés."

Her mom replied, "I'm glad you all are helping her."

Ricky, Gabriela, and John were looking at different web pages and taking notes in their notebooks. Occasionally they took a screenshot. Ms. Tejada watched for a while.

Ricky asked, "Did you know Darwin went to South America? He studied birds—finches—and saw things that were the same and different about them."

John turned to Gabriela, "Come here and help me read this article. It's in Spanish about the Galápagos Islands."

The teens worked for another hour. Before leaving, they looked over the pictures they had taken. Chantal showed them the photos of the map, and the boys asked her to tell them the places where the boat was in each one. They helped her say the names of the towns and practice sentences like "The Beagle sailed to Cape Verde" and "The Beagle is in Cape Town." Gabriela then pointed at some of the bird pictures and said, "Look at the beaks. This one is long. That one is short and thick. Darwin noticed the beaks changed to match the food the birds ate."

As they were preparing dinner later, Ms. Tejada asked her daughter to tell her more about the project. "When I was in school," she said, "we would read some books and write a report. We'd work by ourselves."

Gabriela explained, "This is better, Mami. We are working on this in our science and geography classes. For the final project, we are going to do a screencast about Darwin's voyage. It's kind of like a PowerPoint with sound. We have to put the photos we take with the tablet into a computer program, and then we can record information about each one. What's good is that we can record over what we say if we make a mistake. Each one of us has to speak part of the time. That's why we were helping Chantal practice. But we have four more days before we have to finish."

Gabriela went on to explain how the teachers on her middle school team were supporting the project. Mr. Mohan, the ESL teacher, coteaches with the science teacher, Ms. Kitima. In class, he explains the vocabulary and helps when they read texts. He helps them form sentences to express their ideas when they have to speak or write. In their current unit, Ms. Kitima teaches them about biodiversity. She uses a lot of photographs and video clips, and they did an experiment where they had to try to get food that birds eat—worms in soil, seeds on branches, and nuts on the ground—using different utensils, like tweezers, nutcrackers, and straws. Mr. Gándara, the social studies teacher, has bookmarked web pages for the geography tasks of the project. He found some in Spanish and French, in addition to pages in English. He also reads aloud parts of the diary that Darwin kept when he was sailing and explains what Darwin found. In ESL class with Mr. Mohan, the students read some of the diary entries closely and take notes.

"John no está en ESL pero estudia francés. Él puede ayudar a Chantal un poco," Gabriela concluded.

"You make a good team," said her mom.

We have written this book to share TESOL's vision and present The 6 Principles for Exemplary Teaching of English Learners®—a core set of principles that should undergird any program of English language instruction. TESOL believes that all languages and cultures have equal worth and promotes multilingualism and multiculturalism. Respect for all languages and cultures is a core value. We recognize that many people around the world want to learn English for a variety of personal, academic, and economic reasons, so TESOL, the leading organization of English language teaching professionals, offers its best guidance in this book on how to do so, based on research findings and practitioner knowledge.

The sustained, popular interest in learning English around the world has created a need for a common understanding of second language learning theory and effective instructional and assessment design. In this book, we provide research-based knowledge about second language acquisition and effective pedagogical approaches so that educators can make informed decisions about the teaching and learning process. Learners today need advanced language and literacy skills to communicate with diverse audiences for various purposes along with critical-thinking and problem-solving skills. Our goal is to empower teachers of multilingual learners of English to reflect critically on their current practices, make adjustments as needed to best prepare their students for our globally connected world, and share their expertise with colleagues.

You will find that TESOL's vision, The 6 Principles, and accompanying practices are applicable to all contexts and all audiences. That said, this book, the first in the series, focuses on elementary and secondary classrooms in the United States where students learn English as a new language while also studying the subject area curricula, often through English. We mention specific U.S. policies and programs, but many educators in K–12 classrooms around the world will be able to apply The 6 Principles and their related practices to their own settings as well. The vignette that opens this chapter offers a snapshot of effective instruction that enables students to collaborate around an academically challenging project, using their home language resources, technology, and instructional materials to develop academic English. Although the students in the vignette attend a U.S. school, the situation could be replicated in many places. Some vignettes and cases in this book highlight the implementation of The 6 Principles in other countries.

A Note About Terminology

When referring to students, we use *multilingual learners of English*; in specific instances, we mention *newcomers* and *students with limited or interrupted formal education* (SLIFE).

For teachers with the prime responsibility of teaching English as a new language to these students, we use *English language teacher or English language specialist* interchangeably and *English language development* (ELD) *teacher, dual language teacher,* and *bilingual teacher* as appropriate. We also use *teachers of multilingual learners of English* to refer collectively to all teachers who have these students in their classrooms.

For the instructional programs, we use *English language development* (ELD) *program, dual language program,* and *bilingual program* as appropriate. ESL (English as a second language) is no longer commonly used in U.S. schools.

TESOL (Teachers of English to Speakers of Other Languages) refers to the international professional association. It can also refer to teaching English to speakers of other languages, meaning those who have studied the field and have a certificate (as in TESOL professional), as well as their coursework and university programs in the field.

We refer to the language spoken by an individual's family as the *home language*, although it is also known as the *native* or *first language*.

The glossary provides definitions of these terms and other relevant ones. Appendix A is a chart of the common acronyms related to English language teaching used in the United States.

The Need for The 6 Principles in K–12 Programs

The 6 Principles are universal guidelines and establish the foundation for exemplary teaching of multilingual learners of English. These principles are particularly relevant to the educational context in the United States in the 21st century for several academic and sociocultural reasons:

Multilingual learners of English are a significant subgroup of students in U.S. schools, and they have a pressing need to learn academic English. The majority of students in the United States study in English-medium classes for most of the school day. They need to understand academic English to access and be successful with grade-level curricula. Students in grades K–12 who are identified as not yet proficient in English (known as *multilingual learners of English*) have represented 10% of the total population in pre-K–12 schools since the 2009–2010 school year (National Center for Education Statistics, 2022). This statistic indicates that the stream of students is constant, with new learners of English entering U.S. schools each year. The term *multilingual learner of English* is a temporary designation, however, and most students reach proficiency between 5 and 7 years from the time they begin learning English until they exit English language assistance programs. Nonetheless, educators report that the number of students who struggle with the academic language used in school is considerably higher than the number of learners in these language programs because some learners who have exited the programs (*former English learners*) have not yet attained all of the academic English skills that would allow them to participate successfully in all of their content courses and demonstrate their knowledge on high-stakes assessments.

> Have you noticed changes in your multilingual learner population?

Many elementary grade–level and secondary content-area teachers are underprepared to teach multilingual learners of English effectively. English language development (ELD) teachers, bilingual teachers, and dual language teachers (subsequently identified inclusively as

English language teachers) are well trained to teach in English and about the English language. But essential courses on second language acquisition, ELD techniques for integrating language and content, teaching reading to multilingual learners of English, and cross-cultural communication are not the norm for others studying to be teachers in U.S. schools (National Academies of Sciences, Engineering, and Medicine, 2017). Among teachers who reported having at least one multilingual learner of English in class, only 10% of them had a major, minor, or certification in English as a second language (ESL), and less than half had taken any course on how to teach these students prior to their first year of teaching (National Center for Education Statistics, 2021). Because so many teachers are not required to take such courses to obtain a teaching certificate, school districts bear the responsibility to provide professional development in these topics.

National standards for teacher education institutions recognize that teachers need to understand how to work with diverse learners, including multilingual learners of English, and that they should keep students' culture and language differences in mind to create inclusive learning plans (see Council for the Accreditation of Educator Preparation, 2022). However, the standards do not outline the specific coursework that should be taught or the depth of treatment. Given the demands of state content standards and the high numbers of multilingual learners of English in our schools, future teachers need resources such as The 6 Principles for details on how to teach the academic language and literacy skills necessary for their subject areas to students who are not yet proficient in English.

Not all teachers know which students in their classes are multilingual learners of English. Consider the following responses to the question "Is that student a multilingual learner of English?"

- "I don't think so. Her mom speaks English."
- "He shouldn't be. We can understand each other without any trouble."
- "No, he was born in the U.S."
- "We don't know. Her home language survey said she speaks English, though the family speaks Bengali at home. She wasn't tested for English language proficiency."
- "Of course. Her first language is Mandarin, and she rarely speaks in class."
- "He must be. He speaks English with a strong accent."
- "I doubt it; they're doing fine in my algebra class."

English language specialists hear unsound explanations like these from some teachers when they speak about specific students. Such statements reflect the fact that these teachers tend to rely on their own casual interpretations of what it means to be a multilingual learner of English. In fact, speaking with an accent, being silent in class, and being able to perform math tasks are not reliable indicators of whether a student is a multilingual learner of English. Parents and children are often proficient in several languages, and sometimes a student's current caregivers did not raise the student. Many educators also do not know that most multilingual learners of English in K–12 settings were born in the United States (Bialik et al., 2018).

English language specialists identify students according to a more formal definition, one defined by law. This definition does not equate a student's status as a multilingual learner with being born outside the United States, having a home language other than English, or speaking with an obvious accent. Rather, the formal meaning of the term is that the student has not yet reached the level of English language proficiency that the state has defined as sufficient to succeed academically in the curriculum. Teachers should consult their district's identification and redesignation criteria, as well as their students' English language proficiency scores, to know with certainty which students are multilingual learners of English. With that knowledge and targeted professional development, they can provide better instruction to their students.

Since 2002, educational reforms in the United States have increased the academic rigor of instruction, but most of the resulting accountability measures have not been developed with multilingual learners of English in mind. We have high standards for learning in our schools and want to hold school districts accountable for helping students meet these standards. The situation for multilingual learners of English, however, is not straightforward. These students must do double the work in school by learning academic English while studying the core content areas of mathematics, science, history, English language arts, and other subjects. They are not given time to develop their English skills to intermediate or advanced levels of proficiency before they must participate in high-stakes assessments. They often take subject-area tests that have been designed and normed on English speakers and, except in a few states, conducted in English. These tests are not valid or reliable for multilingual learners of English (Abedi & Linquanti, 2012). Not surprisingly, the achievement gap between these students and students who are proficient in English on national exams of reading, mathematics, and science has not narrowed in the past 20 years (U.S. Department of Education [USED], n.d.). The long-term effects of the achievement gap include lower graduation rates among multilingual learners of English; in the 2019–2020 school year, only 71% of multilingual learners of English graduated, compared with 86% of all students (USED, Office of English Language Acquisition, 2023b).

Education reforms have had mixed consequences for programs designed to serve multilingual learners of English. Policymakers and the general public generally do not understand the process of second language acquisition, nor do they realize that teachers and other staff might not have the training or experience needed to fully meet the needs of multilingual learners of English. As a result, they may falsely blame the learners and their families when schools and districts do not perform well on state tests. At times, poor test performance has led to schools being taken over or closed down, with staff leaving or shifted elsewhere (Menken, 2010).

Misconceptions about learning a new language and learning through a new language can be countered, however. More districts regularly monitor the language proficiency growth and academic progress of their multilingual learners of English and include the data in school improvement conversations. With these analyses, educators can adjust programs, instruction, professional development plans, and resources as indicated. Some federal and state funding is available to help schools and teachers strengthen their programs and instruction so students can develop the necessary academic language and literacy skills to access core content curricula.

The COVID-19 pandemic upended some expectations and assumptions about schooling. When schools around the world began closing in March 2020, English language teachers had to pivot quickly and find ways to teach their students remotely. Traditional means for delivering instruction no longer worked. But not all teachers had the skill set and equipment to use digital tools and platforms, so they had a steep learning curve. Professional development also had to transition to virtual formats, and educators had to build online communities to provide support to their peers.

Furthermore, the divide between students who had technology devices, adequate internet access and bandwidth, and support for distance learning at home and those who did not (many of whom were multilingual learners of English) was striking and led to disparities in learning outcomes (USED, Office of Educational Technology, 2022). Digital inequities, along with the isolation and unmet social-emotional needs of learners, exacerbated achievement gaps between multilingual learners of English and students who are proficient in English (Pier et al., 2021). The need to bridge the technology gap between students from diverse backgrounds to ensure that all learners can benefit from the technological innovations is ongoing. We have had to figure out the types of support our students require to manage the challenges of remote learning and ways to engage them and support their productivity. We have also needed to determine how best to incorporate new technology tools now that we have returned to our classrooms.

How has your instruction changed since the global pandemic?

Out-of-school factors have an impact on student academic achievement. Factors that cause stress and physical or mental illness can lead to negative performance in school. Multilingual learners of English are certainly not the only students affected by these factors, but some factors have particular relevance to their lives. For example, a number of these learners experience one or more of the following: poverty, food insecurity, discrimination, anti-immigrant bias, trauma, and cultural dissonance. Some teachers learn more about the their learners' communities and develop partnerships with leaders to advocate for change (Linville & Whiting, 2020). Others explore social justice issues in their curricular units as a means to reduce some of the stress or help learners make sense of the society around them (Mohammed, 2023). Helping students feel safe and respected in classrooms helps them focus on learning. When teachers explicitly and intentionally integrate social-emotional learning into their teaching practices alongside academic content, they can strengthen students' sense of belonging within the school community and help them develop essential coping skills for handling academic challenges (Frey et al., 2019; Rimm-Kaufman, 2021; Short & Mendoza, 2020).

Ms. Vegas is an upper elementary school teacher in Colombia. She has established an international pen pal video talk partnership with a teacher in Taiwan to help students improve their language acquisition and develop global competencies. For one project, the students discussed social issues and, independently or with a partner, conducted research on one issue. Topics have included poverty, water conservation, and animal welfare. The students use Flip, a video discussion platform, to prepare a 2- to 4-minute talk on the problem and potential solutions. They exchange videos with their pen pals. With Flip, they in turn create a video response to their pen pal's presentation. Ms. Vegas has noticed that this activity boosts students' confidence as they practice English speaking and listening skills through authentic interactions on content-rich topics. The asynchronous nature of the platform allows students to overcome limitations of time and geography, and they find this activity fun and engaging.

Educators seek guidance regarding best practices for educating multilingual learners of English. The use of best practices makes language learning more efficient and satisfying. TESOL, the leading organization of language teaching professionals in the United States, is well positioned to guide educators in the why, what, and how of high-quality teaching. In 1997, TESOL released the first-ever pre-K–12 standards for English as a second language, and its commitment to helping educators implement those standards and subsequent ones has been unwavering (Teachers of English to Speakers of Other Languages, 1997; TESOL International Association, 2006). This commitment has not changed postpandemic.

The stakes are high. TESOL recognizes that high-quality instruction in today's world includes the need for developing advanced literacy skills and intercultural competence, reimagining how to convey information and receive feedback with new and older technologies, personalizing the language learning experience, and differentiating the ways in which we can build our communities of practice. Our elementary and secondary students have university and career goals, so they need to achieve advanced levels of proficiency in English and acquire the content-area knowledge expected of high school graduates. Our programs and practices must help them achieve these goals.

TESOL's Vision for Exemplary Teaching of Multilingual Learners of English

When TESOL conceptualized The 6 Principles initiative in 2017, it sought to address the needs of English language teachers and their learners in a way that would amplify TESOL's vision and disseminate exemplary English language teaching practices. The conviction that knowing more than one language and culture benefits all students is a core value and hallmark of TESOL's vision. The world is an interconnected place, and we all engage with linguistically and culturally diverse people. Technologies and trade have brought us closer together and require skilled cross-cultural communication. Thus, dynamic bilingualism is an asset. Effective education in the 21st century calls for schools to provide opportunities for all students to learn about other cultures and to learn world languages (Commission on Language Learning, 2017). Knowing more than one language has individual and societal benefits, and diversity typically fosters creativity (Marian & Shook, 2012). Understanding different perspectives, life experiences, and world views enriches us and builds intercultural competence (TESOL International Association, 2006).

> "Knowledge of more than one language and culture is advantageous for all students." *(Teachers of English to Speakers of Other Languages, 1997, p. 5)*

In TESOL's vision, multilingual learners of English can be successful in school and beyond. In our schools, these learners can share their viewpoints with English-speaking peers, teachers, administrators, and other members of the school community, who can in turn reciprocate and share their own perspectives. Learners can achieve advanced levels of English proficiency; thrive in English-medium content-area courses; become language-ready for higher education, careers, or other personal goals; and maintain their home language and culture while adding English to their language repertoire. We heartily believe these targets can be reached in effective English language learning programs that demonstrate the following characteristics:

Curricula for multilingual learners of English are rigorous, relevant, and designed and delivered with second language learning in mind. For many years—indeed, for most of the 20th century—multilingual learners of English in the United States were relegated to language development classes, with few opportunities to receive grade-level content instruction until they reached advanced levels of proficiency. When educational practices changed, particularly in the 1990s, these students were often on the receiving end of watered-down curricula and lower expectations than those for students who had proficiency in English. That situation should not be the case today. The standards and curricula for our learners need to be rigorous and relevant to their educational goals. Instructional practices such as the use of scaffolds, extended time, home language supports, and other aspects of differentiation help students gain access to the curricula and accommodate their proficiency levels. At times, newcomers and students with interrupted or limited educational backgrounds may need specialized courses to support their learning. Overall, however, we need to have not only high expectations for our students but also targeted professional development for our teachers so they can best serve their multilingual learners of English as they progress through the second language acquisition process (California Department of Education, 2010; USED, Office for Civil Rights & U.S. Department of Justice, Civil Rights Division, 2015a).

Multilingual learners of English, including learners with special needs, have access to all programs and services. In the United States, multilingual learners of English must have access to ELD services and grade-level content. School districts have a legal obligation to ensure that these learners can participate meaningfully and equally in educational programs and services (USED, Office for Civil Rights & U.S. Department of Justice, Civil Rights Division, 2015a). The programs offered to these students must pass a three-pronged legal test: They must (1) be based on sound education theory and principles, (2) be implemented with adequate personnel and resources and appropriate instructional practices, and (3) demonstrate that language barriers are being overcome within a reasonable period of time so that multilingual learners of English attain parity with English-speaking classmates in instructional programs (*Castañeda v. Pickard*, 1981). Furthermore, multilingual learners of English who are dually identified with a learning disability must receive both ELD and special education services, and language proficiency should not be a factor in determining eligibility for gifted and talented programs (Burr et al., 2015; USED, Office of English Language Acquisition, 2017).

All educational personnel assume responsibility for the education of multilingual learners of English. Helping multilingual learners of English succeed in school must be the job of all teachers—not solely the ELD or bilingual ones. Academic language as used in school settings to meet rigorous standards, curricula, and assessments is more challenging to learn than social language (as detailed in Chapter 2). These students must develop literacy skills for each content area in their second language as they simultaneously learn, comprehend, and apply content-area concepts through their second language (Short & Echevarría, 2016). Indeed, multilingual learners of English must do double the work in schools—learning English and learning content—but they are not given double the time (Short & Fitzsimmons, 2007). Apart from a 1-year grace period for language arts assessments, these learners are evaluated using the same tests as their classmates who are proficient in English, no matter what their English proficiency level is. The learners therefore need to maximize the time spent learning both academic English and content throughout the school day, which can happen only when all their teachers target both areas in their lesson objectives and plan instruction accordingly (Echevarría et al., 2024; Himmel, 2012).

All educational personnel

- respect, affirm, and promote students' home languages and cultural knowledge and experiences as resources;
- celebrate multilingualism and diversity;
- support policies that promote individual language rights and multicultural education; and
- help prepare students to be global citizens.

Our goal is for multilingual learners of English to be successful wherever and whenever they use English. However, we also want them to have opportunities to maintain and further develop their own language and be part of a community that respects their cultures (Canagarajah & Wurr, 2011; García & Kleyn, 2016). In many parts of the world, children learn a second and even a third language, sometimes at home and sometimes at school. We should celebrate and encourage this relatively normal practice of learning more than one language. We know that being bilingual or multilingual generates cognitive and societal benefits and is valuable in many careers. We should never try to eliminate a student's home language or culture. Instead, teachers and administrators must welcome diversity in their schools and gain skills during their training that enable them to work with linguistically and culturally diverse learners and their families (National Academies of Sciences, Engineering, and Medicine, 2017; Nieto & Bode, 2021).

We know from recent research on translanguaging, in fact, that strategic use of a student's home language in the English-medium classroom can facilitate both content understanding and academic English language development. When students use all of their linguistic resources, they participate more in class, make sense of new information, and apply knowledge more fully in learning tasks (Ebe et al., 2021; García et al., 2017; Paterson, 2021).

> What has improved for multilingual learners of English since you started working in schools?

TESOL professionals are recognized as specialists with accurate knowledge, skills, and dispositions for providing high-quality English language teaching. Our profession has struggled over the years with the false notion that if you speak English, you can teach English. Having native-speaking English skills does not ensure someone will be an effective English language teacher. TESOL professionals study a range of topics, including second language acquisition theory, ELD and sheltered instruction methods, and teaching reading to non-native speakers of English. They know how language works as a system, how to plan and differentiate instruction for multilingual learners of English and others who struggle with academic literacy in subject area courses, how culture affects learning and communication, how to assess students with emergent levels of English literacy, and how to interpret and apply results of language assessments. They stay up-to-date with research and policy once they are practicing teachers (see López et al., 2013; TESOL International Association, 2018a). In many U.S. K–12 public schools, teachers of English as an additional language must have either an ELD or bilingual teaching certificate or license or an elementary or content-area teaching certificate or license with an ELD endorsement. In a number of states, teachers must pass a professional exam as well.

TESOL professionals are valued by colleagues and other educators for their expertise and consulted in instructional, programming, and policy decision-making. Because of their knowledge in the fields of second language learning, ELD methodology, and cross-cultural communication, ELD, bilingual, and dual language teachers are valuable resources for colleagues and administrators in schools and districts. Through collaborative endeavors such as professional learning groups, school improvement teams, and textbook selection committees, their expertise serves as a resource for providing the best possible programming, instruction, and materials for multilingual learners of English. TESOL professionals can help colleagues adjust their teaching and testing practices according to the proficiency levels of the students in their classes and design interventions for newcomers and long-term multilingual learners of English. They can advise fellow teachers and administrators about the students' cultures and support them in communicating with parents (Benegas & Stolpestad, 2020; Cambridge English, n.d.; TESOL International Association, 2018a; Valdés et al., 2014).

Policies, programs, and practices are based on current research and accurate information. Policymakers and administrators must rely on research as they establish policies, develop or refine programs, and promote instructional and assessment practices. Building a program around anecdotes and myths will not result in student success. Students do not master academic English just by being exposed to it. Just because students speak English does not mean they are proficient in all four language domains at an advanced academic level. Over the past 35 years, research has become more rigorous, and we know more about how students learn a second language. This learning takes time and investments in resources. Skimping on these needs will not yield the educational or economic outcomes that schools seek and society needs (National Academies of Sciences, Engineering, and Medicine, 2017; Williams, 2021).

The 6 Principles for Exemplary English Language Teaching

The 6 Principles put forth in this book are not revolutionary or groundbreaking concepts in language learning. They are well-established guidelines drawn from decades of research in language pedagogy and language acquisition theory. We present them in seemingly simple statements, yet they carry substantial weight because how well they are implemented can make the difference between student success and struggle. The 6 Principles must be taken together, as a cohesive whole. One cannot just know one's learners, for example, and then not act on that knowledge when planning instruction.

Figure 1.1 provides a brief explanation of each principle, and subsequent chapters show educators of multilingual learners of English how The 6 Principles may be realized inside and outside the classroom.

FIGURE 1.1	The 6 Principles for Exemplary Teaching of English Learners

Exemplary teaching of English learners rests on the following 6 Principles:

1. **Know your learners.** Teachers learn basic information about their students' families, languages, cultures, and educational backgrounds to engage them in the classroom and prepare and deliver lessons more effectively.

2. **Create conditions for language learning.** Teachers create a classroom culture that will ensure students feel comfortable in the class. They make decisions regarding the physical environment, the materials, and the social integration of students to promote language learning.

3. **Design high-quality lessons for language development.** Teachers plan lessons that are meaningful for students, promote language learning, and help them develop learning strategies and critical-thinking skills. These lessons evolve from the learning objectives.

4. **Adapt lesson delivery as needed.** Teachers continually assess as they teach, observing and reflecting on learners' responses to determine whether the students are reaching the learning objectives. If students struggle or are not challenged enough, teachers consider the possible reasons and adjust their lessons.

5. **Monitor and assess student language development.** Language learners learn at different rates, so teachers regularly monitor and assess their language development in order to advance their learning efficiently. Teachers also gather data to measure student language growth.

6. **Engage and collaborate within a community of practice.** Teachers collaborate with others in the profession to provide the best possible support for multilingual learners of English with respect to programming, instruction, and advocacy. They also continue their own professional learning.

A Look Back and a Look Ahead

More people are learning English every day. It is critically important that their teachers make informed decisions about their instructional and assessment practices. This book supports teachers in this work.

In Chapter 1, we have

- explained TESOL's rationale for identifying core principles for exemplary teaching of multilingual learners of English and the pressing need for their implementation in K–12 classrooms in the United States;

- shared TESOL's vision of effective education, which includes honoring home languages and cultures, recognizing TESOL professionals as specialists in language education, and ensuring that multilingual learners of English have access to challenging, rigorous curricula; and

- introduced The 6 Principles, which are discussed in detail in Chapter 3. These principles help teachers create conditions in the classroom that promote language learning and plan and deliver lessons that keep learners' needs, interests, and backgrounds in mind.

Teachers of multilingual learners of English need to understand that language development is dynamic and not always linear and that how well we communicate depends on our purpose and audience. One aspect of making choices related to language teaching methods and techniques involves knowing how people learn second languages and what inhibits or facilitates the learning process. Chapter 2 explores what academic language is in schools, how students' levels of language proficiency influence their performance of tasks in English, and various factors that support learning English as a new language. The goal is that when teachers apply The 6 Principles in their classrooms, they will do so knowledgably and with their learners' needs in mind.

Additional resources pertaining to this chapter are available at www.the6principles.org/K-12.

2 WHAT TEACHERS SHOULD KNOW ABOUT ENGLISH LANGUAGE DEVELOPMENT TO PLAN INSTRUCTION

The 6 Principles are not new concepts. Rather, they build on the findings of several decades of research on second language acquisition and English language teaching. They are consistent with the recommendations found in several syntheses of research on educating language minority students in U.S. schools (August & Shanahan, 2006; Baker et al., 2014; National Academies of Sciences, Engineering, and Medicine [NASEM], 2017). More importantly, they represent an assets-based approach, in which the home languages and cultures of multilingual learners of English are viewed as resources to draw on and make a valuable part of the classroom for the benefit of all students.

Before we delve into The 6 Principles and their implementation in the classroom in Chapter 3, a brief discussion of the main concepts of second language and literacy development will be useful. We have all experienced learning our home language, although not all of us have learned a second or third language. In this chapter, we explore what it takes to learn a second language, what a progression through levels of proficiency looks like, and the vital role that language plays in school.

Multiple times every day, teachers make instructional decisions about how to convey information to multilingual learners of English and how to determine whether they understand the material and are making progress in their language development. Yet most teachers do not think of themselves as language teachers. When asked how they identify themselves, they often respond, "I'm a math teacher" or "I teach social studies." In these responses, they imply that their content expertise frames their teaching responsibilities and that teaching language to students is not their task.

Every teacher, though, relies on language as a tool to develop students' content knowledge. They explain, lead discussions, assign readings, and expect students to complete written assessments. Each of these teaching tasks entails knowledge of language as much as knowledge of the content. As a result, every teacher who relies on language as an instructional tool *is* a language teacher. We want to encourage every teacher to recognize this fact, take ownership of this role, and design their lessons with language learning in mind.

Language is a means of communication to share information and ideas, convey understanding and creativity, and build cooperation. It develops through use and interaction. Students construct language; as they do so, they learn to use language in ways that others use when communicating with them. An individual's language competence is the accumulation of all of their previous language uses. The more frequent and varied learners' opportunities are for language use, the more functional, complex, and flexible their language ability becomes.

In this chapter, we provide foundational knowledge for language teaching, including language components and skills. We discuss how academic language can develop in K–12 schools and the importance of knowing students' proficiency levels in academic English for designing appropriate instruction. We then explore English literacy skills instruction for multilingual learners of English and strategies that promote literacy development. Additionally, we examine essential and beneficial conditions for language learning and factors that may influence progress. For example, when teachers know that language develops through use and interaction, they can plan lessons that encourage students to use language actively and draw on their home language as a resource. Finally, we explain how teachers can foster learners' self-identity as competent bilinguals or multilinguals through asset-based pedagogical approaches such as culturally responsive teaching, technology integration, and attention to social-emotional learning (SEL).

Foundations of English Language Acquisition in K–12

Knowing how the language acquisition process works and the time it takes for an individual to become proficient can help teachers make instructional decisions with regard to the planning and delivery of a lesson. They might modify their speech by speaking more slowly and using more cognates and fewer synonyms with students beginning to learn a new language, for example. With more advanced students, they might speak at a normal pace and use more complex sentences. If a learner makes an error in English, a teacher's response should be based on whether the error is normal for a given proficiency level or whether it indicates something that has been learned incorrectly or not at all. Not only are effective teachers of multilingual learners of English conscious of their role, but they are also willing and intentional about how they handle this role. They have reasonable expectations for learners because they understand the time, effort, and practice that it takes for someone to learn a new language.

Overview of Language Components and Language Skills

Learners' ability to use language revolves around the four language skills of reading, writing, listening, and speaking and their interaction of these skills for the purpose of communication. Competence in language use involves five basic language components: (1) phonology (i.e., to identify and distinguish individual sounds); (2) morphology (i.e., to recognize the meaningful parts and structure of words); (3) syntax (i.e., to understand the rules of arranging words to make phrases and sentences); (4) semantics (i.e., to comprehend meanings of words, expressions, and symbols in a language); and (5) pragmatics (i.e., to interpret how language is used to convey concepts in a given context). *Grammar* refers to the system of rules for a language and includes phonology, morphology, semantics, and syntax.

Using examples, Table 2.1 summarizes how the five language components correlate with the receptive, or interpretive, skills (listening and reading) and productive, or expressive, skills (speaking and writing).

Table 2.1	Descriptors of Language Components and Language Skills			
Component	**Receptive Language Skills**		**Productive Language Skills**	
	Listening	**Reading**	**Writing**	**Speaking**
Phonology	• Distinguish between voiced and voiceless consonants aurally (e.g., /b/ vs. /p/). • Recognize stress patterns in spoken words (e.g., *product* vs. *production*).	• Identify phonological features in words (e.g., words that rhyme in poems). • Count the number of syllables in a word (e.g., *cup* has one syllable, *motivate* has three syllables).	• Understand how the alphabet letters represent individual sounds in spelling (e.g., *dog* has three sounds [/d/, /o/, and /g/]). • Differentiate words that look and sound similar but have different meanings (e.g., *too* and *two*).	• Identify different speech patterns and tones. • Differentiate accents or dialects in speech (e.g., American English vs. British English).
Morphology	• Identify affixes aurally and recognize how they change meaning of words (e.g., *read* vs. *reread* where the prefix *re* means "do again"). • Recognize how irregular plurals affect spoken form (e.g., *people* vs. *birds*).	• Analyze how morphological changes in words (e.g., prefixes and suffixes) affect the meaning (e.g., *cat* refers to the animal, while *cat* with suffix *s* refers to how many of that animal). • Recognize pronunciation variations for irregular verb forms (e.g., *swim* vs. *swam*).	• Adapt spelling when adding affixes to words (e.g., *happy* vs. *happiness* vs. *happiest*).	• Use correct pronunciation when adding suffixes (e.g., *ed* in *rained* vs. *helped* vs. *wanted*). • Modify speech when conveying singular vs. plural forms (e.g., *pen* vs. *pens*).
Syntax	• Comprehend complex sentence structures in spoken language (e.g., subjunctive mood, passive voice). • Recognize sentence types and linguistic structures in spoken English.	• Analyze and understand complex sentence structures in academic texts. • Interpret sentence structures used for different rhetorical effects (e.g., anaphora vs. parallelism).	• Apply grammatical rules to construct clear sentences. • Utilize varied sentence structures to diversify writing styles for different audiences (e.g., descriptive vs. persuasive).	• Speak using accurate sentence structures according to purpose or intent (e.g., hypothesis vs. opinions). • Employ varied sentence structures for engaging storytelling.

Component	Receptive Language Skills		Productive Language Skills	
	Listening	Reading	Writing	Speaking
Semantics	• Grasp nuanced meanings and connotations of words in speech (e.g., *stubborn* vs *determined*). • Recognize figurative language and idioms in spoken discourse.	• Infer meanings of unfamiliar words from context in reading. • Analyze the use of metaphors, similes, and symbolism in literature.	• Use precise and contextually appropriate vocabulary in writing. • Create mood and tone through word choice.	• Convey the intended meaning of ambiguous or nuanced words through context. • Employ figurative language (e.g., idiom, simile, metaphor) in speech.
Pragmatics	• Understand indirect speech acts (e.g., sarcasm, politeness).	• Understand implied meanings and the intended messages for the audience in a written context.	• Adapt writing style for different purposes and audience (e.g., emails to friends vs. formal letters).	• Adjust speech according to context and audience (e.g., formal language in business meetings, informal language with friends).

Source: American Speech-Language-Hearing Association (n.d.); Fromkin et al. (2015); Hazen (2015)

To help learners use these language components and develop the related skills, effective teachers prompt students to interact frequently. They provide regular opportunities for students to use oral and written language throughout the school day in varied modalities. They also encourage students to use and build on all of their language resources, including relevant and strategic use of their home languages (Echevarría et al., 2024; Ellis & Shintani, 2014; Paterson, 2021). With this approach, students can constantly tap into their linguistic knowledge to study, infer, and regulate their use of language skills.

Specific examples of how teachers help students practice language skills in the classroom include the following:

- Encourage pair work and small-group activities for listening and speaking.
- Provide language frames and models so that students can learn to articulate language functions (e.g., they know what expressions to use if they want to agree or disagree, build on another student's idea, or provide support for an opinion).
- Give students time to formulate and practice responses before interacting.
- Prompt students to annotate texts with their own explanations and responses to promote reading comprehension.
- Ask students to notice language forms in texts and use them in their responses.
- Assign quick-writes to stimulate language use and promote writing fluency.
- Remind students to discuss ideas and plans before they start a writing task.

In short, effective teachers multiply opportunities for students' active engagement with the material through frequent speaking, listening, writing, and reading practice (Baker et al., 2014; Council of the Great City Schools, 2023; Dodge & Honigsfeld, 2014; Gibbons, 2015; Short & Echevarría, 2016; Zwiers, 2014).

Developing Academic Language Proficiency in School

Roberto, come on up here. Here is your patch of dirt, right here on the floor. I want you to stand in your patch of dirt here, and you are going to be a plant. You are going to be a plant, and you are going to grow. He is a nice, happy plant, wouldn't you say? Plants grow if they are feeling happy, and they make seeds. But what happens if the plant grows too big for its small place, and it gets very crowded where the big plant is? Can the big plant just walk away to some place with more dirt?

(Second-grade science teacher)

For our class activity, we'll create a timeline of major events of the Civil Rights Movement in U.S. history. Work together in pairs to research and organize the events chronologically. During our discussion, we'll highlight the historical significance of each event and its contribution to the development of the United States.

(Ninth-grade history teacher)

Teachers who grew up speaking English and were educated in classrooms where all students spoke English proficiently may overlook the prominent role of language in their lessons. Like the teachers in the preceding vignettes, they may hold an expectation that every student will be able to follow teacher talk, ask questions, answer in intelligible speech, and participate in classroom discussions. Likewise, they may have an expectation of shared cultural experiences and a common ground of beliefs and assumptions. With learners who are not yet proficient in English in the classroom, however, teachers can feel at a loss when they realize how much they rely on English to teach.

> Record 15 minutes of your own teaching, observe a class, or watch a video of classroom instruction. Note how you (or the teacher you watch) and students rely on language to communicate meaning. What is the teacher saying, word for word? What language do the students hear and produce orally or in writing? In addition to language, in what other ways is meaning being conveyed? Reflect on the role of language in the instructional segment.

Social and Academic Language

Students learning English through informal communication tend to master social language first—much sooner than they can communicate in formal ways. Social language is conversational and requires mainly listening and speaking, a vocabulary of a few thousand words, and the mastery of frequently heard utterance patterns. Students' mastery of social language does not indicate proficiency in academic language. In contrast, students who learned English as a foreign language through grammar drills and academic reading likely have not acquired much proficiency in social language. Formal academic language, however, is more challenging to learn and is what students need to use in school.

The distinction between social and academic, or informal and formal, language is not binary. First, different skills are involved. Social language is conducted primarily through listening and speaking, whereas academic language also requires a large amount of reading and writing. Second, development from social to academic language unfolds along a continuum, with elements mastered gradually, over years of practice.

The Continuum From Social to Academic Language

Three students and their teacher are describing the same photograph in a language arts textbook. Notice how academic language has more complex sentence structure and more varied vocabulary.

More Social

FELIPE: Here, two people at an old building. She's up there. She's looking down. He's looking up. He's saying something—like, Girl, you're great. I like you. Can you come down?

ZHIHUI: I see a picture that's in black and white. I see a building and a balcony. I also see the sun shining in, which means that it's the morning. I see Romeo looking up at Juliet, and Juliet looking down at Romeo.

BARIKA: This is a scene from the play *Romeo and Juliet*. I see a backdrop with a sky. The female lead role is Juliet, who is standing on the balcony of a palace. The balcony and the wall look antique. The picture has a dramatic feeling

TEACHER: This is a black-and-white photograph of a theater stage. It captures the famous balcony scene in the play *Romeo and Juliet*. The stage set shows the classical architecture of a weathered palace at dawn. The breaking light casts shadows on the main characters. Although Juliet is on the balcony and Romeo is on the ground, their eyes are locked as they are absorbed in their conversation.

More Academic

Although children can acquire the basic social language they need by actively engaging in oral communication with peers and adults, this form of language acquisition is insufficient for the vast majority of English learners in school. The task of acquiring a new language to the degree that one needs to succeed academically or professionally in that language is surprisingly lengthy and complex. Fully appreciating the complexity of this undertaking can be difficult for anyone who has not tried to learn a new language.

Academic English Proficiency in School

The ability to use academic language is important for anyone studying content in English or planning to pursue a career that uses English. This ability is integral to a student's academic success within the type of standards-based curricula found in U.S. schools and is the core of TESOL's *PreK–12 English Language Proficiency Standards* (TESOL International Association, 2006). Academic language is the language used in textbooks, informational texts, scholarly papers, instructional videos, academic presentations, and lectures. Table 2.2 displays the main characteristics of academic language at the conceptual, discourse, sentence, and word levels. To be considered proficient in academic English, multilingual learners of English need to approach the academic language skills of their grade-level peers.

Table 2.2	Characteristics of Proficient Academic English	
Characteristic	Explanation of Characteristic	Examples
Conceptual Level		
Conceptual Complexity	• The treatment reflects the following cognitive functions: describing, explaining, comparing, classifying, sequencing, justifying, analyzing, evaluating, and synthesizing.	• *This is what it looks like …* • *This belongs in the category of …* • *This is an important choice because …* • *These phenomena are related in this way.*
Development	• Adequate details are provided. • Claims are supported.	• *This means that …* • *For example, …* • *The sources of this information are …*
Abstraction	• Concrete events and objects are treated as representations of abstract concepts.	• *Expertise is a key aspect of professional identity.*
Figurativeness	• Abstract terms are assigned attributes of concrete things or live beings. They can move, communicate, or have intentions.	• *A solution surfaced.* • *The position commands respect.* • *The analysis was deceiving.*
Detachment	• The speaker or writer separates from the message to suggest objectivity and logical reasoning.	• *Research shows that …* • *The evidence points to …*
Discourse Level		
Organization	• Ideas follow a logical progression. • The topics are controlled. • The connections between ideas are marked.	• *First,… Second,… Then,… Finally,…* • *Nevertheless, consequently, likewise*
Cohesion	• Words and sentences are linked. • Key words are repeated strategically. • Pronouns match their referents.	• *Visual representations can help us solve math problems. For example, a number line is one form of visual representation. It can show…*
Conciseness	• Information is densely packed. • Meanings are nuanced.	• *Currently, the annual mean growth rate of carbon dioxide in the Earth's atmosphere is 2.1 parts per million.*
Genre	• The conventions of different genres are observed.	• *Opinion essay, news article, journal article, interview, technical report*
Sentence Level		
Precision	• Sentences are complete, and each is formed with care. • Qualifiers are frequent.	• *It is mostly true. Results could improve. The best solution may be…*
Syntactic Complexity	• Phrase and sentence structures are varied and developed. • Sentences are long.	• *When we are working more than ever before to be able to afford the purchases we are choosing to make, we are spending less time with the people who make our lives happy.*
Density	• Information is packed into elaborate noun phrases.	• *Several justifiable grievances against the released draft of the proposed health care law were raised.*

Characteristic	Explanation of Characteristic	Examples
Grammar	• Sentences adhere to the rules of formal grammar. Grammatical features that are less common in social language appear often (e.g., passive voice, embedded clauses, modal auxiliaries, range in verb tense and aspect).	• *Lawmakers were given …* • *Feedback should have been considered.* • *Had there been more discussion, …*
Mechanics	• There are no spelling errors, and accurate punctuation is used.	
Word Level		
Exactness	• Words are intentionally selected from a set of vocabulary alternatives based on their frequency, connotations, and suitable collocates.	• *Alternatives for go down: happiness decreases; the price drops; the plane descends; stocks plummet*
Conciseness	• Ideas are condensed into technical terms. • Extra words are omitted to avoid wordiness.	• *climate agreement, protagonist, absolute value, parallelism* • *Due to the fact that vs. Because* • *In the event that vs. If*
Variety	• Word repetition is avoided except for key words and for effect.	• *Alternatives for pretty: attractive, appealing, lovely*
Clarity	• The pronunciation of words reflects knowledge of sound patterns and word stress.	• *The White House vs. a white hóuse* • *bénefit, benefícial, beneficíary*

Source: Anstrom et al. (2010); Short & Echevarría (2016); WIDA (2014); Zwiers (2014)

To develop learners' proficiency with academic language, teachers need to understand the role of language in school. They must consider the differences between social and academic language, as well as the characteristics of academic English. They need to account for standards that define English language proficiency for different contexts and purposes. In monitoring their students' progress toward proficiency, teachers also need to consider research-based levels of language development and reasonable time frames for their students to achieve proficiency.

Standards for English Language Proficiency

Various language proficiency standards define language proficiency for different contexts and different purposes around the world (e.g., Council of Europe, 2020). In the United States, English language proficiency for K–12 students is guided by federal law (Every Student Succeeds Act, 2015). The law requires each state to have English language proficiency standards defined for listening, speaking, reading, and writing skills. The standards should address different proficiency levels and align with each state's academic standards.

The purpose of these standards is to ensure that learners "attain English proficiency and develop high levels of academic achievement in English" and that "all English learners can meet the same challenging State academic standards that all children are expected to meet" (Every Student Succeeds Act, 2015, Sec. 3102, 1–2). Practically speaking, this means that multilingual learners of English must develop functional, grade-level use of English so they can be successful academically in content courses that align with state standards. Each state must choose (1) the English language proficiency standards that best serve as a benchmark for its learning standards in the content areas and (2) the proficiency test that assesses the extent to which each student has attained these standards.

It is important for teachers to recognize that English language proficiency in the U.S. K–12 context is a tool for moving students toward meaningful participation in grade-level instruction; proficiency is not the exclusive educational goal. It is *not* the goal for learners to be indistinguishable from monolingual speakers of English, nor is it for them simply to blend in within the English-speaking classroom. The standards of English language proficiency for K–12 U.S. schools focus on what students can do with language in content-based instruction.[1]

Levels of English Language Proficiency

Language development is not unlike the physical growth of children: It is continuous, incremental, and unnoticed except during or following periodic growth spurts. Children who grow in a healthy manner—interacting with other speakers and employing language frequently for a variety of purposes—develop new language gradually. Each day, they can comprehend and produce more words, add to their stock of formulaic language expressions, and surprise us with their utterances and increasingly sophisticated phrases. They can communicate meaningfully about a greater variety of topics and in more nuanced ways.

For the purposes of instruction and assessment, experts have organized language development into proficiency levels and described what language use typically looks or sounds like at every stage of development for each of the four language skills (i.e., listening, speaking, reading, and writing). In the United States, most states identify four or five levels of English proficiency, with a final level that represents grade-level language functionality. These levels are intended to guide teachers in their observations of students and their instructional planning (Nutta et al., 2014; TESOL International Association, 2006; WIDA, 2020).

Table 2.3 summarizes the growth that occurs in utterance variety and control, vocabulary use, and communicative functions and registers as learners progress from Level 1 to Level 6 of English proficiency. Utterance variety and control refers to a learner's ability to form phrases and sentences with varying complexity. Developing this control requires attention to forms (e.g., verb tenses, noun plurals) and abundant opportunities for practice and use. Vocabulary use relies on word knowledge—both a wide range of words and an understanding of types of words (e.g., nouns, verbs, adjectives). More broadly, vocabulary use includes terms for concrete and abstract concepts, function words (e.g., modal verbs, pronouns, conjunctions), multiple-meaning words, fixed expressions, idioms, and more. Communicative functions and registers represent the purpose for using language (e.g., to compare, describe, or justify) and the degree of formality needed for specific social situations.

Multilingual learners of English need the ability to form phrases and sentences with varying complexity. They usually begin with memorized chunks (e.g., *I got it, that's easy, what's this*) and progress to one- or two-word responses and simple phrases (e.g., *this part, the red one, can't see, show me, I have it*). Over time, they develop a repertoire of common phrase structures (e.g., *in the picture/book, look at this/that one, it's good/nice, read/do it with me*). They then combine these phrases into longer utterances (e.g., *I like to play soccer with my friends. I'm coloring the circle blue*). But they are still a long way from being able to control complex utterances such as *When I color over the blue circle with a yellow crayon, I get a green circle; I found the answer by taking 2 away from 14, which is 12*; or *If I had a garden, I would plant all kinds of fruit trees so I'll have sweet treats to eat.*

---

[1] TESOL International Association (2006) developed English language proficiency standards for pre-K–12 learners. These standards were based on the WIDA Consortium's 2004 English language proficiency standards and helped inform WIDA's 2007 English language proficiency standards (WIDA, 2004, 2007). ELPA21 is another consortium with standards used in several states.

Descriptions of language development at each level can help teachers identify learners' current levels and chart their progress toward proficiency.

Table 2.3	English Language Development Levels		
	Utterance Variety and Control	Vocabulary Use	Communicative Functions and Registers
Level 1	Relies on memorized phrases	Uses a small vocabulary of high-frequency words	Engages in a few types of familiar exchanges; requires native language or nonverbal supports for academic tasks
Level 2	Produces a variety of memorized phrases and a limited range of sentence patterns	Uses mostly high-frequency words and some content words	Participates in very simple verbal and written interactions; performs academic tasks with native language or other supports
Level 3	Forms a range of phrase and sentence patterns	Uses high- and mid-frequency words, plus a few hundred content words	Interacts in most everyday situations, conveys information, and asks questions; performs academic tasks with modifications
Level 4	Forms a wider range of utterance patterns with growing accuracy	Uses mid-frequency words as well as hundreds of technical and content words and some idioms	Participates in social interactions; expresses meaning in multiple related sentences; distinguishes formal and informal registers; performs many academic tasks
Level 5	Forms a variety of utterance patterns into connected discourse with growing accuracy	Uses several thousand technical and content words as well as frequently used idioms and fixed expressions	Participates in extended discourse; switches purposefully between informal and formal registers; performs a wide range of communicative functions and academic tasks
Level 6 (Exited EL status, at grade-level language ability)	Fluently produces grade-level utterance patterns with accuracy	Uses grade-level vocabulary, including a variety of idioms and fixed expressions	Performs grade-level communicative functions, using informal and formal registers appropriately; performs academic tasks independently

Note. The levels and descriptions in this table are intended to be illustrative. Some states use fewer levels. States set their own benchmark for proficiency and subsequent reclassification of students from current multilingual learners of English to former multilingual learners of English.

The conditions for language acquisition vary for language learners, and students do not pass through these proficiency levels in an identical manner. Language development is not an all-or-nothing ability but a lengthy, developmental trajectory. Teachers must keep in mind the time that students have had to learn English. Some learners show evidence of language gains in bursts, whereas others plateau, especially in the absence of regular interaction with proficient speakers, challenging curricular material, and beneficial feedback. The levels indicate a hypothesized progression to functional grade-level English language proficiency. This is a rigorous expectation for multilingual learners of English, who are acquiring the language while they are learning grade-level content in English.

It is important to realize that a student's overall level may not directly correspond to uniform proficiency across all skills. Students may, for example, receive a Level 2 as a composite score, indicating a beginning level of language proficiency. However, upon closer examination, it may become evident that the student is at Level 1 in writing and Level 3 in speaking. Some students progress faster in speaking than they do in writing. And, of course, much of language development is latent, takes place in the mind, and is often difficult to characterize in terms of observable language use. With careful attention, teachers can learn to recognize the markers that indicate language development:

- increased length of utterances (e.g., oral or written phrases and sentences)
- greater variety of utterance patterns
- broader choice of words and greater awareness of their appropriateness to convey intended meaning
- greater variety of topics to discuss
- increased comprehensibility of the ideas being communicated
- increased appropriateness of the level of formality (i.e., register) to audience and occasion
- decreased use of hesitation phenomena (e.g., *ah, hm, er*)
- reduced use of filler expressions (e.g., *stuff like that, you know*) and formulaic phrases

Collect several samples of the oral or written language of a multilingual learner of English. If possible, compare different samples from months apart. Evaluate the changes that you recognize by looking carefully for the markers of language development:

- increase in the mean length of utterances
- greater variety in the types of phrases and utterances
- broader choice of words
- increase in the comprehensibility of what is being communicated
- reduction in formulaic phrases, patterned language, hesitation sounds, and filler expressions
- broader choice of register (degree of formality)

Students who rely on sentence fragments, repetitive structures, and formulaic expressions are usually less proficient than those who produce a lot of detail and variety in their language, choose their words carefully, and can adjust the way in which they express themselves, depending on the conversation partner or communicative situation.

Time Frame for Reaching Proficiency

We do not yet know definitively how long it takes to achieve English language proficiency in U.S. schools (NASEM, 2017). The research base is growing, but we do know that the length of time depends, in part, on the assessment and achievement benchmarks used to define English language proficiency, and these vary by state and even by year. The time frame also depends on the populations of learners, their grade of school entry, their initial English proficiency, the language support program in which they are enrolled, and whether they have a learning disability.

The majority of identified multilingual learners of English in public elementary and secondary schools are born in the United States, and they start kindergarten or first grade with varying knowledge of English (Zong & Batalova, 2015). Longitudinal research (Greenberg Motamedi, 2015) conducted in seven districts in the state of Washington with high percentages of these students, high levels of poverty, and low academic achievement shows that the average number of years needed for kindergartners to achieve English proficiency and be reclassified as former multilingual learners of English was between 3 and 4 years, but between 10% and 15% of the learners were still not proficient after 8 years. Those who started kindergarten with advanced English proficiency took 2 1/2 years, on average, to achieve full proficiency, and those with disabilities took 5.5 years, on average.

The study also found that multilingual learners of English who started learning the language in Grades 2 through 5 took longer to reach reclassification (4.2 years on average), but almost 20% were not yet proficient after 8 years. Many of these learners spent as much time moving from beginner to advanced levels as they did moving from advanced to grade-level proficiency (Greenberg Motamedi, 2015). As students move up in proficiency level and in grades, they have more to learn, so developing proficiency takes longer.

Looking specifically at students who receive special education services, we see that the number of multilingual learners of English with disabilities in the United States grew by nearly 30% between the 2012 and 2020 school years (U.S. Department of Education, 2022). The proportion of long-term multilingual learners of English with learning disabilities is especially high in secondary grades, which may be because many of these students face ongoing challenges in passing the writing and reading subtests of the language proficiency assessment (Rhinehart et al., 2022).

In sum, acquiring proficiency in English, and in academic English in particular, is an involved, long-term enterprise that takes years of instruction and deliberate practice—more than 4 years for most students. The work does not stop when students can use social language fluently. The goal is to reach advanced, grade-level proficiency within the standards adopted by a given state. However, this goal does not mean that students should only study language until they are proficient in English. These learners must also have content courses in their daily schedule. When planned well, the mix of language and content instruction facilitates students' English language development. Keep in mind that being a multilingual learner of English is a temporary designation, whereas being a competent multilingual is a lifelong asset, worthy of every teacher's support.

The Role of Language in School

Given all of this information about developing students' proficiency in academic English, effective teachers recognize that teaching linguistically diverse students consists of three critical components (see Fig. 2.1):

1. They must depart from predominantly oral and text language-based instruction and use a full repertoire of resources for making information comprehensible. These resources include pictorial, gestural, experiential, interactional, and linguistic supports.

2. They must employ strategies to help students draw on their own available resources, such as linguistic, social, experiential, cognitive, and strategic knowledge.

3. They must become aware of the target language features that students need to develop to be fully functional in the classroom and with the specific content they are learning, and they need approaches to explicitly teach these target language forms at the same time that they teach content.

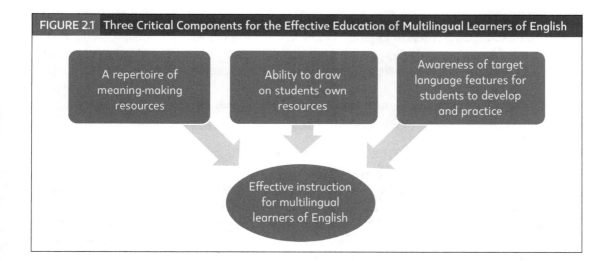

FIGURE 2.1 Three Critical Components for the Effective Education of Multilingual Learners of English

When we observe students' language use in different grades, we see that all students become more proficient with language over time. Effective teachers adjust to this development and match their own language production to their students' linguistic abilities of their students. For example, a kindergarten teacher speaks differently from a third- or sixth-grade teacher. The following classroom vignettes illustrate this.

Point the flashlight on the word like. *Good. Give the light to Amanda. Amanda will point to the word* and. *Good. Give it to Sophia. She is going to point to the word* go. *Very good. Give it to Victoria. She is going to point to the word* will.

(Kindergarten teacher, Ms. Lopez)

We are learning today about the main idea of the story and how to find the supporting details. But you know how I am. I don't only want you to find the supporting details. I want you to tell me why they are the supporting details. Olivia, what is a supporting detail?

(Third-grade teacher, Mr. Yeung)

As we are reading today, if you feel that you want to underline or annotate the text to help you better understand, please go ahead and do that at any time. If you want to underline evidence to cite in your answer, do that because that's what good readers do.

(Sixth-grade teacher, Mr. Willoughby)

All three teachers use language appropriate for the grade level. Notice that the kindergarten teacher, Ms. Lopez, uses short, familiar utterance frames, which she keeps repeating with just minor variations so that students can focus on the task and not struggle with her instructions. She uses only words that are among the most frequent in the English language and that young children who have a vocabulary of a few thousand words will know.

The utterances of the third-grade teacher, Mr. Yeung, are longer, but he still starts them with the basic subjects (*we, you, I*) and uses only two less common, technical terms (*main idea, supporting detail*). He repeats the key term *supporting detail* and immediately invites a student to explain it.

When addressing sixth graders, Mr. Willoughby speaks in long sentences that do not start with the subject. Not only are his utterances syntactically complex, but they also begin with dependent clauses, making them much more challenging to comprehend. In addition, Mr. Willoughby includes four technical terms (*underline, annotate, evidence, cite*).

Constantly monitoring students' understanding and using instructional language to match their English language proficiency are hallmarks of high-quality teacher communication. Many teachers do this routinely when they instruct English-speaking students in different grades; however, with multilingual learners of English, they need to be able to make adjustments even more skillfully, much as they would when teaching in a different grade. Teachers need to be mindful of target language features and steer students toward noticing, practicing, and using these features frequently in the classroom. They must also steadily advance the students' language skills over time, not using, for example, the simple present verb tense all year long, but instead expanding verb tenses to past, future, conditional, and so on.

Literacy Skills Development for Multilingual Learners of English

Students in K–12 settings cannot achieve full competence in English without grade-level academic reading and writing skills. The vocabulary used in extemporaneous oral communication is a small subset of the English vocabulary. Grade-level vocabulary and the full mastery of language forms can be achieved only by engaging with formal written and recorded texts. To read well, multilingual learners of English need to develop code-based skills, such as phonological awareness, and language-based skills, such as knowledge of semantics and syntax.

Learning to read is a dynamic process. Second language literacy learning is very similar to learning to read in a language one already knows. Differences in the new language's writing and spelling systems are more relevant to the process than whether the learner speaks and understands the language (Goldenberg, 2020). Research on literacy development shows that one does not have to have oral language knowledge of a new language to learn to read it; one can develop reading, writing, listening, and speaking skills simultaneously (Genesee et al., 2006). Research also indicates that literacy instruction and intervention programs that are effective with students who know English can be effective with multilingual learners of English too, with modifications such as the development of background schema and oral language skills (Goldenberg & Cárdenas-Hagan, 2023).

> In what ways should literacy instruction for multilingual learners of English differ from teaching reading and writing to students whose home language is English?

Over the years, extensive research into reading, which is also called the *science of reading,* has pinpointed crucial components needed to excel in reading. For example, the National Reading Panel (National Institute of Child Health and Human Development, 2000) has identified five foundational components of reading instruction for teachers to support school-age readers: phonemic awareness, phonics, fluency, vocabulary, and comprehension. It is equally important for students to develop verbal reasoning skills so they can construct meaning from text, apply content knowledge to enhance comprehension, understand metaphors and analogies, and make inferences (Council of the Great City Schools, 2023). Specifically, for second language learners, two major syntheses of research (August & Shanahan, 2006; Genesee et al., 2006) found that

- second language learners need to develop oral language proficiency as well as the five components identified by the National Institute for Child Health and Human Development;
- academic literacy in the home language facilitates learning to read and write in a new language; and
- second language learners need explicit and augmented vocabulary development.

For these reasons, current practices in some states that exclusively prioritize phonics, spelling, and basic comprehension (which are only part of the validated corpus of research studies known as the aforementioned science of reading) are not sufficient for serving any learner, particularly not for multilingual learners of English who are developing critical oral language skills and background knowledge while reading in English. Students need background knowledge to make connections and inferences with what they read, and they need oral language supports to make meaning of new words, phrases, sentence structures, and genres.

To develop these literacy skills, learners must engage in extensive and intensive reading. Extensive reading, which often involves learners reading on their own, ensures that learners encounter a wide range of vocabulary and language forms. Intensive reading is supported by the teacher through explicit and systematic instruction and provides opportunities for building depth of knowledge of target words and linguistic forms, as well as the multiple encounters and multimodal practice needed for learning that lasts (Cloud et al., 2009; Day, 2020; Herrera et al., 2014).

Literacy-Related Learning Expectations

Because reading and writing skills are so important to academic success, teachers of multilingual learners of English welcome guidance on what to expect from the students and how to assess their progress. Table 2.4 displays examples of classroom activities that support learners in literacy-related skills development as they progress up the grades and develop more proficiency in English.

Table 2.4	Literacy-Related Learning Expectations by Grade
Grades	Examples of Literacy-Related Learning Expectations
K	• Recognize and write their own name. • Follow along in a picture book while the teacher reads aloud. • Copy letters. • Begin to understand basic punctuation (periods). • Write a simple sentence about familiar topics, with scaffolds.
1	• Identify basic sight words and use them in sentences. • Read and comprehend simple stories independently. • Write short stories to describe characters, settings, and main events. • Begin to use correct spelling and punctuation in writing. • Discuss characters, settings, and main events in stories.
2–3	• Identify main ideas and key details in stories. • Develop narratives with a clear beginning, middle, and end. • Compare and contrast characters or events in different stories. • Write book reports or summaries of informational texts (e.g., about animals).
4–5	• Analyze the authors' purpose in texts. • Use evidence from the text to support opinions or arguments. • Write persuasive essays with claims and reasons. • Use graphic organizers to summarize characters' attributes and actions in stories. • Analyze themes in texts.
6–8	• Cite evidence to support analysis and inferences. • Analyze how authors contribute perspectives in texts. • Evaluate the credibility of sources and detect arguments. • Engage in peer review for writing.
9–12	• Analyze authors' style and word choices. • Write papers with a clear thesis statement and citations. • Engage in literary analysis. • Create multimedia presentations. • Conduct research projects using multiple sources.

Asset-Based Literacy Instruction for Multilingual Learners of English

Multilingual learners of English possess the immense potential to develop English language proficiency through grade-level literacy skills (e.g., academic writing and reading). Their exposure to different languages can enhance cognitive flexibility and adaptability, helping them develop the ability to think about and analyze language structures. As teachers nurture the literacy skills of their learners, they also embrace the diverse strengths and unique backgrounds that each learner brings to the process. Effective teachers are aware of opportunities to celebrate their students' assets and resilience and to foster a learning environment that addresses challenges with knowledge, creativity, compassion, and a commitment to promoting literacy success.

Here are some considerations for providing literacy skills instruction for multilingual learners of English:

- **Familiarize students with the English writing system.** Multilingual learners of English vary in how much knowledge they have about the English writing system, particularly if their home language uses an entirely different form of writing. Writing systems vary in the linguistic features of the language that they mark, such as vowel or consonant sounds, sound length, tone, and stress. Writing scripts vary from alphabetic (e.g., English, Russian, Greek, Korean) to those with only consonants (e.g., Arabic, Hebrew) to syllabic (e.g., Bengali, Gujarati, Thai) and logographic (e.g., Mandarin). Teachers can intentionally exhibit specific language features that the English writing system encodes to support their learners.

  - **Alphabetic vs. logographic.** In the English writing system, individual letters usually represent distinct sounds, allowing a more direct phonetic representation of words. Students who are transitioning to the English alphabet may need explicit phonics instruction to decode and sound out new words. The English writing system, for example, demands attention to both consonant and vowel sounds but not to word stress, consonant length, or tone (Borgwaldt & Joyce, 2013; Weingarten, 2013).

  - **Punctuation and text formatting.** Each written language has its own set of punctuation rules and formatting conventions (e.g., the use of capitalization). As opposed to left-to-right English texts, some languages such as Arabic organize text in a right-to-left direction. Multilingual learners of English may require continued practice on how these rules and conventions operate in writing.

- **Teach English spelling rules.** Because pronunciation often does not match spelling in English, students may struggle when learning to read. Consider the spelling variations for sounds that are the same (*you, do, threw, through, shoe, ewe, queue, flu, true*). Although English has many dialects in which pronunciation is systematically different, the spelling of words remains the same regardless. Consequently, recognizing letters of the alphabet is a very small part of learning to read in English, in contrast to the much larger part that it plays in those languages (e.g., Spanish, Italian, Finnish, Turkish) where the sound-letter correspondence is more predictable and consistent.

  - **Phonological awareness.** To read in English, students need considerable practice in hearing and segmenting sounds (i.e., phonological awareness), mapping sound patterns to spelling patterns (i.e., phonics), and memorizing sight words. Silent letters in English words (e.g., *e* in *cake* and *w* in *wrist*) often make it difficult for multilingual learners of English to predict how a word is pronounced based on its written form. Digraphs (i.e., two letters representing one sound) in English—such as *sh* and *ch*—and tricky pairs of letters—such as *gh* in *yoghurt*, *gh* in *night*, and *ph* in *phone*—do not always appear in spelling and sound patterns of other languages.

Further confusion happens when the same sounds in English can be spelled in multiple ways (e.g., *there, their, they're*).

- **Grow English word knowledge.** An important element in the readability of texts and second language literacy development overall is the vocabulary coverage—that is, the number of different words in a text. Effective word acquisition can be understood through three dimensions: breadth, depth, and accuracy. The dimensions collectively represent how learners expand their vocabulary knowledge over time. As one of the most widely spoken languages globally, English has constantly been enriched by other cultural contacts and languages. As of today, new words are still coined in the English language, and many commonly used English words originated or were adopted from other languages. Common English words that come from different languages and cultures include *lemon* (Arabic), *ballet* (French), *ketchup* (Chinese), *cartoon* (Italian), and *manga* (Japanese).

Teachers play a crucial role in supporting their learners' word acquisition by providing diverse and rich language experiences in K–12 classrooms and encouraging students to notice the versatility of languages.

  - **Breadth of vocabulary knowledge.** Breadth refers to the size of a learner's vocabulary. Word knowledge is incremental: With each new encounter, learners can add new details, associations, and multiple meanings to a word. Multilingual learners of English with a wide breadth of vocabulary have a large repertoire of words at their disposal in different situations and registers (e.g., formal meetings, casual talks) to communicate with others. Vocabulary learning begins with learning labels for concrete objects, followed by using a small handful of modifying words that can cluster with those object names to express a more complete idea (e.g., *car – blue car – car here – car go – my car*). Although students can usually learn the names of concrete objects easily, the most important words to prioritize for teaching are those that can be applied most frequently across all types of uses.

  Among these are the function words that play a role in grammar and help learners connect ideas. These function words are auxiliaries (*be, do, have*), modal auxiliaries (*can, may, should*), prepositions (*in, with*), pronouns (*it, they, who*), articles (*a, the*), determiners (*some, few*), conjunctions (*and, so*), and conjunctive adverbs (*consequently, finally*). Productive vocabulary knowledge also includes knowing word parts (i.e., prefixes, suffixes, and roots), as well as identifying cognates (words that are similar in spelling or pronunciation and have related meaning in one's home language).

The box "Types of Words to Learn" (on the following page) offers examples of vocabulary lists developed in accordance with research findings. These tools can help teachers strategically build students' word knowledge and support their academic success.

Types of Words to Learn

- **High-frequency words.** The 2,800 most frequently used word families cover 90% of all words spoken and written in English. The New General Service List (www.newgeneralservicelist.com) provides a current source for this vocabulary.

- **Sight words.** These are the most frequently written words, which every learner should recognize automatically—without needing to sound them out—to build speed and fluency in reading. The Essential Word List (Dang & Webb, 2016) was made for beginners for English language learning (www.edu.uwo.ca/about/faculty-profiles/stuart-webb/_docs/essential-word-list.pdf).

- **General academic words.** Some academic vocabulary is less subject-specific. These terms are cross-curricular and thus useful in every discipline. A current source is the New Academic Word List (www.newgeneralservicelist.com/new-general-service-list-1), which includes 960 headwords. Other sources include the Academic Word List (Coxhead, 2000), which has 570 high-incidence and high-utility academic word families, and the Academic Vocabulary List (Gardner & Davies, 2014), which has 3,000 core academic words.

- **Content vocabulary commonly used in school texts.** These terms are specific to the content area and grade level. A notable collection of these terms can be found in *Words Worth Teaching* (Biemiller, 2010), which focuses on the meanings known by children in K–2 and grades 3–6. Core Vocabulary Word Zones (TextProject, n.d.) lists the 4,000 word families that are used most frequently in core content areas.

- **Depth of vocabulary knowledge.** Depth refers to the level of understanding and familiarity with the words learners know. A word is gradually networked into a semantic web in the learner's brain. Think about a concept like pollution. To discuss, read, and write about it, students need to know related words, such as *smog*, *trash*, *litter*, *clean*, *dirty*, *healthy*, and *unhealthy*. Depending on the purpose for studying pollution, students may need to know *cause*, *effect*, *happen*, *result*, *source*, and *solution* as well.

  Depth of word knowledge also entails knowing which words occur together to form expected collocations. For example, in English we say *do homework*, not *make the homework*. We *share our thoughts* but we do not *divide our thoughts*. We eat *fast food* but not *slow food*.

- **Accuracy of vocabulary knowledge.** Accuracy concerns the precise and appropriate use of words. It involves using the types of words in context correctly and selecting the right words to convey intended meanings. Understanding nuances is integral to vocabulary knowledge accuracy. For example, learners need to know synonyms may have different connotations that are close but not the same, such as *happy* versus *gleeful*. Also, accuracy refers to how effectively learners can discern words that change meaning depending on the context. For instance, the word light can mean the opposite of heavy or can refer to illumination. One challenging area for vocabulary accuracy is the use of fixed expressions and idioms, which requires memorization of multiword units with vague meanings. Fixed expressions and idioms cannot be easily interpreted from their individual words. Many fixed expressions are ubiquitous but become familiar (*What was that again? To be perfectly honest with you; Actually, the thing about it is that…*). Idioms, by contrast, are the ultimate challenge; they are opaque, are rarely taught to language learners, and make sense only if produced exactly word for word (*Cat got your tongue? Turn the other cheek*).

- **Apply vocabulary knowledge to text selection and instruction.** Research indicates that comprehension of a text read independently depends in large part on how many words a reader knows in the text (Nagy & Scott, 2000). For example, knowing 80% of the words in a text might seem reasonable, but in reality reading comprehension is virtually impossible with vocabulary knowledge at that level. For minimal reading comprehension, a reader should know 90% of the words, and for adequate comprehension, they need to know 95%. To learn vocabulary or content information from a text, the typical reader needs to understand 95% of the words in the text. For unassisted reading for pleasure—the most sustainable and rewarding reading activity—most readers should have 98% vocabulary coverage. These facts have important implications for teachers of multilingual learners of English:

  1. Reaching such a high percentage is difficult for multilingual learners of English working with grade-level texts unless they are at an advanced proficiency level. Therefore, to learn language through reading, students need texts in which they know almost all the words, with few exceptions. Their language development is best served when they read books with few unknown words per paragraph or a single unknown word in every third line. To achieve this high level of vocabulary coverage, teachers need to make sure these learners have access to modified texts that are suitable for their age and interest but not overwhelming in the number of unknown words (Jeon & Day, 2016; Nakanishi, 2015; Nation & Webb, 2011; Schmitt et al., 2011).

  2. When assessing the percentage of unknown words in a text, teachers need to recognize that multilingual learners of English are often able to sound out words fluently without knowing the meanings of those words. For language learners, being able to decode— that is, sound out—text is distinctly different from comprehending it. Some teachers have students read aloud, but a better way to gauge vocabulary coverage is to ask the students to read shorter passages in the beginning section of the text (about 100 words) and have them mark unfamiliar words. If they indicate more than 10 words as unfamiliar, the students need alternative texts or additional supports. Teaching students to preview texts so they can identify and gauge the ratio of unknown words when they select books for independent reading is also useful.

  3. In classrooms, students have to work with texts above their independent reading levels on occasion—sometimes to complete a task when other resources are not available and sometimes to grapple with a rigorous, grade-level text as a challenge. Teachers should be aware that in these situations, they must provide explicit instruction and scaffolds so the students can be successful in these endeavors.

What to Do If There Are Too Many Unfamiliar Words in a Text

Ask a student to read a short passage of about 100 words at the beginning of a text and to mark any unfamiliar words. If the number of unfamiliar words exceeds 10, consider doing the following to support the student:

- Mark the key passages for the student to focus on instead of reading the whole text.
- Find alternative readers with controlled vocabulary.
- Supply a home language edition or audio text, or a text with similar content in the home language, for students to read first for comprehension; then have them read the English text.
- Supply bilingual editions, and mark strategically the sections to read in either language.
- Elaborate texts by inserting brief, comprehensible explanations of unknown words.
- Simplify texts by replacing some of the unknown words and sentence structures.
- Provide a bookmark that glosses the target vocabulary in the text.

- **Use oral language supports.** Oral language requires skills in listening and speaking for someone to comprehend and process information. Multilingual learners of English benefit from oral language opportunities that can facilitate their understanding of written language. In classrooms, oral language often serves as a scaffold for comprehension. If students understand a story when listening to it, they will find it much easier to comprehend the story when reading it again on their own. When teachers provide texts to read that are within learners' oral language abilities, they can transfer knowledge from listening to reading.

  Reading comprehension becomes extremely challenging if the text is beyond learners' oral language abilities, even when they can decode the words with apparent fluency. Therefore, teachers must talk with their learners about the content of texts before and after reading. By doing so, they will also ensure that oral language and reading comprehension develop simultaneously (Baker et al., 2014; Helman, 2016; Herrera et al., 2014).

- **Motivate students to read.** Some multilingual learners of English may not have had many home experiences with pleasure reading, so motivating them to read might be as straightforward as introducing them to engaging text. Some students are motivated by particular topics or genres that teachers may need to discern. Some texts that fit a proficiency level might be intended for a younger audience and thus unappealing; other texts might be too far above a learner's reading ability level and thus frustrating. The effort teachers make to find suitable texts is worth it because sparking students' motivation to read and kindling their self-efficacy in reading widely are important for language development (Herrera et al., 2014; Protacio & Jang, 2016; Turkan et al., 2012).

- **Build and activate background knowledge.** *Background knowledge* refers to the information and conceptual understandings or schemas that readers bring to their comprehension of texts. To construct meaning, students need to integrate new knowledge with what they already know (Duke & Cartwright, 2021). Studies have shown that second language learners' content familiarity can compensate for inadequate linguistic knowledge at most proficiency levels. Conversely, lack of schema and relevant background will impede reading comprehension even for advanced multilingual learners of English or for seemingly fluent readers (August & Shanahan, 2006; Smith et al., 2021).

  When teachers know what each learner is knowledgeable and passionate about, they can match their students with texts that enable them to use their background experiences to help with comprehension and build their linguistic knowledge. This knowledge of their learners will also help teachers recognize when students are not able to manage texts on their own and need additional support before, during, and after reading (Herrera et al., 2014; Lesaux et al., 2006). If students do not know much about the topic or theme of a text, teachers can help build that knowledge by making connections to related topics students know or experiences they have had (Echevarría et al., 2024).

Ways to Keep Multilingual Readers Engaged

- Help students become strategic readers and learn to make informed choices about their reading, such as selecting language preferences, types of readings, and developing reading strategies.
- Provide audiobooks in learners' home language and English when available.
- Provide students with a diverse selection of high-quality reading materials that are appropriate for their age and English proficiency levels, including books in their home languages.
- Teach students strategies to select books according to their interests and vocabulary knowledge.
- Use scaffolds (e.g., think-alouds, recasting) and visuals (e.g., pictures, graphic organizers, word walls) to help learners comprehend reading materials.
- Encourage parents of young children to read to them at home in the home language and have the children read to the parents as well.
- Encourage parents of older children to ask questions about what they are reading and make connections to other texts, stories, or experiences.

- **Promote cross-linguistic transfer.** Cross-linguistic transfer—that knowledge of one language can influence the learning and use of another language—can play a significant role in developing the literacy skills of multilingual learners of English. Knowing how these learners' home languages can be used to develop literacy skills, teachers can optimize the benefits by
    - providing access to books and reading materials in the home language(s) to promote regular reading practice;
    - encouraging writing activities (e.g., journals, creative writing) in both English and home languages;
    - recognizing that code-switching (switching between languages) is a natural part of language development for multilingual learners of English; and
    - celebrating students' linguistic assets by acknowledging the diversity and richness of languages spoken and written around the world.
        - » **Metalinguistic awareness.** Learners develop metalinguistic awareness, one aspect of cross-linguistic transfer, when they reflect on language as a system. Multilingual learners of English can recognize and discuss different components and rules that make up their home languages and analyze linguistic patterns such as individual speech sounds, word and phrase meanings, sentence structure, discourse, grammar, and writing conventions. In turn, they can compare and analyze the structures and patterns of English. Teachers can enable such comparisons and analyses or direct students' attention to similarities and

differences when they are sensitive about variations of linguistic features between their students' home languages and English.

> » **Translanguaging.** Translanguaging is a strategic process by which an individual chooses to use one language or another, orally or in writing, for a specific communicative purpose. Research on translanguaging has revealed that multilingual learners of English have one complex linguistic system that can include two or more languages, such as English and Spanish, rather than two separate systems. Certain knowledge, skills, and strategies—such as phonological awareness, listening and reading comprehension skills, and narrative skills—can be shared between the languages or can transfer from one language to another (García et al., 2017). Being able to translanguage gives these learners agency; they can call on this resource flexibly to develop their literacy skills and communicate successfully with others (Seilstad & Kim, 2020).

Factors Affecting English Language Development

We would all like to know the best way to teach a new language to any learner. However, although an entire field of research (second language acquisition) is dedicated to examining this topic, we do not yet have a definitive answer. A dozen theories focus on the neurological, psychological, cognitive, and linguistic processes by which people learn languages other than their home language. Yet these theories have not necessarily focused on ideal ways of teaching a particular variety of a particular language—in this case, academic English—in a particular context—in this instance, U.S. K–12 schools (Lightbown & Spada, 2014; MacSwan, 2018; Valdés et al., 2014; Williams et al., 2015). Despite the range of theories, we have learned from decades of research findings that some conditions are essential and others are beneficial for acquiring a new language. Some individual variables play a role as well.

Essential Conditions

Essential conditions are those that must be present for second language acquisition to occur. Teachers can play a role in promoting some of these conditions. Essential conditions include the following:

- **Normal home language development.** Language is a complex neurophysiological function. It can be thought of as software that runs on the hardware of the brain (Anderson & Lightfoot, 2002). Second language acquisition is facilitated by the software of the first language. In other words, a learner's acquisition of their home language established neurophysiological processing that plays a key role in how they handle input in a new language. Normal first language development indicates that all is well with the learner's neurophysiology to allow them to acquire additional languages. So, teachers should inquire about students' experiences with their home language development and view rich home language development as a strong foundation for learning new languages (Baker, 2014; Kohnert, 2013).

- **Motivation.** Motivation prompts individuals to pursue and sustain an effort toward a goal, and language learning requires a great deal of effort over a period of many years. Language learning activities must be inherently pleasurable, or the eventual goals must be so positive that the learner considers them worth the struggle. Motivation cannot be successfully sustained externally, with threats and rewards. Therefore, teachers should work with each learner to understand and optimize internal sources of motivation (Dörnyei & Ushioda, 2011; Muir & Dörnyei, 2013).

- **Facilitative emotional conditions.** Learning cannot succeed if students feel anxious, worried, threatened, or overwhelmed. When they experience negative emotional conditions, learners shut down and are unable to take risks with language or attend to language forms. We learned quite a bit about this factor during the global pandemic. Social-emotional distress led to lower academic outcomes (Sutton & Lawson, 2023). A welcoming, safe, and relaxed environment is indispensable for language learning. Helping students manage their emotions in the classroom, supporting them so they can overcome anxiety or negative emotional responses, and developing their social-emotional skills are essential teaching responsibilities (Jagers et al., 2019).

- **Usable input and feedback.** Input refers to how teachers present information. The term is related to *comprehensible input*, which denotes language that is only one level above the language that the learner already knows (Krashen, 1985). Input beyond a learner's understanding can become usable when a teacher supports meaning through other means, such as visual aids, gestures, and home language summaries. Another form of input that is key to acquisition is feedback. Without feedback, learners cannot be certain that the language they produce is understandable in its meaning, form, or pronunciation. A large body of research addresses the many useful varieties and relative efficacy of different types of feedback (Ellis, 2017; Ellis & Shintani, 2014; Nassaji & Kartchava, 2017). Some types of feedback include clarification requests, explicit correction, reformulations, metalinguistic signals, and recasts. Prompting speakers to repair their own speech, also called elicitation of self-repair, is the most productive form of feedback.

- **Deliberate practice.** Practice is the collective name of activities whose goal is to systematically develop second language skills (DeKeyser, 2010). These activities are not drills that demand imitation and repetition; rather, practice is a much broader range of activities that lead to fluency, accuracy, and automaticity of specific subskills. Students need to interact with others to test out their use of language for communication, and they need to interact with texts to check for comprehension and construct meaning. Knowing language rules cognitively is not the same as applying them in real time, fluently, consistently, and without conscious awareness. Teachers need to plan activities that help students explicitly practice the skills, vocabulary, and grammar they are studying. Mastering a second language requires a complex set of skills that takes thousands of hours of systematic, deliberate practice to develop (DeKeyser, 2010). When students become proficient in a new language, they no longer focus on basic skills, and they are able to use language naturally and automatically.

The foundation of effective instruction is monitoring and ensuring that the essential conditions of second language acquisition are met and sustained for every learner.

Beneficial Conditions

Beneficial conditions contribute to second language learning and work to the advantage of learners who have access to them. Some beneficial conditions depend on the context of language learning; others can be enhanced by instructional practices.

- **Relatedness of home and new language.** When we say that the home language is closer to the new language—in this case English—we mean that the home language and the new language have similar speech sounds and phonological features, have many cognates (i.e., words that have similar form and meaning), have the same basic word order, and use the same writing system. In such cases, learning a new language is significantly easier. In contrast, learning a new language that is quite different from the home language, such as learning Swahili when the home language is Bengali, is more difficult and typically takes longer.

- **Home language oracy and literacy skills.** Many first language skills are transferrable to the second language, including a large conceptual vocabulary (August & Shanahan, 2006). Although the names of concepts and related terms are different in the second language, understanding the concepts themselves can scaffold word learning in the new language. Other areas of language transfer include phonological awareness, understanding the meaningfulness of print, and use of cognitive and metacognitive skills. When students have these skills in their home language, learning the new language is easier.

- **Avid reading.** Being a motivated, avid reader in the home language helps a learner acquire a second language. Practiced readers decode words automatically. They are able to hold their focus on texts for long periods of time. These skills are preliminary for being able to allocate working memory to the task of word learning by not struggling with the decoding task. Avid readers also read more, which means that they encounter more words and meet each word more often, which can result in a larger vocabulary and deeper word knowledge. These are reasons why extensive reading promotes literacy development. Skilled readers master transferrable reading comprehension strategies in the home language, too, such as summarizing or quickly identifying main ideas and supporting details (NASEM, 2017).

- **Prior foreign language learning.** If a student has experience with learning a foreign language or is bilingual, learning English will be easier. Bilingual students bring to the learning process prior experiences, self-efficacy, and strategies that helped them succeed previously (NASEM, 2017). They are able to draw on the language that they consider to be closer to the target language. They do not necessarily understand the differences between the language (or languages) they speak and the new language, but they draw effectively on their intuition and are ready to "give it a go" (Rutgers & Evans, 2017).

- **Cultural knowledge and the ability to read social situations.** Having knowledge of the culture helps one understand, in part, how language is used in that culture. Communication depends on gleaning meaning from contexts and assumptions and being attuned to nonverbal cues. Being able to process situations, gestures, or unarticulated intentions correctly helps a person infer the real meaning of messages (Lynch, 2011). Language is also dynamic, and words, for example, can be coined or used in different ways by members of a community (e.g., slang used by teenagers). Students who already understand the culture or have teachers who serve in the role of culture facilitator have an advantage.

- **Personality factors.** Research has identified a number of personality factors that facilitate language learning, such as courage (shaking off fear, being willing to take risks), positivity (reacting with positive emotional responses to experiences), tolerance for ambiguity (experiencing partial understandings as *The glass is half full*), and willingness to communicate in specific situations (Williams et al., 2015).

- **Regular access to competent speakers of the new language.** Although all types of interaction are useful for language learning, students gain more from interacting with teachers and proficient peers (Sato & Ballinger, 2016). Sometimes teachers assume that students have access to interaction with native speakers if they live in an English-speaking country; however, this is not always the case. Each student's circumstances are different. Students should spend time at school and away from school engaging with others who are proficient in English.

- **Having purposes and frequent opportunities to use the new language.** Having reasons and occasions to use the new language is closely related to the previous condition of having access to competent speakers of the language. But this condition matters even more than that one for language learning. Regardless of the educational context, with careful lesson planning, teachers can set students up with collaborative learning tasks, such as pair work and small-group work, or group projects that integrate using the new language with curriculum topics that will benefit most students' language development.

- **Integrative motivation in the speech community.** This type of motivation deserves a separate mention from motivation for language learning in general (Gardner, 1985). Students who identify with a speech community (i.e., a group of people who share a common language or linguistic norms and expectations for the use of language) work harder because of their desire to be a member of that community (Pavlenko & Norton, 2007). Some examples of a speech community include shared interest groups, professional communities, social media groups, and book clubs. This condition is powerfully supported by active measures to make multilingual learners of English and their families feel included and integrated in English-speaking communities.

- **High-quality instruction.** Effective teachers provide instruction that includes all of the necessary conditions for second language acquisition, leverages beneficial conditions, and mitigates the challenging factors for language learning (NASEM, 2017). Chapter 3 offers a wealth of ideas for providing high-quality instruction that facilitates learning academic English.

> Which of these essential and beneficial conditions could you incorporate into your learning environment?

Challenging Conditions

Most of the conditions that we have discussed so far are within a teacher's or learner's control and can enhance language learning, but several additional factors merit special consideration. These factors may hinder second language learning for school-age students, so teachers should recognize them and try to minimize their impact with specialized instruction and suitable interventions.

- **Older learners.** The age at which a learner's exposure to the new language begins matters for the eventual outcome of language learning. Age effects have been the subject of much research since the 1960s. Research suggests that there are some limits on late-onset learners' development of native-like pronunciation, but that type of proficiency is not the educational goal for most second language learners. Where age has the most influence is in secondary school settings because new learners of academic English have less time to acquire the language than younger learners, and older learners have much more to learn to reach the level of the academic language proficiency of their peers. Nonetheless, dynamic bilingualism is achievable even for these learners (Birdsong & Vanhove, 2016; DeKeyser, 2013).

- **Social-emotional factors.** As we have discussed, the challenges that social-emotional factors present to second language learning can manifest themselves in many forms, including trauma, posttraumatic stress, anxiety, and depression. Since the pandemic, more teachers are learning about ways to implement SEL skills in the classroom, and schools are working with families to understand the home and cultural context and create intervention plans (Pentón Herrera & Martinez-Alba, 2021).

- **Special needs.** Some multilingual learners of English struggle to read in English or acquire the language more slowly than others. Although effective instruction with appropriate learning opportunities can ameliorate the delays for some, others may have speech and language disorders or learning disabilities. Effective teachers actively screen for and monitor these students, consider whether there is a language delay or disability, and may initiate the special education referral process. For multilingual learners of English with special education status, the law is clear that they need services for both English language development and their learning disability. The recommended approach is to use multi-tiered, evidence-based interventions that are culturally and linguistically responsive (Hoover et al., 2016; Kangas, 2021; NASEM, 2017; U.S. Department of Education, Office of English Language Acquisition, 2017). Teachers should also understand that if a multilingual individual has a learning disability, it will appear in both the home language and the target language.

- **Limited and interrupted formal education backgrounds.** One group of learners who face enormous disadvantages by definition are students with limited and interrupted formal education (known as SLIFE)—particularly if they lack literacy in their home language. It is imperative to identify these learners' educational needs separately from issues related to English language learning and advocate for intensive, accelerated, supplemental instruction that is designed to close gaps in literacy and content learning (Custodio & O'Loughlin, 2017).

- **Long-term multilingual learners of English.** A number of multilingual learners of English fail to achieve the language proficiency needed to exit the English language development program even after many years of instruction in U.S. schools. Becoming a long-term multilingual learner of English can be the result of several factors, such as poor instruction, weak home language skills, transiency, or special education needs. Teachers should be aware of the potential long-term negative effects when learners experience difficulties with initial adjustment, switch program types, transfer from school to school, or do not receive appropriate services when dually identified (NASEM, 2017).

Table 2.5 lists essential, beneficial, and challenging conditions for second language learning in K–12 schools. The list serves as a reference for understanding the various factors that can influence and shape the acquisition of a new language. The factors in bold in the first two columns represent those conditions that teachers have some influence over in their classrooms. The other factors represent individual characteristics. The third column reflects factors that students come to school with, but they can be addressed in part with specialized programming and interventions.

Table 2.5	Conditions for Second Language Learning in K–12 Schools	
Essential	Beneficial	Challenging
• Normal home language development • **Motivation** • **Facilitative emotions** • **Usable input and feedback** • **Deliberate practice**	• Relatedness of home language • First language skills • **Avid reading** • Prior foreign language learning • **Cultural knowledge** • Personality factors • **Access to competent speakers** • **Purpose and frequent opportunities to use the language** • Integrative motivation in a speech community • **High-quality instruction**	• Older learners • Social-emotional factors • Special needs • Limited and interrupted formal schooling • Long-term multilingual learners of English

Note. Bolded conditions are those conditions that teachers have some influence over in their classrooms.

When teachers pair their understanding of the conditions for second language learning with knowledge of each student's background, educational history, and personal characteristics, they can maximize the conditions that they control or shape. Chapter 3 explains in detail the process of designing instruction that can optimize essential and beneficial conditions of second language acquisition and mitigate the challenging factors to the extent possible within a specific teaching context.

> Consider additional factors that may affect second language learning. What challenges do you face when you plan instruction?

Obstructive Beliefs About Teaching and Learning English and Constructive Responses to These Beliefs

No discussion of the conditions for second language learning would be complete without giving attention to an important, deep-rooted challenge: the beliefs that some educators hold about teaching multilingual learners of English in U.S. schools. Without a doubt, teachers' beliefs influence the ways in which they make consequential decisions about how to approach the design and delivery of instruction. Unfortunately, a great number of misconceptions circulate about teaching these students, and these notions do not match up with current research (Klinger et al., 2016). Moreover, research findings on second language acquisition are often not shared with teachers in ways that are constructive for teaching and learning.

Table 2.6 presents a summary of obstructive beliefs about teaching and learning English, paired with research-supported constructive responses to these beliefs. By embracing the knowledge presented in the right column, teachers will plan instruction more effectively to develop students' academic language skills.

Table 2.6	Obstructive Beliefs About Teaching and Learning English and Constructive Responses
Obstructive Beliefs	**Constructive Responses**
The role of the English language teacher is to develop students' English language proficiency through English-only instructional contexts.	Students' home languages can enhance cognitive capacity, and self-efficacy is a strong source of motivation for second language learning. Effective teachers try to develop all of their students' competencies.
Students are either motivated to learn English or they are not, and students who are not motivated will not learn.	Motivation is key to successful language learning. Teachers can build a climate to support students' motivation and should explicitly consider how their instruction can enhance it.
Students should start learning English at a very young age. The younger the better for learning a new language.	Young and older learners bring different assets to the language-learning experience. Everyone should be encouraged to learn a language at any age. Realistic expectations, abundant time, and many opportunities for practice are the most important factors for learning.
Young students pick up language unconsciously and effortlessly. All they need is immersion in English.	Young students need a positive environment in which they have frequent opportunities to play with language, use it with conversation partners, and engage in meaningful, developmentally appropriate literacy activities that are scaffolded to support their success.
The fastest way to acquire advanced proficiency in English is through immersion.	Immersion may promote certain aspects of language (e.g., pronunciation, acquisition of social language). Immersion is not sufficient, however, for learning academic English, especially reading and writing.
Older adolescents and adults are rarely able to master a new language.	Older learners can acquire high levels of proficiency in a second or third language. They are capable of comprehensible and accurate language production.
Students either have the aptitude for learning foreign languages or they do not. Learning English is not for everyone.	All individuals who acquired a first language can learn a new language. Even those who cannot hear can acquire additional languages. With the right method of practice, every student can be successful.
The role of the teacher is to simplify language input so students can comprehend it.	When learners are at the early stage of acquisition, the teacher's use of simple and clear language can increase their comprehension. However, for learners to advance, they need to encounter and use language of growing complexity. Teachers should match the appropriate language to the student's proficiency.
Students cannot comprehend grade-level content in English until they develop English language proficiency.	Students can and must acquire grade-level content while also learning the academic English in which the content is presented. Delaying content instruction hinders students from advancing through the grade levels.
Students should use English all the time, even at home with their families.	For many families, using English in a family situation may be completely unnatural. If parents are not proficient in English, using the language they know best in interactions with their children is preferable. Home language skills and a large vocabulary developed through rich conversations and shared reading with family members can support greater success with the second language as well as balanced bilingualism.
Students should focus on memorizing words and phrases.	Students should focus on using the language purposefully. Routine and patterned language is typical for beginners, but students need to construct and be creative with language to develop proficiency.

Sometimes these beliefs manifest themselves explicitly; other times they remain unstated, yet they guide teachers' decision-making and actions. Recognizing obstructive beliefs in our own actions is important. For example, we may spend a great deal of time teaching students about sentence structures but not allow them ample opportunity to use and practice these forms in the classroom. We may limit our language teaching to highlighting a few vocabulary items and expect that students will memorize them on their own. We may expect students to pick up language mainly from teacher presentations. We may oversimplify our speech and the content we teach. Reflecting on our own teaching in light of these obstructive beliefs is a productive start. Helping to dispel these beliefs and promoting constructive responses in our own classrooms and among our colleagues are worthwhile next steps.

Additional Considerations for Supporting Language Development in the Multilingual Classroom

Supporting language development goes beyond merely teaching a new language; effective teachers embrace the richness of linguistic diversity and recognize the unique assets that multilingual students bring to the classroom too. This section explores ways to bolster students' learning of a new language through culturally responsive teaching, technology integration, and SEL practices. (See Chapter 3 for more discussion.)

- **Culturally responsive teaching.** Culturally responsive teaching is a pedagogical approach that leverages the cultural competence and linguistic assets of students from diverse backgrounds to inform appropriate instruction and promote engagement in learning (Au, 2009; Gay 2018; Hammond, 2015). Culturally responsive teachers help learners kindle an ideal self that incorporates multilingual competence as integral to success. Their learners are not afraid to take on this challenge, and they possess the strategies to achieve language learning goals.
  - **Acknowledge and value learners as individuals.** We must always remember to consider each learner as an individual. The way in which we use language is personal. Our identity is delicately wrapped in how we speak and interact with one another (Douglas Fir Group, 2016; Norton, 2013). Each of us is easily recognized by our voice, the characteristic intonation of our speech, our particular speech habits, and our accent. How other individuals relate to our language use is important for our self-worth and bears powerfully on any potential relationship that we establish. The way in which we use language may serve to create common ground, or it can become a source of *othering*. Othering is a mental judgment of an individual as "not one of us"; it positions a person as an outsider to the community, "a cultural other" (Sanderson, 2004). Effective teaching ensures that every student in the classroom community knows that their home language is valued and their multilingual ability is an advantage, even as they are developing proficiency in the new language (Cummins, 2001). When we respect our students as individuals and encourage them to share their language and culture, we welcome them to take part in all aspects of a community.
  - **Recognize that student identity is tied to language.** Effective teachers are aware that learning languages is a process of self-exploration and self-discovery, and they understand that motivation to learn a language is bound up with the work of shaping identity (Cummins, 2001; Dörnyei, 2014; Norton, 2013). Such teachers recognize that identity is dynamic; it can be shaped and formed by discourse communities, and, in turn, membership in these communities motivates learners to

communicate in the valued ways of those groups. Integrating and including learners in the discourse community shapes their identity and motivation to realize their ideal self.

- **Technology integration.** In recent years, the integration of technology into educational settings has opened new horizons for multilingual learners of English in U.S. schools. Recent research has highlighted the potential impact of technology-based instruction to transform learning—with interactive platforms, applications, and games—on language acquisition and differentiation for students. Dvorskiy and Gudkova (2023) discussed the significant role that technology can play in language acquisition. For example, they explored the advantages of using online language learning platforms (e.g., Busuu, Drops, Duolingo), language learning applications (e.g., Quizlet), and virtual language exchange programs. They reported how technology increases language learning experiences by supplementing traditional teaching techniques and boosts students' enthusiasm for language acquisition.

  - **Provide engaging literacy experiences with interactive apps.** Çinar and Arı (2019) investigated the effects of Quizlet, an online vocabulary application, on vocabulary acquisition skills and mindsets toward English lessons. Seventy-one high school students participated in the study, with one group receiving Quizlet-based training and the other receiving traditional classroom instruction. Compared with the control group, the Quizlet-trained experimental group displayed considerably superior vocabulary learning and retention scores. Furthermore, when using Quizlet, students' mindsets toward English learning improved, demonstrating the importance of technology in enhancing language acquisition and motivation.

  - **Offer adaptive learning opportunities tailored to learners' needs.** Technology enables teachers to effectively individualize instruction, develop personalized learning plans, and cater to diverse learning needs (Brinks Lockwood, 2018). A research study by Lee and Martin (2020) investigated the application of the flipped classroom model in preservice English as a second language teacher education within a Computer-Assisted Language Learning course. For the flipped classroom sessions, the teacher candidates watched instructional, content-oriented videos outside of class and engaged in collaborative learning activities during class time. Other sessions followed a traditional model in which instructors delivered instructional content directly. The results indicated several advantages of using the technology-supported flipped classroom method, including fostering learner autonomy, giving participants a sense of ownership, and successfully developing knowledge at learners' own pace. Furthermore, the approach reduced the cognitive load by chunking content in instructional videos into appropriate segments, allowing learners to comprehend the information more easily. Participants reported increased engagement and interaction with peers due to the combination of hands-on learning and support.

  - **Use digital platforms to enhance language skills.** Technology can assist multilingual students in improving their reading, writing, speaking, and listening skills, which they must practice and master to become proficient in English. Harper and colleagues (2021) found that multilingual learners of English at beginning and intermediate proficiency levels in middle school who used Rosetta Stone® Foundations for individualized practice improved their listening, speaking, and reading-aloud scores significantly more than control students who did not use the software did. Nadzrah and colleagues (2017) investigated using blog communities to improve learners' language competency in reading and writing. The study included first-year university students who had low proficiency levels of English and participated actively in blog posts and conversations. The online platform fostered meaningful interactions and language exercises, which developed users' language abilities considerably.

Although several of these studies involved university-level students, successful applications to K–12 settings have occurred since the COVID-19 pandemic. What is important to remember, however, is that teachers' guidance is crucial for maximizing technology-based learning benefits to empower multilingual learners of English, enhance language acquisition, and shape the future of language education when the technology supports are combined with effective pedagogy and equitable access.

- **Social-emotional learning.** The practices of SEL can be integrated into teaching to enhance students' academic success and well-being (Elias, 2019; Hoffman, 2009; Pentón Herrera, & Martinez-Alba, 2021). With culturally responsive SEL practices, teachers can establish a learning environment that engages multilingual learners of English in recognizing authentic feelings, developing healthy identities, and acknowledging diverse perspectives (Lau & Shea, 2022). When students feel safe and have a sense of belonging, they are more motivated in the learning process. In the United States, a widely adopted SEL framework includes five core social-emotional competencies (i.e., self-awareness, self-management, social awareness, relationship skills, and making responsible decisions) that work in tandem to foster students' learning and development (Collaborative for Academic, Social, and Emotional Learning, n.d.). The following examples illustrate the integration of these five competencies with language development.

  - **Promote self-awareness.** Promoting self-awareness for multilingual learners of English entails guiding them to actively reflect on their language learning process and identify specific areas of strength and growth in their language skills. For instance, teachers can encourage self-reflective activities (e.g., journals, progress tracking) to help learners develop a sense of ownership over their language learning process. Classroom practices can include helping students explore their emotional reactions to a text and discussing how readings relate to their real-life experiences (Pentón Herrera, 2020).

  - **Foster self-management.** Learners with well-developed self-management skills demonstrate effective emotional regulation, goal-setting, and planning in their language learning. In the classroom, teachers can foster these skills by providing various opportunities. For example, teachers can offer checklists, rubrics, expectation lists, and learning tools (e.g., sentence stems and frames) to help students organize and track their progress on assigned tasks (e.g., writing argumentative essays, preparing a 5-minute presentation). Teachers may use a feelings thermometer as a check-in tool to allow learners to reflect on and manage strong emotions (Elias & Tobias, 2018).

  - **Raise social awareness.** This competence refers to learners' ability to show empathy toward people from different backgrounds and to understand diverse perspectives. One effective way to achieve this competence is by affirming and valuing learners' linguistic assets in projects and class discussions on topics related to cross-cultural experiences. For example, learners can share how they translate cultural expressions and vocabulary words from their home language to English for their chosen topics

(Cummins, 2015). Another example is encouraging learners to discuss social norms of characters in multicultural literature.

- **Develop relationship skills.** To foster effective connections and collaboration with others, learners require essential relationship skills, including conflict resolution and teamwork. Teachers can promote these skills among multilingual learners of English through activities such as cooperative learning, role-playing, assisting learners in developing team norms, and other collaborative endeavors (Sprenger, 2020).
- **Support responsible decision-making.** Establishing a sense of autonomy and agency can help students make thoughtful choices in their language learning experiences. Teachers can support learners in developing responsible decision-making skills. For instance, providing multiple options for completing assignments allows learners to utilize their linguistic repertoire and makes them feel more comfortable with showcasing their understanding, which can help them meet the learning goal. (See Lawrence, n.d., for more resources.)

A 21st-Century Goal: Dynamic Bilingualism

Knowing two or more languages is a strength and a sought-after 21st-century skill. Multilingual learners of English are poised to be fully proficient in more than one language, and the optimal long-term outcome for these students is dynamic bilingualism. Dynamic bilingualism is the ability to adapt to communicative situations and use more than one language flexibly and strategically to make meaning, depending on the audience, conversation partner, or topic (García et al., 2017). One aspect is translanguaging, which includes the flexibility to switch between languages to accomplish tasks with others. Translanguaging can be a practical choice; it can serve to help others and convey solidarity or group identity.

Dynamic bilinguals are fully functional with communicative partners who use either or both of their languages. They can cross linguistic boundaries with ease and participate in knowledge communities beyond these borders. Dynamic bilinguals are an invaluable asset in the community. They begin as emerging bilinguals—that is, multilingual learners of English who also maintain and continue to develop their home language. With support, they can experience their dual language skills as a functional resource and a recognized element of an ideal identity.

> How can students use their home language to learn in your classroom?

TESOL supports multilingualism and multicultural literacy as an educational goal for all multilingual learners of English and promotes instructional approaches for the teaching of English that align with that goal. The following three vignettes show students who use their home and new language flexibly and strategically, gaining not only content knowledge but also confidence in the classroom.

In the first vignette, Anita, a Hungarian-English bilingual, shares her homework with her second-grade class. Her task was to talk about a decision her family made together, add details, and illustrate the event with a drawing. Anita elects to use both languages to do so.

Translanguaging in Grade 2

Ms. Connors:	*Tell us how your family decided on this trip.*
Anita:	*I wanted to go to the ocean. So I told my mom, "Anyu, mennyünk a tengerpartra. Oda ahol a játszótér van. Ahol lehet hintázni." And my mom said, "Az egy nagyon jó hely, csak messze van." Then my dad said, "We can go to the ocean much closer." My brother said, "Oda ahol a nagy sziklák vannak." So we went there where all those rocks are and there is lots of sand also. You can dig with your fingers into holes and find razor clams. That's how my family decided on that trip.*
Ms. Connors:	*I really like how you told us this in the words that everybody in your family used. So you wanted to go to a far-away beach. Is that what you said?*
Anita:	*I really like a beach with a playground, but it's far away in Maine. We went to a beach that's closer. It doesn't have swings and slides, but you can go there in an afternoon.*
Ms. Connors:	*Show us your picture, and tell us about the words you wrote.*
Anita:	*This is my family on the beach—my mom, dad, and my brother. I wrote anyu, apu, and Robi. Here is the ocean, the sun, and the sand. Tenger, nap, homok. And the razor clams that my dad got. They are called kagyló, but I just put clam. I am going to ask my mom how to write kagyló. Then, we are going to share the picture with my Magdi mama.*
Ms. Connors:	*Your Magdi mama must be very happy because you can write to her in Hungarian. Say those words again slowly, in your teacher voice. We can try our best to repeat them after you. Then, you can tell us how well we did.*

In the next vignette, Mateo, a dynamic bilingual sixth grader, is working on a word problem with Diego, who is a multilingual learner of English. Mateo chooses to use Spanish to teach Diego, a newcomer who doesn't know much English yet.

Translanguaging in the Math Classroom

Mateo:	*El primer ejemplo dice: A car uses 3 gallons of gas to go 96 miles. Express the miles to gallons as a ratio using different formats. Entonces, un auto usa 3 galones de gasolina en 96 millas. Vamos a escribir la relación entre galones y millas diferentes formas.*
Diego:	*Una forma es decir la razón 3 a 96 y otra forma as 3:96.*
Mateo:	*The ratio 3 to 96, which we can also write as 3:96. Another way to say it is 96 miles per 3 gallons and 32 miles per gallon. 96 millas por 3 galones y 32 millas por galón.*
Diego:	*Sí, otro formato es la fracción 3 sobre 96, y también en fracción común, 1/32.*
Mateo:	*Okay, we can use the fraction 3 over 96 and the simplified fraction 1 over 32.*

In the third vignette, Ana, a bilingual fourth grader of Mexican heritage, volunteers to read to the class a book of her choice in Spanish. She reads the text in short segments and explains to her classmates in English what is happening in the story, highlighting for them some key Spanish words they may want to learn.

Dynamic Bilingual Book Sharing in Language Arts

[Ana reads aloud from the Spanish-language version of the storybook Abuela *by Arthur Dorros, then explains what she has read in her own words.]*

Ana [reading aloud)]: *"Ella es la madre de mi mamá. En inglés 'abuela' se dice grandma. Ella habla español porque es la lengua que hablaba la gente del lugar donde nació antes de que ella viniera a este país. Mi abuela y yo siempre visitamos diferentes lugares."*

Ana [to class]: *So the little girl is saying that she calls her grandmother* abuela, *which is Spanish for grandmother. Because her grandmother came from a country where they speak Spanish. She and her grandma,* abuela, *I mean, are always visiting different places. You can see in this picture how they get on the bus to go together to visit a new place. They are sitting together, happy and dressed up very nicely.* ¡Me gustan sus vestidos de colores! ¡Van en un camión! *They are riding a bus.*

As teachers, one of our main responsibilities is to act mindfully to ensure that students feel accepted and included, regardless of accent or dialect or any perceived idiosyncrasy of language use. Effective teaching ensures that all students in the classroom community know that their home language is valued and that their multilingual abilities are an advantage, even as those abilities are developing (Cummins, 2001).

A Look Back and a Look Ahead

Chapter 2 has presented foundational information about second language learning, highlighting the following ideas:

- Competence in a language involves understanding and using five basic language components—phonology, morphology, syntax, semantics, and pragmatics—while reading, writing, listening, and speaking.

- The English language has a prominent role in instruction in U.S. schools, and programs are tasked with moving students to proficiency to meet their federal obligations. Multilingual learners of English can learn content through multimodal means, and they bring their own preexisting resources for learning to the classroom as well.

- The development of English language proficiency entails the control and length of utterances, the growth of vocabulary, and the mastery of language functions and registers. Academic English is an important variety of the English language that requires grade-level mastery of listening, speaking, reading, and writing skills.

- Multilingual learners of English bring a wealth of diverse strengths to their literacy development. Depending on their home language literacy, English learners may need to learn a new writing system. They may need to learn oral language and basic vocabulary at the same time that they are beginning to read. Keeping these learners motivated to read requires matching them with meaningful texts that hold their interest and do not contain too many unfamiliar words.

- Successful second language acquisition depends on five essential conditions: normal home language development, motivation, facilitative emotional conditions, usable input and feedback, and deliberate practice. Effective instruction must guarantee these as well as incorporate beneficial conditions: frequent interaction, avid reading, skills transfer from home language literacy, and strategy instruction. High-quality instruction maximizes comprehensible input by building on the language that students already know, giving them feedback frequently, and scaffolding their comprehension with multimodal input. Teachers promote motivation in the classroom by supporting student collaboration in a unified classroom community.

- Not all learners have the same challenges. It is easier to learn a new language if you have learned one before, if your first language is similar to English, and if you are literate in your first language.

- Multilingual learners of English need educators' backing to imagine and realize themselves as successful, high-functioning individuals whose abilities to communicate in multiple languages are valuable to the whole community.

- Educators can support language development by creating an inclusive learning environment that embraces students' diverse cultural backgrounds, leverages the power of technology, fosters social-emotional support in learning, and encourages students to navigate multiple languages fluently.

Chapter 3 illustrates classroom practices for The 6 Principles that undergird exemplary teaching of English learners:

1. Know your learners.
2. Create condition for language learning.
3. Design high-quality lessons for language development.
4. Adapt lesson delivery as needed.
5. Monitor and assess student language development.
6. Engage and collaborate within a community of practice.

As you read that chapter and explore The 6 Principles and related practices, apply the ideas about second language acquisition that Chapter 2 has presented. The 6 Principles derive from research-based understandings about how language develops in K–12 multilingual learners of English. Let those understandings about language acquisition serve as an essential backdrop as you move through Chapter 3.

We also encourage you to reflect on your own practice as you read about The 6 Principles. Consider what you know about your students and which aspects of their backgrounds may influence their second language development (Principle 1). Reflect on how you organize your classroom and bolster the positive conditions for language development (Principle 2). Evaluate how you keep students' language proficiency levels in mind when you plan and deliver lessons, and think about the ways in which you convey content knowledge. Do you use a large repertoire of nonlinguistic resources, embed mini-lessons of applicable English language functions and forms, and incorporate tasks that require students to interact and use language in authentic ways? (Principle 3). Reflect on what happens while you implement your lesson and how you make necessary adjustments through differentiation, scaffolding, or background building to improve student comprehension or task performance (Principle 4). Consider how you go about continually monitoring and giving feedback on your students' output of academic language on a class assignment or a summative assessment to ensure your students make timely progress in their language development (Principle 5). Finally, reflect on how you continually develop and strengthen your teaching through collaboration within a community of practice (Principle 6).

Additional resources pertaining to this chapter are available at www.the6principles.org/K-12.

3

THE 6 PRINCIPLES FOR EXEMPLARY TEACHING OF ENGLISH LEARNERS

Multilingual learners of English in the United States represent a wide range of backgrounds. Students come to school with many different needs and abilities, and the number of current and former multilingual learners of English is rising in U.S. schools. As a result, almost all K–12 teachers in U.S. schools have some of these students in their classes. Former multilingual learners of English are still language learners—most critically, in the area of academic English—and they sometimes still need instructional support in the classroom. Teachers of these students include English language development (ELD) and bilingual teachers, grade-level classroom and subject-area teachers, special education teachers, dual language teachers, bilingual teachers, and reading teachers, among others. Many ELD teachers are coteachers in grade-level and subject-area classrooms as well. Teachers who do not have an ELD or bilingual teaching certificate or endorsement, or targeted professional learning, may need specific guidance to work with students learning academic English at the same time that they are learning subject matter content in school.

As we discussed in Chapter 2, all students who have learned their home language can learn a new language, but doing so takes time, persistence, and deliberate and ongoing practice. Students need frequent opportunities for interaction so they can test their emerging language skills and receive feedback on their oral and written utterances. As we elaborated on in Chapter 2, research has identified essential and beneficial conditions for language acquisition that teachers can influence in the classroom, as well as challenges related to individual student factors that teachers should keep in mind.

Despite the challenges that teachers face in educating learners to a high level in both the English language and content knowledge, experienced teachers have achieved excellence by following key principles for effective English language education. This book presents these core tenets as The 6 Principles for Exemplary Teaching of English Learners®. This chapter describes each principle and identifies helpful classroom practices for teachers to implement and support that principle. The chapter also presents numerous examples that flesh out the practices and illustrate how they may be implemented in K–12 classrooms.

The 6 Principles for Exemplary Teaching of English Learners and Classroom Practices

1. **Know your learners.**
   1a. Teachers gain information about their learners.
   1b. Teachers embrace and leverage the resources that learners bring to the classroom to enhance learning.

2. **Create conditions for language learning.**
   2a. Teachers promote an emotionally positive and organized classroom.
   2b. Teachers demonstrate expectations of success for all learners.
   2c. Teachers plan instruction to enhance and support student motivation for language learning.

3. **Design high-quality lessons for language development.**
   3a. Teachers prepare lessons with clear outcomes and convey them to their students.
   3b. Teachers provide and enhance input through varied approaches, techniques, and modalities.
   3c. Teachers engage learners in the use and practice of authentic language.
   3d. Teachers integrate language and content learning.
   3e. Teachers design lessons that incorporate culturally responsive teaching practices.
   3f. Teachers plan differentiated instruction according to their learners' English language proficiency levels, needs, and goals.
   3g. Teachers promote the use of learning strategies and critical thinking among students.
   3h. Teachers promote students' self-regulated learning.

4. **Adapt lesson delivery as needed.**
   4a. Teachers check student comprehension frequently and adjust instruction according to learner responses.
   4b. Teachers adjust their talk, the task, or the materials according to learner responses.

5. **Monitor and assess student language development.**
   5a. Teachers monitor student errors.
   5b. Teachers strategically provide ongoing, effective feedback.
   5c. Teachers design varied and valid assessments and supports to assess student learning.
   5d. Teachers analyze and interpret assessment data for multilingual learners of English.

6. **Engage and collaborate within a community of practice.**
   6a. Teachers are fully engaged in their profession.
   6b. Teachers collaborate with colleagues.
   6c. Teachers develop leadership skills that enable them to become a resource in their schools.

Kim Kanter is a kindergarten teacher in south Florida. She has been teaching for 10 years and loves her job. One of her students, Juan Carlos, is having a difficult time adjusting to the classroom routines. Juan Carlos comes from a migrant family and is learning to speak English. To help manage his behavior, Kim asks Juan Carlos's father to meet with her. Kim proposes that she write home about the child's behavior daily. She suggests that on days when Juan Carlos has misbehaved, his father should enforce a small consequence.

"What should I do?" the father asks.

"Oh, maybe you can keep him from going on the Web," says Kim.

"We don't have internet services," the father replies.

"Well, then, don't let him ride his bicycle," answers Kim.

"Juan Carlos doesn't have a bicycle, Miss Kanter."

"Well, then, keep him indoors. Don't let him go outside to play."

"Miss Kanter, we don't have air conditioning. It's too hot to stay in the house all day."

Teachers can best adapt instruction to students they know well. Learning about students is time well spent. Basic information includes a student's name, the pronunciation and spelling of the name, home country, address, guardians' or parents' telephone numbers, emergency contacts, and health history. How will the student arrive and depart from school every day? Is the student an immigrant, a refugee, or a migrant, or was the student born in the United States? What languages does the student speak? And how much schooling has the student had? If school records exist, teachers can ask for translation assistance to determine the accumulated amount of instruction that the student has received. This information will help the teacher determine a learning plan and can clarify misconceptions such as those Miss Kanter had.

Values, traditions, social and political relationships, shared history, geographic location, language, social class, and religion determine many aspects of personality and lay out pathways for dealing with the world (Nieto & Bode, 2021). Learning about students' cultures helps teachers form reciprocal relationships with them more easily. This dynamic connection is pivotal for nurturing a productive and impactful learning environment. Beyond teachers having an understanding of their students, such relationships benefit students as well because they can become familiar with their teachers' personalities, teaching methods, and classroom expectations. The two-way interaction fosters effective communication and builds a foundation of trust and empathy to facilitate instruction. Figure 3.1 indicates areas for teachers to explore when getting to know new students and designing a learning plan for them.

FIGURE 3.1   What Teachers Need to Know About Their Learners

- Home country
- Home language
- Cultural background
- Level of proficiency in the four English domains (listening, speaking, reading, writing)
- Home language literacy level
- Home language oral proficiency
- Educational background
- Special needs
- Access to supportive resources

- Level of digital literacy and access to digital tools
- Learning preferences
- Cultural knowledge
- Life experiences
- Interests
- Gifts and talents
- Life goals
- Social-emotional background
- Sociopolitical context of home country

PRACTICE 1A   Teachers Gain Information About Their Learners

Teachers gather information regarding their students' linguistic and educational backgrounds, employing these insights as part of their teaching strategies and interpretation of assessment scores. This information ensures teachers can place students accurately at appropriate language learning levels and provides better ideas of what students can do with their language skills. Teachers also seek to learn about students' families, cultures, and geographic backgrounds as a resource for classroom learning. The fast growth of digital technologies has reshaped the data-gathering, organization, management, and analysis procedures in many districts and classrooms, helping educators process information more quickly, make better decisions, and support students.

The first and most important step in getting to know your learners is learning how to pronounce their names. Esther Park, a high school teacher in Virginia for 15 years, shares an engaging and thoughtful lesson titled "Teach Us Your Name" on her website (www.mrspark.org/free). The lesson is free to download.

Examples of Practice 1a

Teachers review student records and gather additional information on their backgrounds. Many local school districts and state agencies have developed systems to assist teachers in collecting the basic information outlined in Figure 3.1. Such information provides a holistic understanding of students' backgrounds and may help teachers create personalized plans for supporting their students' learning. Student records usually include a student's attendance and disciplinary records, grades, family address and contact information, and health records. Teachers may also use parent surveys to learn more about their students' special interests and skills, social and emotional needs, and academic support at home. Breiseith (n.d.) provides ideas for gathering information about your students.

Teachers gather information about new students' language skills from the registration process. A district or school administers a home language survey during school registration to identify potential multilingual learners of English. All families enrolling in school take the survey, not just those assumed to be multilingual. The survey typically includes three key questions:

1. What is the language primarily used at home, regardless of the language(s) spoken by the student?
2. Which language does the student speak most often?
3. What is the language that the student first acquired?

Students identified with a language other than English are then screened with a state-approved English proficiency language test (e.g., Initial English Language Proficiency Assessment for California, WIDA Screener) that measures their reading, writing, listening, and speaking skills. Some districts also interview parents about their child's prior education and may assess the child's numeracy and math skills and/or home language literacy. This information is used to either place multilingual learners appropriately into the language program in the district or determine that they do not need language services. Sample home language surveys in various languages can be found in Chapter 1 of the U.S. Department of Education, Office of English Language Acquisition's (2017) *English Learner Toolkit for State and Local Education Agencies.* Henry and colleagues (2017) provide a tool that districts can use to self-assess their home language survey process.

Teachers help students construct a personal profile, using digital tools as available. Students may include their self-portraits, personal drawings, written journal entries, and an interest inventory in their personal profiles. These profiles could be on paper or online. One effective way to have students create these profiles is for the teacher to set up a Google Forms survey at the beginning of the academic year. The survey could include questions about students' home language proficiency, preferred learning styles, how they use English and the home language outside of school, and specific challenges they face. These questions can be in students' home languages, and online translation tools can help teachers understand the responses. This tool organizes answers into a spreadsheet designed to track patterns among students easily and point out individual responses, automating the process rather than relying solely on teachers to analyze the data. In addition, the survey data help teachers plan lessons and ensure a personalized approach that successfully engages and supports each student.

Teachers organize and share information about learners. The collected information should be available to all the student's teachers. Districts often have a shared digital database that all teachers can access, allowing for an efficient and accurate collection and retrieval of details such as preferred names, English language proficiency levels, interests, learning styles, and other key information. It is important for districts to provide common guidelines for sharing information. As possible, gather a student's teachers together to communicate what you have learned to help determine an educational plan for each student.

PRACTICE 1B Teachers Embrace and Leverage the Resources That Learners Bring to the Classroom to Enhance Learning

Teachers purposefully tap their learners' prior knowledge in their teaching. They try to determine what gifts and talents students bring to the classroom, what interests motivate them, what life experiences they have had that relate to the curriculum, and what else in their backgrounds has influenced their personalities and beliefs.

Examples of Practice 1b

Teachers collect resources about students' home cultures and languages. Online resources will provide the most current information about a student's culture. Multiple sources are helpful. Speak with staff or community partners who share the same culture. Bear in mind that culture is not monolithic, nor is it stagnant. Not all individuals from a common geographic area share a common culture.

Teachers engage with parents or guardians to gain knowledge about students' experiences. Home visits (in person or virtual), parent coffee chats, translation services, and a warm smile can help put families at ease. Because teacher questioning may be intimidating for families who are vulnerable in a new and strange country, assure families that the information you seek about their children is only for the purpose of providing the best education plan for them. Technologies used in some districts enable teachers to communicate informally with families through texts that the teachers type in English and the program translates into a family's preferred language.

Teachers guide students in an autobiography project. As part of beginning-of-the-year community building, help all students gather and organize information about their lives—in words and pictures or through multimedia. For instance, students might use various mediums such as written narratives, drawings, and digital presentations to share their linguistic backgrounds, hobbies, and favorite things and events. Have students share their information with each other in pairs. Help students who are less proficient in English talk about themselves with the class. Encourage them to use their home language as needed.

Ms. Kaye, an elementary school teacher in Guam, designed the lesson "My Favorite Things" to get to know her students at the start of each school year. With her first- and second-grade classes, she first sings a simplified version of "My Favorite Things" from The Sound of Music *to introduce the concept. She next leads a brief class discussion and invites students to talk about their favorite things. She introduces target verbs such as* enjoy, like, *and* draw, *using facial expressions (e.g., doing something with a smiling face), gestures (e.g., thumbs-up or thumbs-down), and visual representations. As needed, she provides simple definitions and examples. Students then act out something they enjoy.*

After teaching the vocabulary, she instructs her multilingual learners of English to think about their favorite thing and draw a picture representing it. Students then come to the front of the class to introduce themselves and say what their favorite thing is while displaying their drawing. Ms. Kaye provides scaffolds to assist her students in using complete sentences, such as Hello, my name is _____ *and* One of my favorite things is _____. *As each student presents, Ms. Kaye provides positive reinforcement and directs classmates to listen attentively. To wrap up the lesson, she displays the lyrics of "My Favorite Things" with images for the unfamiliar items (e.g., whiskers, mittens) and engages the class in singing a portion of the song together, emphasizing pronunciation and rhythm.*

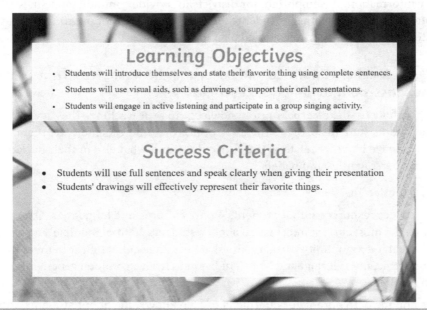

Learning Objectives

- Students will introduce themselves and state their favorite thing using complete sentences.
- Students will use visual aids, such as drawings, to support their oral presentations.
- Students will engage in active listening and participate in a group singing activity.

Success Criteria

- Students will use full sentences and speak clearly when giving their presentation
- Students' drawings will effectively represent their favorite things.

Image used with permission.

Teachers act as cultural mediators for students. When we provide opportunities for students to discuss differences or conflicts among cultures and analyze the variations between the mainstream culture and other cultural systems, we enable students to learn about and honor other cultures and clarify their ethnic identities. We help students develop positive cross-cultural relationships and teach them to avoid perpetuating prejudices, stereotypes, and racism. Our goal is to create a learning environment in the classroom that encourages learners from diverse backgrounds to celebrate and affirm their peers, work collaboratively for mutual success, and dispel powerlessness and oppression (Gay, 2018; TESOL International Association, 2018b).

Principle 2. Create Conditions for Language Learning

Ms. Anderson prepared a plan for her eighth-grade social studies class to assist a group of her multilingual learners of English, many of whom are Middle Eastern immigrants and refugees with different levels of English proficiency. For the unit on ancient civilizations of Egypt and Mesopotamia, she saw an opportunity to apply the power of digital storytelling to create an engaging language learning activity relevant to her students' lives and interests. Ms. Anderson arranged the desks in groups to foster collaboration and meaningful discussions. She adorned the walls with captivating posters featuring historical images and inspiring quotes, creating an immersive and motivational learning environment. She used diverse multimedia resources, websites, and books about ancient civilizations to cater to students' various learning styles.

To begin the unit, Ms. Anderson introduced the project, emphasizing how digital storytelling would allow students to apply their language skills and express themselves creatively while exploring their selected historical topics. She highlighted the opportunity for students to showcase their cultural insights, making the project personally meaningful to each student. She set achievable milestones throughout to celebrate their small successes, fostering a positive and rewarding learning journey. For the digital storytelling task, Ms. Anderson demonstrated user-friendly platforms for their Chromebooks: StoryMap JS, which enables students to create interactive maps with narration, and Book Creator, which allows them to craft multimedia-rich e-books with embedded text, images, and audio. Ms. Anderson was eager to see the digital storytelling projects her students would create. She believed this dynamic and interactive approach would leave a lasting impact, fostering a love for history, language learning, and creativity.

Multilingual learners of English come from many countries; speak many different languages; and may or may not be eager to leave the comfort of their home countries, friends, and family members to live in the United States. Teachers can respond to these understandable anxieties by creating a classroom culture that will ensure that new students feel safe and welcome in the class.

PRACTICE 2A Teachers Promote an Emotionally Positive and Organized Classroom

Teachers apply their knowledge of the positive conditions that promote language learning as they make decisions regarding the physical environment and the social integration of new students. They then plan for instruction that will engage new learners and ensure their success. They also recognize that a sense of emotional safety and belonging is crucial for effective learning. They design the classroom environment to not only support academic activities but also provide spaces that encourage emotional expression and peer collaboration.

Examples of Practice 2a

Teachers ensure that new students receive a warm welcome from their classmates. Although new students may not yet understand English, they can interpret facial gestures, and everyone can learn one another's names. A smile is understood in all languages.

Teachers design appropriate work spaces. Many classrooms have moveable furniture. To ensure that students can interact easily with others, ask for help, and work together on assignments, arrange classrooms with tables or desks in pairs or groups of four to facilitate communication among learners. Many schools have tablets for all students, but if not, a section of the room can have computer workstations. Designating some open space for activities that require movement, such as a task in which students physically form a timeline of key dates for an historical event, is useful.

When new students arrive, position their desks adjacent to those of other students and make sure the new students have the materials necessary to participate in class, such as a notebook and pencil or pen. Assign a nearby peer to help a new student utilize online learning tools: the equipment, classroom learning management systems, and apps. Tour the school with new students to point out locations of lockers or cubbies, bathrooms, the cafeteria, the gym, art and music rooms, the main office, the nurse's office, the counseling office, and other important areas.

Teachers organize the physical environment of the classroom to help students learn and use the new language. In elementary classrooms, wall spaces and bulletin boards are useful for displaying the alphabet, relevant vocabulary (with graphic support), and illustrations that communicate content information. In classes with beginners, classroom objects are labeled in English and ideally in learners' home languages. The side of the board is a convenient place for listing the day's schedule, perhaps with icons to communicate the time for reading, science, music, and other subjects. In secondary classrooms, listing some common sentence starters and language frames or critical reading strategies on the wall can be helpful. At all school levels, teachers should set aside one place in the room for posting the language and content objectives, and they can present the day's lesson outline electronically or written on the board. A classroom library with independent reading material is valuable.

Teachers organize online learning platforms with learners' access to technology and supports in mind. In today's schools, fueled by advancements in instructional technology, many students have experienced instruction via remote learning. When this situation arises, teachers need to consider what technology students have available at home and how they can get technical and academic support if needed. Teachers may have to build an online classroom culture by creating discussion norms with students and setting expectations for attendance and participation. Furthermore, clear task explanations can reduce confusion and empower students to navigate their online learning experience more confidently. Teachers can also facilitate students' online learning by organizing the learning management system files and modeling how to use apps and other programs. (See Hellman, 2021, for more ideas on how teachers can facilitate this use of technology.)

Teachers identify a mentor for each student. Peer mentoring helps new students learn classroom routines as they are guided throughout the day. The student mentor can help interpret the schedule for the new student, perhaps using pictures or gestures to communicate. Choose mentors carefully, with an eye to selecting learners with patience and compassion. The role should be celebrated and viewed positively in the classroom. Mentors can be even more important to have in a remote-learning environment. Mentors need guidance and support from the teacher.

Teachers use clear, patterned, and routine language to communicate with new learners. Teachers' use of patterned speech and language learning routines can be very helpful, particularly with beginners. This practice is seen in action when a kindergarten teacher sings the same "It's Clean-up Time" song each day, a middle school teacher routinely introduces new vocabulary in only two or three ways, and a high school teacher provides oral and written directions with a demonstration when introducing a subject-area assignment.

Teachers invite and support the use of students' home languages and cultures to build rich understandings. Classroom displays, books, and other resources reflect connections between home and new cultures and languages. Teachers connect content learning with students' current and prior understandings—for instance, they identify home language cognates in a science lesson, have their students study the rainforest by looking at pictures from students' home countries, or use culturally familiar goods to study economic trading practices.

Teachers facilitate social-emotional practices. We know that student well-being plays a role in academic performance. Teachers can incorporate activities such as regular check-ins, emotion identification, empathy building, sharing circles, and positive affirmations into classrooms to encourage students to explore different feelings and constructive ways to manage emotions in different situations (Lau & Shea, 2022).

PRACTICE 2B Teachers Demonstrate Expectations of Success for All Learners

Student achievement is affected by teachers' expectations of success. A teacher with high expectations will exhibit positive behaviors toward students, motivating them to perform at a high level because of the personal relationship enjoyed between teacher and student. A teacher who has little expectation of student success does not communicate positive emotions or build personal connections that lead to higher achievement in school. Multilingual learners of English have been subject to low expectations from many in the school community. Their peers realize that they are unable to communicate well in English and may be unaware of their proficient communication skills in another language. To overcome potential biases, teachers must hold high expectations in terms of behavior, effort, and learning goals and communicate these expectations clearly to all their students—both multilingual learners of English and their classmates.

> What is the culture of your school community regarding expectations for multilingual learners of English?

Examples of Practice 2b

Teachers demonstrate the belief that all students in the classroom will learn language and academic content to a high level. They state these expectations clearly and consider in advance how they will scaffold learning to ensure that all students are engaged and successful. They have plans to meet the needs of individuals, and they consistently implement those plans in accordance with clear expectations. (See Practice 3b for a discussion of scaffolding.)

Teachers praise students for effort and persistence to communicate how success is achieved. Praise is most useful when teachers are specific in their comments. Saying *Good job* does not communicate exactly what the student did that was good. A better comment might be *I like your organization of the math problem on the page. Your computation is clear and complete. Tell me what helped you the most in completing this math problem.* Praise of this sort will most likely lead the student to replicate the effort in math computation. Teacher language that values risk-taking and effort promotes a growth mindset (Dweck, 2006): *You got better because you practiced; You thought hard about that; Your effort is paying off; You figured it out!*

Teachers use a wide variety of instructional approaches to appeal to diverse learners. When teachers create conditions for learning, they consider student preferences and best practice based on second language acquisition research. This means that, at times, teachers may choose small-group or individualized learning or let students choose their partners. They may break down complex content and tasks into incremental, step-by-step processes. They may use alternative formats, such as computers, video, demonstrations, reenactments, and role-play. They may augment learning with art or music or engage in cooperative learning projects. These choices depend on learners' needs and interests.

Teachers promote students' self-efficacy in learning. Teachers who work intentionally with students to attain goals show commitment to ongoing improvement and student success. One way teachers can do this is by guiding students to take ownership of their learning by setting realistic goals, tracking progress, and reflecting on their own growth, reinforcing a sense of accomplishment as they strive for success. Such practices can engage students in self-directing their learning goals and foster college readiness (Conley & French, 2014).

PRACTICE 2C Teachers Plan Instruction to Enhance and Support Student Motivation for Language Learning

Learning a language is difficult and takes a very long time. There may not be a big incentive for young learners to dedicate time and effort to learn English if there is no early payoff. Adolescents may lose interest in language learning activities because they see English as outside their own cultural comfort zone or a threat to their identity. As the research we discussed in Chapter 2 makes clear, we know that motivation is an important condition for language learning, so teachers need to expend effort to engage their learners and motivate them to work persistently at learning a new language.

Examples of Practice 2c

Teachers prompt students to make connections from their learning to their own lives. When multilingual learners of English make connections between their lives and what they are learning, they feel like they are part of the classroom experience and can internalize their understanding of classroom concepts better. For example, elementary teachers may ask students to interview family members to gather information for constructing a family tree. Older students may relate their cross-cultural experience when reading stories that share elements of diverse cultural practices and historical contexts.

> *Loray James teaches third grade in a dual language classroom. This year her class has five students whose families have emigrated from Guatemala. The children have varying levels of language proficiency, but all of them are below grade level in their reading and writing skills. Loray decided to teach a social studies unit based on the agriculture, weather, vegetation, food, and customs of Guatemala. Her multilingual learners of English contribute to the topic by sharing family pictures, recipes, and descriptions of the places they lived in Guatemala. Loray has never seen her language learners participate so enthusiastically in their learning. They love reading the books that she found about their country.*

Teachers build a repertoire of learning tasks that students enjoy and experience as inherently motivating. Teachers continually add new teaching ideas to their knowledge base and select from them strategically to inspire students to learn. Some examples include game-like activities, tasks structured as play, experiential activities, storytelling, simulations, experiments, rehearsed performances, role-plays, songs, chants, and real-world case studies. When student choice plays a part in the selection of learning tasks, students are more involved and motivated to learn. When students are familiar with the activities, they can focus more on the content than on the directions.

Teachers use technology applications to craft engaging activities that develop a stronger connection to language learning. Thoughtful lessons enhance motivation for language learning, especially personalized lessons and interactive tasks that align with students' interests and needs. Including visuals, audio clips, and sample sentences may make learning more vivid and accessible, boosting students' interest and curiosity. Incorporating gamified features such as quizzes, games, and collaborative tasks also develops a sense of competition and collaboration. Teachers may also provide real-time feedback and track progress, giving students a sense of accomplishment as they observe their growth over time.

Teachers help students focus on a well-defined project with a future outcome to motivate and structure their behavior. Problem-based and project-based learning improve classroom dynamics by engaging learners in an important group task with a well-defined outcome. Teachers choose projects or problems that have connections with students' lives—for instance, testing water samples in the school fountains, growing vegetables hydroponically in city environments, designing a new playground, or saving the town's remaining Gingko trees. When students can relate classroom content to real-world applications, they are more likely to see the relevance of what they are learning, which makes the tasks more motivating.

Teachers expect student ownership and support students' engagement with learning. When students are engaged in their learning, they process concepts more deeply. They are open to thinking out loud, venturing opinions, seeking comprehension, entering discussions, and questioning to examine ideas. Teachers promote student ownership when, for example, they establish peer-to-peer discourse opportunities, either in person or via remote learning, or when they ensure that student choice is considered in classroom learning opportunities.

Principle 3. Design High-Quality Lessons for Language Development

Mary DeCosta teaches world history in a high school in a large city in California. Ten students in her class of 24 are multilingual learners of English, and 6 more are former multilingual learners of English. All 16 are Spanish speakers. As a cumulative project for the unit on the Renaissance period, students will prepare a report on an enduring contribution from the arts or sciences of that time. Rather than assigning written reports, Mary has decided that this class will create videos with an annotated list of sources. Mary writes out the unit objectives, explains them clearly, and lets the students know that they can conduct the research by using English or Spanish sources. She also shows student-made videos from her U.S. history class that model the academic language register that she expects from her students. In addition, Mary meets one-on-one with her multilingual learners of English and asks them to describe what they are expected to know or be able to do at the end of the project.

To design high-quality lessons, teachers must plan carefully. They must include specific language development goals to advance students' proficiency over time, and they should target other learning objectives as well to make lessons meaningful and relevant. Explicitly teaching to these goals, selecting appropriate materials, designing tasks for students to practice and then apply the knowledge they are gaining, and providing scaffolds and supports to enable participation and achieve success are critical for maximum learning to occur.

Students are not sponges absorbing new information; rather, they need to be active participants constructing meaning and making connections to what they know and have experienced. Effective teachers design lessons that promote the development of learning and thinking strategies. Mayer (1992) lists three mental processes that are necessary to meaningful learning:

1. selection of information to be learned and added to working memory

2. organization of information into a coherent whole

3. integration of organized information into the prior knowledge structures of the learner

Careful lesson planning can support the application of these mental processes when students are learning a new language and new content.

PRACTICE 3A Teachers Prepare Lessons With Clear Outcomes and Convey Them to Their Students

Teachers can guide students to a lesson's essential language learning and content more efficiently if teachers and students are both aware of the intended outcomes of the learning experience. All teachers should have language and content objectives in each lesson. Learning strategy objectives are also beneficial.

Examples of Practice 3a

Teachers determine language and content objectives for their lessons. Consider the following when planning:

To determine content objectives, ask these questions:

- What specifically do I want my students to know or be able to do with the informational content by the end of the lesson?
- Is my objective grade-appropriate?
- Does my objective derive from a state content standard of a subject students are studying?
- Is my objective cognitively challenging?

- How can I communicate the objective to my students?
- Is my objective measurable?
- What contextual supports can I provide for learning?

(Echevarría et al., 2024)

To determine language objectives, ask these questions:

- What specifically do I want my students to be able to say, read, or write by the end of the lesson?
- What specific language structures and vocabulary are necessary to convey the content?
- What grammatical forms do I want my students to use and understand?
- What language functions do my students need to use to be successful in this lesson?
- How can I communicate the objective to my students?
- Can my objective be measured?
- What contextual supports can I provide for learning?

(Echevarría et al., 2024)

To determine learning strategy objectives, ask these questions:

- What learning strategy will I teach or demonstrate to help my students learn more efficiently?
- How can my students practice this strategy?
- Is my objective measurable?
- Is my objective age-appropriate?
- How can I communicate my objective to my students?

(Levine & McCloskey, 2013)

Teachers communicate learning objectives to students. Simply telling students about the learning objectives is not sufficient for many multilingual learners of English. It is always preferable to write the objectives down, read them aloud, and then demonstrate what a successful outcome might look or sound like (Echevarría et al., 2024). For example, given the language objective *Orally explain the solution to a math problem using past tense and sequence words*, a teacher might demonstrate how to describe the completion of a math problem in this way: *This is how I completed the math problem. I had to use subtraction because _____. First, I _____. Then I _____.* Content objectives can be successfully communicated in a similar manner. However, it may be helpful to show exemplars (e.g., sample essays, a poster exhibit, a well-documented science lab report) of the eventual outcome of the lesson or unit objectives.

Sample Language and Content Objectives

Grade and Subject	Language Objective	Content Objective
Kindergarten social studies	Students will use adjectives to describe the physical environment. (*The [object/ landform/plant] is [adjective].*)	Students will read a map and identify natural resources.
Grade 4 science	Students will explain cause and effect in a lab report, using ___ *happened because ...* or ___ *is the result of ...*	Students will conduct an experiment to determine factors that affect plant growth.
Grade 7 language arts	Students will propose an alternate ending for the story with a partner.	Students will identify the main plot and setting in a short story.
High school algebra	Students will explain orally how to graph a linear equation, using sequence words.	Students will solve linear equations.

Note. English language arts teachers sometimes ask how language objectives differ from language arts objectives because their curricular content is language. We suggest that these teachers divvy up the language content. They can write language objectives to focus on the language forms and functions necessary to process or demonstrate knowledge of the content. Language functions are the purposes for which language is used (e.g., to describe, propose, compare, determine cause and effect). Language forms are the grammatical structures of words and sentences (e.g., irregular past tense verbs, comparatives and superlatives, complex sentences, adverbial clauses). The teachers can then write language arts content objectives to focus on reading and writing skills (Echevarría et al., 2024; Levine & McCloskey, 2013).

Teachers review learning objectives at the end of the lesson. The teacher and the students will benefit from reviewing what they have learned at the end of the lesson. By returning to the language, content, and learning strategy objectives at the close, students can reflect on their learning, and teachers can assess whether their goals were met. Teachers might ask students to complete an exit ticket, rate their level of understanding (e.g., 1 = I know it, 2 = I'm getting there, 3 = I need more time and support), or tell a partner what they learned or questions they still have.

PRACTICE 3B Teachers Provide and Enhance Input Through Varied Approaches, Techniques, and Modalities

Comprehensible and enhanced input is necessary for communicating with language learners. To prepare to meet this need, teachers ask themselves questions regarding the implementation of the lesson:

- How will the new information be conveyed to my students?
- Will they listen to it, read it, or engage in research or an inquiry task to discover it?
- How can I support the input with context and scaffolding?
- How can I be sure that my students understand my input?

Examples of Practice 3b

Teachers use comprehensible input to convey information to students. Comprehensible input is of primary importance for progress in the target language. Whether oral or written, comprehensible input helps learners understand the meaning of what is being communicated. Teachers can adjust language input in multiple ways to aid learners in processing new information and to promote understanding. There are many strategies and techniques teachers can use to increase comprehension, both in terms of their actions and instructional decisions and in terms of the tools they use to convey knowledge. Table 3.1 provides examples of these actions and tools; multiple strategies are often used in a given lesson.

Table 3.1	Strategies and Techniques for Improving Comprehensibility
Teacher Actions	**Tools for Comprehensibility**
<ul><li>Gesturing and using facial expressions</li><li>Illustrating and using visuals</li><li>Adjusting rate and complexity of speech</li><li>Enunciating clearly and using intonation and stress to emphasize information</li><li>Using repetition</li><li>Simplifying or elaborating</li><li>Relying on high-frequency vocabulary</li><li>Embedding definitions and explanations</li><li>Preteaching key words</li><li>Preteaching text genres and structures</li><li>Building background or activating prior knowledge</li><li>Explaining in the home language (or asking classmates to explain)</li><li>Writing down key words for students to see during an explanation or video</li><li>Providing written summaries in the home language</li><li>Modeling, demonstrating, and acting out</li><li>Conducting think-alouds</li><li>Giving students more time to process new information</li></ul>	<ul><li>Visual aids, such as<ul><li>» maps, charts, graphs, and graphic organizers</li><li>» presentation slides</li><li>» drawings, illustrations, and photos</li><li>» physical objects</li><li>» video clips</li></ul></li><li>Manipulatives and other hands-on materials</li><li>Multimedia, including interactive videos and programs with embedded supports and comprehension checks</li><li>Audiovisual supports, such as<ul><li>» real-time transcription software</li><li>» text read-aloud tools</li><li>» closed captions (in English or home language)</li></ul></li><li>Translation tools</li><li>Highlighted or bold text</li><li>Bilingual glossaries</li><li>Picture dictionaries</li><li>Simplified English and home language summaries</li><li>Texts at different reading levels</li><li>Study guides</li><li>Anchor charts and word walls</li><li>Exemplars of student work</li></ul>

Source: Coelho (2012); Echevarría et al. (2024); Gibbons (2015); Levine et al. (2013)

Typically, but not always, learners are first provided with comprehensible oral language input, especially if they have not yet acquired literacy in another language. If multilingual learners of English are already literate in another language, teachers may offer both oral and written input. The dual modalities complement each other and provide further support for meaning, especially for older learners.

School language uses an academic register, which is the register of academic texts and instruction. As we learned in Chapter 2, academic language is denser and more complex than social language. It has many abstract terms and offers limited support by means of graphics, pictures, or other forms of scaffolding. Consequently, multilingual learners of English typically acquire social, or conversational, language first if they have sufficient amounts of accessible input. Social language is the language of the playground, the school lunch table, hallway chats, and social media posts. Learners can use the gestures, high-frequency vocabulary, and context of the social conversation to clue in to the meaning of the utterances. (See Chapter 2 for a thorough discussion of the components of academic register and the distinction between social and academic language.)

Bilingual and dual language classrooms provide multiple opportunities for multilingual learners of English to receive comprehensible input. The home language is accessible through classroom peers, teacher explanation, or technology. Content subjects taught in the home language may be reviewed in English. Having knowledge of the content enhances a learner's ability to make hypotheses about the meaning of the input.

Teachers adjust their language to enhance input to students. When teachers enhance input, they make it more usable for multilingual learners of English, who may then perceive target features of the language more clearly. The enhancements used by teachers may be verbal or visual. For example, teachers

- speak clearly;
- speak at a slower rate for beginners and at a normal rate for advanced learners;
- use varied repetition;
- use gestures as clues to meanings;
- use word stress, intonation, and pauses purposefully (perhaps with exaggeration);
- recast learners' language in ways that approach the target usage;
- contrast forms (e.g., academic vs. creative writing, public speaking vs. casual conversation);
- use fewer pronouns in extended talk;
- avoid idioms, jargon, and slang;
- avoid rapid language and vowel reduction;
- write down key words as they speak; and
- elicit oral production or elaboration from learners.

> Be sure to face students when conveying information orally. Facial expressions and gestures aid in comprehension, and your voice will be clearer. You can gain their attention better, too.

Teachers use multiple sources of input. When teachers add visuals, graphic organizers, and vocabulary or audio supports to written text, they increase the comprehensibility of the material. Peer reading offers further assistance to students who are struggling with text. Other sources of input include

- movies, video, and internet sites (carefully curated);
- online programs, apps, and other technology;
- paired talk or paired reading;
- peer tutoring;
- small-group discussion; and
- presentations accompanied by visuals, charts, and peer support.

Teachers utilize technology to personalize input to meet student needs. Technology tools can create an individualized learning experience and give students some autonomy to determine the supports they need to comprehend new material that they encounter in a digital mode. Here are some examples:

- Some online reading programs offer links to definitions or translations of words in a story. Students decide whether or not they need to click the link to understand a word.
- Students may listen to text read aloud, in English or perhaps their home language, while they follow along on their screen. They may pause where desired or listen to the text multiple times.
- Microsoft Learning Accelerators, particularly Reading Coach and Immersive Reader, offer customizable reading levels, interactive vocabulary support, multimodal learning experiences, progress tracking, and scaffolding techniques (TESOL International Association, 2023).

- Edpuzzle, an online educational technology platform, provides options for teachers to add audio voice-overs to video content, which can include descriptions, explanations, or other supports in English (perhaps at a slower rate with simpler sentence structure) or in the student's home language. Closed captioning is possible as well.

- With the flipped learning approach, students watch videos of instruction at home the day before the class and can pause or replay as needed. During class, they are more actively engaged in discussion and activities and can ask questions about the content.

These features are valuable for multilingual learners of English in contexts where additional linguistic support may be necessary.

Teachers communicate clear instructions to carry out learning tasks. Teachers use and teach consistent classroom management practices and routines throughout the school year in an effort to help students understand what is expected of them in a classroom and throughout a lesson. Teachers use simple directions with patterned language that they repeat each time. For example, teachers may gain the attention of students through patterned hand clapping or simple attention-getting schemes (*One, two, three, eyes on me*). They use the same gestures with each direction (saying *Turn to page 33* while holding up the text). They use signals for behavioral management as well, such as placing a hand behind an ear (to indicate *Listen*) or pointing to the eyes (to indicate *Look*).

Remember that multistep directions can be broken down into step-by-step procedures, with each step modeled as needed, depending on the learners' language proficiency, and written, oral, and pictorial clues can further aid comprehension. If we want students to perform a task well, we have to begin by showing them *how* to do it.

When introducing a new activity, teachers often use familiar content so students can concentrate on the procedure and learn the steps. Then teachers use that activity with new content.

PRACTICE 3C Teachers Engage Learners in the Use and Practice of Authentic Language

We know that language skills grow through interaction. Students are motivated to attend and participate in classroom conversations and knowledge construction when teachers deliver lessons that engage them with relevant and meaningful content and include speaking, listening, reading, and writing activities. In these activities, students need to use authentic language and practice it in authentic ways. Inauthentic language activities like decontextualized substitution drills, rote memorization, and static scripted dialogues will not prepare students for the advanced communication skills they need in the 21st century, nor will they motivate students to put in the time and effort necessary to become proficient in the new language. (See Chapter 2 for further discussion of more considerations for supporting language development in multilingual classrooms.)

Examples of Practice 3c

Teachers elicit output from students. Listening, speaking, reading, and writing are interrelated processes that rely on and develop in conjunction with one other in a dynamic way. Listening to oral language input is a receptive process, as is reading. Both processes require an active and engaged mind to construct meaning from the speech or the text. Speaking and writing are productive processes. Students use their evolving knowledge of English to express their thoughts and ideas. For most students, speaking helps them develop the ability to write in the target language.

Speaking a new language requires a high level of focus on grammar forms, vocabulary selection, and fluency to make the message understandable to the listener. Speaking helps learners notice a mismatch between what they *want* to say and what they *can* say. If the listener does not understand, the learner modifies output to make meaning more clear.

One simple way to increase student talk in class is to ask more open-ended questions. By asking questions such as *Why?* and *How?* or by prompting students to elaborate (*Can you tell me more about that? What else did you learn?*), teachers elicit longer utterances rather than a one- or two-word responses. Another strategy is to increase wait time. Many teachers wait only 1 or 2 seconds after asking a question before answering it themselves. Instead, pause 4 or 5 seconds to allow for basic recall questions and longer (7–10 seconds) for more complex questions.

Learning to write is similar to learning to speak, but the immediacy is not always present. In many classrooms, students' academic writing is not read and responded to as quickly as an utterance is in a conversation. Nonetheless, students need to practice writing a variety of texts and get feedback. Wide reading offers students models for their own writing.

To design activities that will elicit authentic output, teachers need to consider how language is really used in academic classrooms and other settings where students will need to use English. We do not want students sitting silently listening to a teacher for the whole period. Instead, they must actively practice using English and participate in tasks such as group discussions, daily writing assignments, and literature circles.

Teachers create opportunities for learners to be active participants. Language is best learned while *doing* something—by being actively engaged with it as a listener, speaker, reader, or writer and applying it through deliberate practice. Conditions teachers have created in the classroom environment as part of Principle 2, such as arranging desks in groups and posting anchor charts and word walls, will facilitate student participation. For virtual instruction, assigning students purposefully to breakout groups and using tools like Flip will encourage interaction.

Teachers may establish collaborative groups in their classrooms as a way to include all learners in the classroom conversation. Groups that are carefully constructed, with attention to gender, personality, language proficiency, and knowledge levels, can promote productive classroom talk. Tasks that groups are assigned should enable students to practice elements of language they have been studying. Features that lead to successful group work (Frey & Fisher, 2009; Gibbons, 2015) include

- providing clear expectations,
- teaching group procedures,
- establishing and modeling a clear outcome,
- integrating content and language learning,
- requiring talk, and
- building small-group skills (e.g., active listening, taking different perspectives, providing constructive feedback to peers).

To support multilingual learners of English in achieving a high level of proficiency, teachers help them make their talk accountable. Accountable talk requires that students explain their thinking with evidence; they justify a claim or opinion. It also requires that they listen, reflect, and respond constructively to others while raising issues or solving problems (Michaels et al.,

2013; Zwiers, 2019). Teachers can assist in productive classroom talk by posing questions and prompts such as the following:

- Explain what you mean.
- So, you are saying …
- Do you agree or disagree with that?
- Why do you think that?
- What have we discovered?
- What do you think?
- Who can add on?

Some of our students may be newcomers with no or limited proficiency in English. If we think back to the discussion of asset-based instruction in Chapter 2, we can see how encouraging students to share their knowledge and ideas in their home language lets them use that language as a strategic resource. If they do not know the words yet in English but can convey meaning in their home language, they are not excluded from the academic conversation. They can demonstrate their learning while also being introduced to the English words or forms they do not yet know—in the teachable moment.

Teachers use techniques to promote active language practice at every stage of the lesson. Many techniques assist teachers in providing variety to classroom lessons and encouraging language development (Levine et al., 2013; Vogt & Echevarría, 2022). Different techniques are useful at various stages of a lesson, as illustrated in the examples in Table 3.2.

Table 3.2	Language Practice Techniques Throughout a Lesson
Starting Instruction	• Making predictions • K-W-L chart (Know-Want to Know-Learn) • Four corners vocabulary chart • Anticipation guides • Language experience approach
Building Instruction	• Sentence frames • Directed reading-thinking activity • Reciprocal teaching • Concept maps • T-charts
Applying Instruction	• Dialogue journals • Reader's theatre • Role-plays • Group presentations
Concluding Instruction	• Rubrics • Collaborative dialogues • Comprehension checks • Numbered heads together • Kahoot!

Teachers encourage language learning beyond the classroom. Although some learners may live in areas where English is not routinely spoken, teachers should encourage authentic language learning and practice through activities outside the classroom. School clubs, sport teams, and community or religious organizational activities can offer this authentic practice. Useful input can result from paying attention to the media and the arts (e.g., film, television, music, newspapers, internet). Social media, although not always a source of grammatical accuracy, can help students expand their vocabulary and communicate with others. It offers them a practical and engaging way to acquire words and popular cultural knowledge while connecting with a global community of users. Students can also engage in discussions on online platforms or explore educational content on video-streaming channels. The informal and conversational nature of social media usually allows students to understand how words are used colloquially. In addition, teachers can encourage language interaction through tasks such as interviewing a grandparent, reading to a sibling, and going to the public library. High school students might have a part-time job or internship where they can practice English too.

> Examples, descriptors, and models of many of the strategies mentioned in this chapter can be found in *The GO TO Strategies: Scaffolding Options for Teachers of English Language Learners, K–12* (Levine et al., 2013), a free downloadable resource.

PRACTICE 3D Teachers Integrate Language and Content Learning

In the United States, teachers must integrate language and content learning for school-age multilingual learners of English. Whether they are in a bilingual, dual language, or ELD program, these learners will have some subject-area classes taught in English and will have to take high-stakes tests written in English. Moreover, they do not have time to learn the language first, before studying the core curriculum subjects. Students are expected to be able to read about the content, construct meaning, understand and participate in classroom discussions, make inferences, cite examples of major constructs, and determine cause-and-effect relationships, among other tasks. Content also serves as the vehicle for language development, so teachers with primary responsibility for language development incorporate vocabulary, reading, and writing activities that reflect the content areas that their learners study (Echevarría et al., 2024; Levine & McCloskey, 2013; Staehr Fenner & Snyder, 2017).

Examples of Practice 3d

Teachers become familiar with the language demands of different subject areas. Each content area requires specific vocabulary and syntactic structures that may or may not overlap with generalized knowledge of English. Here are a few characteristics and challenges of the language used in different content areas:

- **The language of history and social studies** has abstract, multiple-meaning vocabulary and complex sentence forms with embedded clauses, logical connectors, and reported speech. Passive voice is common, and subject referents are buried in the middle of sentences. Teaching methodology in the social sciences often relies on textbook readings that are dense and beyond the reading levels of many multilingual learners of English. Teachers of the social studies use abundant scaffolding to help these students read texts, and they employ oral language strategies to convey information. Dialogues, oral history, role-play, historical reenactments, and viewing multimedia are some examples of alternative teaching techniques.

- **The language of mathematics** is specific, precise, clearly expressed, and logical. Mathematical language is a required aspect of standardized testing. Multilingual learners of English can succeed in math when their teachers use extensive oral and written practice of mathematical reasoning in math lessons. Students learn how to initiate and respond to questions and discuss and explain math while using math vocabulary and grammar. The use of visuals, think-aloud modeling, manipulatives, frequent and varied repetition, demonstrations, and small-group work all promote mathematical reasoning and language.

- **The language of science** has specific vocabulary, and concepts require abstract reasoning. However, science has the benefit of offering hands-on learning opportunities. *Doing science*, rather than reading about science, is an effective methodology for multilingual learners of English. By exploring the world around them, students learn how to make observations, ask questions, investigate solutions, and communicate results. The context of the "here and now" provided by laboratory sciences promotes comprehension and achievement. Science teachers are effective instructors for our students when they model and demonstrate; use varied grouping; relate learning to prior experiences; and use manipulatives, visuals, graphs, advance organizers, and active experimentation.

- **The language of language arts** is quite varied and can include aspects of the other subject areas because students read, write, and discuss both fiction and nonfiction texts. Besides concrete and abstract concepts, multiple-meaning vocabulary, and complex sentence forms with embedded clauses, logical connectors, and reported speech, texts include dialogue as written in story or interview formats and in plays. Students will often encounter language that is not modern or commonplace in the United States (e.g., Shakespearean dialogue, global Englishes in multicultural texts). A benefit of the language arts classroom is that students often engage in practice with all four language skills (reading, writing, listening, and speaking) as they work with texts. Language arts teachers also teach grammar, usage, mechanics, and spelling, all of which are useful for multilingual learners of English. Critical-thinking skills (e.g., literacy response and analysis) and opportunities to use creativity (e.g., writing and performing texts across multiple genres; writing scaffolds that clarify the student's *role* as the writer, in addition to the *audience*, *format*, and *topic* [RAFTs]) are supported. ELD curriculum frameworks align with or lead into English language arts frameworks.

Teachers consult with colleagues to support multilingual learners of English in grade-level or content classrooms. Learning what multilingual learners of English are studying (and will be studying in the near future) and what your colleagues perceive as challenges for your students can help you craft pertinent content objectives for ELD lessons. Objectives might center around building background for an upcoming history topic, introducing elements of a short story, or teaching basic math symbols, for example. Language objectives might include preteaching vocabulary or teaching reading and writing skills that will be needed. In addition, ELD teachers can address confusing concepts or clear up any misconceptions regarding information that has already been taught in grade-level and content classrooms. Such collaboration among teachers takes coordination, but working together in this manner can have a positive effect on these learners' academic outcomes (Honigsfeld & Dove, 2019; Martin-Beltran & Peercy, 2014).

Teachers introduce common academic tasks and provide practice opportunities. Teachers can help multilingual learners of English be more successful in their subject-area classes when they instruct them in how to perform common activities. For students who are in middle or high school and new to U.S. schools, this practice is particularly helpful. In these secondary grades, most content teachers expect students to know how to create a timeline and outline, cite evidence from a text, identify operational words in a math word problem, write a topic sentence, complete graphic organizers like Venn diagrams and T-charts, and follow directions for a science experiment because these tasks are regularly taught and practiced in the elementary grades. Even multilingual learners of English who entered school at the elementary level may need more assistance with the academic language involved in completing some of these tasks to a high level.

Helping Students With Academic Tasks

As teachers help students with academic tasks, they should keep several things in mind:

- Steps to complete the task. How can the procedures be conveyed clearly to multilingual learners of English? What familiar information can I use to demonstrate the steps?
- Language embedded in the task. What language (e.g., vocabulary, forms) do students need to know to understand the task and perform it? What scaffolds (e.g., sentence frames) can I provide to guide their language production as they complete the task?
- Purpose of the task. How might this task help students meet a lesson's objectives?

While instructing students in how to do these tasks, teachers are building students' academic language skills as well. Furthermore, they are preparing students for assessments because some of these tasks appear on district and state tests. As students learn about and practice the task, some might use their home language. This allows them to participate and develop a cognitive understanding of the procedures. Over time, teachers should revisit a task and apply it to new learning objectives, at which time they can guide students toward speaking or writing in English to complete it.

PRACTICE 3E Teachers Design Lessons That Incorporate Culturally Responsive Teaching Practices

Culturally responsive teaching is a pedagogical approach that goes beyond just acknowledging students' diverse backgrounds; it recognizes and values the assets students bring to the classroom, such as their lived experiences, home language skills, multicultural knowledge, talents, and dispositions (e.g., perseverance) and taps into these assets during lessons (Au, 2009; Gay, 2018; Hammond, 2015; Lau & Shea, 2022; Stembridge, 2020). Culturally responsive teachers hold high expectations for their students. In doing so, they communicate a belief in their students' abilities and motivate the students to strive for progress. Culturally responsive teachers promote respectful communication and open discussion to different cultural perspectives. Students are encouraged to make connections between what they learn and their own values, beliefs, and worldviews. Teachers can use information about students' social and cultural identities as a basis for lesson activities. When these identities are affirmed and integrated into the school experience, students recognize themselves within the classroom and school community—a powerful form of empowerment.

An eighth-grade multilingual teacher in North Carolina, Mrs. Jacaranda, explores the importance of empathy and acceptance with her students. The lesson begins with students reading aloud the displayed content and language objectives. Students then analyze how dialogue reveals aspects of a character from the book I Am Not Your Perfect Mexican Daughter *by Erika Sánchez.*

Mrs. Jacaranda: Let's read this line again: "She is always apologizing to white people, which makes me feel embarrassed. And then I feel ashamed of my shame." We are going to stop and think about what she means by saying this. Let's use our technique: Stop, Think, Write, Read, and Share.

Students write their thoughts in their dialogue journals and read them to their partner. Translanguaging and sketch noting are encouraged to help students build confidence to participate in discussions.

Mrs. Jacaranda: What does Julia mean when she says, "I feel ashamed of my shame?"

Maria: Porque no cree que su madre necesite sentirse inferior a nadie. Ella debería ser egual to the people. No shame.

Examples of Practice 3e

Teachers plan tasks that are culturally relevant and interesting to students. Relating learning tasks to the cultural heritage of your learners ensures that they will engage with the classwork. For example, students from countries with a culture of oral storytelling will respond well when prompted, "Share your own stories or folktales." Students who value music and dance in their cultures can be asked to choose songs that represent characteristics of the fictional figures being studied. Additionally, teachers can integrate technology into their lessons to foster student engagement with culturally responsive content. They can encourage collaborative projects such as podcasts, video presentations, or multimedia products that address real-world issues from a culturally responsive perspective. For example, students from diverse backgrounds could work on issues that threaten environmental resources. They could explore how their cultures traditionally value and protect the environment and propose environmentally sustainable solutions. Under close teacher supervision, students can create impactful social media content that showcases their cultural connections. This approach enables students to address real-world challenges, connect authentically with their cultural backgrounds, and engage in a rich and meaningful learning experience.

Teachers uncover the funds of knowledge in students' households. Families and their communities have a wide range of knowledge and experiences that they use in their daily lives and cultural practices (Gonzalez et al., 2005). Teachers can find out about these funds through home visits, parent coffee chats, online gatherings, and surveys, then use them in the classroom for concept and skill development and family engagement activities. Students' narratives about family often reflect diverse experiences, such as customs and traditions, immigration or migration journeys, and their connections with home culture, which shape their identity and understanding of their cultural roots.

> What have you learned about culturally responsive teaching that you may incorporate into your instruction?

Teachers select materials that reflect students' backgrounds and interests. When teaching literature, teachers may choose stories from their students' literary traditions: myths, folktales, novels, drama, film, and poetry. For other content areas, speeches, news articles, bookmarked home language websites, and other culturally relevant material may supplement a lesson. Teachers may also choose nonfiction stories (e.g., biographies) that include historical figures with a similar cultural background as their students. Texts may be in the students' home languages or English. To increase motivation, teachers allow students to choose materials for research or independent reading.

Teachers integrate social-emotional learning and culturally responsive teaching. This approach is grounded in the understanding that effective teaching goes beyond simply imparting academic knowledge; it also involves creating an inclusive and affirming learning space where students from diverse backgrounds can thrive both emotionally and academically. The pedagogical approach of integrating culturally responsive social-emotional learning in literacy instruction (e.g., CULTURE model proposed by Lau & Shea, 2022) not only prioritizes the development of literacy skills in multilingual learners of English but also emphasizes the fostering of trusting relationships among peers and between students and teachers, all while nurturing students' social-emotional skills (e.g., developing empathy, having positive social interactions, learning self-awareness).

Teachers create space for translanguaging. Multilingual learners of English may use the languages they know strategically to access content and participate in their classes. When they embrace translanguaging, teachers send a powerful message to their students that multilingualism is not a hindrance, but rather a valuable resource in the classroom. Translanguaging invites the sharing of diverse perspectives and enables students to engage in class activities with depth and meaning. Learners, especially those at the beginning stage of developing English proficiency, can fluidly draw from their linguistic repertoire and use language tools (e.g., bilingual picture dictionaries, digital translation resources) to enhance their comprehension of literary texts, scientific articles, or concepts in mathematics. Mohamed (2021) provides more practices that can be used to incorporate translanguaging into the classroom.

PRACTICE 3F Teachers Plan Differentiated Instruction According to Their Learners' English Language Proficiency Levels, Needs, and Goals

Differentiated instruction is an instructional approach that provides students with multiple pathways to learning by offering supports and enrichment. The academic and linguistics needs of multilingual learners of English in K–12 classrooms sometimes differ from the needs of students who are proficient in English. Teachers who differentiate instruction first learn the needs of their learners through observation and interaction, then plan and deliver instruction based on those needs to ensure all students can participate in class.

Delivering academically rigorous instruction is an important tenet in U.S. schools. Teachers are discouraged from watering down the curriculum. Differentiation requires that teachers scaffold instruction for student success rather than reduce the complexity of instructional goals (Tomlinson, 2014). Teachers may adjust the supports they provide (e.g., using a word bank or texts at different reading levels), the task or product (e.g., beginners write one paragraph and advanced students write five paragraphs), or student groupings (e.g., small groups, pairs, one-on-one with the teacher) as needed for a given lesson and learning objective (Fairbairn & Jones-Vo, 2019). A key goal of differentiation is to provide equitable access to content for all learners.

Examples of Practice 3f

Teachers build scaffolding into lessons for different purposes. Various forms of scaffolding help all students succeed. Teachers structure learning in incremental steps and provide assistance to the level that the learner needs to be successful. The prime goal of scaffolding is, however, for students to work independently, so the teacher gradually removes assistance as students acquire skills and expertise. The assistance may be in the form of a knowledgeable peer, annotations in a text, outlines or other organizers for summarizing concepts, bilingual dictionaries, or interactive features in computer programs. Some programs that track and analyze student performance can offer targeted learning scaffolds (e.g., audio supports, images, vocabulary definitions) as well as additional exercises for further practice.

Teachers employ grouping patterns designed to promote peer support, engagement, and comprehensibility. Buddy pairs and small groups are the most common forms of social assistance for multilingual learners of English. Many teachers carefully choose the groups' makeup so that students have opportunities to participate fully and feel supported in their learning. Sometimes, groups are arranged by home language or reading ability, or with a mix of language proficiency levels.

Consider a group project reporting on a NASA space mission like the Curiosity Rover on Mars. Teachers can assign different tasks according to group mates' language skills. Some students could explore information on the internet, others could do text research, and others might create outlines of all collected information or assemble visuals from multiple sources. The material could then be organized for a TV talk show, with a "host" and "guest experts" asking or answering questions about the mission. In this activity, all students would learn the content, and they would contribute to the group effort at their varied skill levels.

Teachers provide supplemental materials. Teachers may use texts at a lower reading proficiency level or home language texts on the same topic or content, in print or online. They may rewrite the text to simplify grammatical structures or decrease density, add definitions and more background to a text, or provide summary translations. They may also introduce alternative activities for students who are not yet reading at the level of the text, such as oral reports, online searches, and oral interviews.

Teachers plan for appropriate challenge, depending on learner language proficiency levels. Teachers prepare to modify the language level of oral instruction if necessary and incorporate modeling and demonstrations in their lessons to support comprehension. They aim for cognitive rigor yet may develop a range of activities for student practice. By knowing their learners' interests and levels, teachers can design lessons that challenge all learners to advance in their learning.

PRACTICE 3G Teachers Promote the Use of Learning Strategies and Critical Thinking Among Students

Multilingual learners of English face the dual challenge of learning a new language and new content material at the same time. Critical thinking is an important element in this learning process. As students learn content, they are encouraged to think logically, analyze, make comparisons, and apply knowledge in new ways. They ask questions; form opinions; and evaluate a statement, an argument, or a piece of writing. They solve problems, make claims with evidence, and synthesize information. To help students attain this high level of critical thinking, teachers need to instruct them in learning strategies, then offer multiple opportunities to practice using the strategies in different contexts. Learning strategies are flexible tools that allow learners to control and direct their own learning. These strategies include conscious, observable behaviors and non-observable mental practices that help students become more efficient in their learning.

Learning strategies transfer to a new language. If students know how to summarize a text in their home language, they will know *how* to summarize (i.e., the process, the purpose, the end result), but they need to learn English words and grammar to do the task in English. Sentence frames and sample summaries may help bridge the language gap.

As part of their geography unit on the tropical rainforest, Ms. Nascimento's Brazilian high school students learned about the journalistic writing style and practiced their summarizing skills. After introducing the five Ws of journalism (who, what, where, when, and why), she planned for the students to use them as a reading strategy to comprehend a news article on how deforestation affects the blue Spix's macaw, a rare bird species in the Amazon region. To build background, the students created four-corner vocabulary charts of key words and watched a clip from the movie Rio, *which features a Spix's macaw character named Blu. They next read an article about the extinction of the Spix's macaw, which they annotated as they found answers to the five W questions. The class discussed the article and made predictions about other impacts of deforestation, then Ms. Nascimento paired the students up to create an infographic organized around the five Ws that would summarize the article. She provided a template for students to use if desired.*

Examples of Practice 3g

Teachers teach a variety of learning strategies for specific purposes. Over time, teachers introduce learners to a range of learning strategies that they can apply as needed to figure out meaning, complete an assignment, or review material. Teachers model the strategies through techniques like think-alouds, real-time text annotations, and role-plays. Different types of strategies have different uses and purposes:

- **Metacognitive strategies** enable a learner to plan for a task, monitor the work, and evaluate effectiveness when the task is complete. They allow the learner to self-regulate, and they have broad generic applications. Examples of these strategies include advance organization, organizational planning, selective attention, self-management, monitoring of comprehension, monitoring of production, and self-assessment (Chamot, 2009). Recent research shows that using metacognitive strategies improves student reading comprehension (Duke et al., 2021).

- **Cognitive strategies** involve critical thinking and often relate to specific types of tasks. For example, note-taking is helpful when listening to oral language input, and word grouping is useful for vocabulary learning. Other examples of these strategies include elaborating on prior knowledge, summarizing, creating images, reasoning by deduction or induction, using auditory representation, and highlighting text (Chamot, 2009).

- **Socioaffective strategies** are important for multilingual learners of English because effective classroom learning involves cooperation with others and students' ability to ask questions for clarification. These strategies also ease the anxiety that accompanies being a language learner in a dominant language group. Examples of these strategies include questioning for clarification, encouraging peers, and using self-talk (Chamot, 2009).

- **Language learning strategies** help students learn the new language on their own. Examples are vocabulary strategies, rehearsal strategies, analyzing forms and patterns of English, paraphrasing, and repetition such as rereading and rewatching (Short & Echevarría, 2016).

Teachers design tasks for students to practice using critical thinking and learning strategies. Despite best intentions, more than half of teacher questions are at the literal or basic comprehension level. They require yes or no answers or responses of just a few words. As a result, these questions do not provoke higher order thinking or elaborated speech. Teachers need to deliberately plan more challenging questions, problem-solving activities, and project tasks and regularly remind students to reach into their learning strategies toolbox to plan and guide their learning. In turn, students need to learn that they purposefully select a strategy or two depending on the situation; they don't use all of their strategies at once.

PRACTICE 3H Teachers Promote Students' Self-Regulated Learning

As successful learners proceed through the grade levels, they become increasingly autonomous and in control of their own learning goals and behaviors. In brief, they learn to self-regulate. Self-regulated learning involves three skills: forethought, performance, and self-assessment. Forethought involves setting goals and thinking strategically about accomplishing key tasks. Students exercise self-control and use self-observation to monitor progress during performance. For self-assessment, they evaluate their performance and regulate their reactions. Self-regulated learners are in control of their learning outcomes (Zimmerman & Schunk, 2012).

Examples of Practice 3h

Teachers facilitate students' setting of meaningful goals for themselves and monitoring their own progress toward those goals. Many teachers accomplish student goal setting through individualized conferences with students that occur on a regular schedule. They may orient students to self-directed learning by helping them sequence steps for tasks and provide checklists or other benchmark tools to monitor progress. Some interactive language learning programs, for instance, have digital tools to help learners independently navigate their educational path. At subsequent conferences, teachers can display evidence of student accomplishment to that point and suggest various goals for future progress. Teachers may then enable students to make their own choices about how to achieve their goals.

Teachers provide self-assessment tools that allow students to evaluate their strengths and weaknesses. For young learners, a smiley or frowny face evaluation at the end of a learning task might be sufficient. For older learners, Likert-type assessments can help them evaluate performance in a variety of areas on a scale of 1 to 5. Rubrics are useful for learners of all ages. They help learners self-evaluate by providing a list of the specific criteria tied to the lesson objectives that will be used to judge a product or presentation. The rubrics model or describe various performance levels, using a scoring scale with numbers, letters, or other descriptive labels. When teachers explain rubrics prior to the learning experience, learners have a clear understanding of what they should know or be able to do at the end of the lesson. Learners can self-assess their performance or provide feedback to peers. These tools give students guidance on what it takes to achieve at a higher level.

Teachers help learners develop effective study habits. Effective study habits are necessary for multilingual learners of English who are mastering content and language simultaneously. Many students, however, do not know which habits are best for learning. Teachers can identify effective study procedures at varying stages of language and learning proficiency and integrate these into the classroom lesson. Modeling and practice over a period of time will ensure that students learn the procedures and are capable of using them. Productive study habits include the following:

- structured note-taking
- use of graphic organizers
- before, during, and after reading techniques
- annotating text
- Question-Answer Relationship
- rehearsing oral presentations
- constructing concept maps

Principle 4. Adapt Lesson Delivery as Needed

Sam Eagle teaches ninth-grade Earth science in a suburban school in Oregon. Half of the students in his class are currently learning English at various levels of proficiency. To catch up on time lost due to a school assembly, he assigned reading the chapter on the rock cycle for homework. In the next class, Sam realized that most students had not done the assignment. When he asked why, many said the textbook was too hard to understand. Sam wanted the students to have background knowledge before they conducted an experiment, so he adjusted his plan for the day. He used the jigsaw technique, dividing the class into six cooperative learning groups. Two groups each read one portion of the text (about igneous, sedimentary, or metamorphous rocks) and responded to some questions he provided. He intentionally designed each group to include at least one proficient reader and one student who performed well in science. Then he created new groups of three in which each group member had read a different section so the students in the triads could teach one another what they had learned from their portion of the text.

The interactions between teachers and learners during classroom instruction provide teachers with a great deal of information about the effectiveness of their teaching. By observing and reflecting on learners' responses, teachers can readily see whether or to what degree the students are succeeding in meeting the learning objective. Often, objectives are not met because of various obstacles, such as the students' lack of prior knowledge, the teacher's incorrect assumptions about lesson delivery, staggering differences in the students' language proficiencies, and pacing problems, among other challenges. If students are not succeeding, teachers need to reflect on the causes and make adjustments during their lessons. Similarly, if the lesson tasks are too easy, the teacher will want to make them more challenging. This decision-making may occur frequently on any given day, and teachers sometimes need to make decisions in a matter of seconds.

PRACTICE 4A Teachers Check Student Comprehension Frequently and Adjust Instruction According to Learner Responses

To teach effectively, teachers need to evaluate what students know and what they do not know in real time. We do not want to wait until the end of a lesson or the end of a unit to discover that our students have misunderstood a key concept or incorrectly learned critical vocabulary.

Examples of Practice 4a

Teachers use teaching practices that ensure better auditory comprehension. Using a structure like 10-2 activities, teachers interrupt their oral input every 10 minutes to provide 2-minute opportunities for students to interact with the new learning. Multilingual learners of English learn best when they are not required to sustain extended periods of concentration while simultaneously attempting to comprehend auditory input. Lessons will be more effective if students have opportunities to interact with others about the input. These 2-minute breaks offer teachers excellent moments for checking learners' comprehension and can be used with all learners throughout the lesson. Examples of 10-2 comprehension checks include Turn and Talk, Think Pair Share, Sketch and Share, and other targeted interactional structures.

Teachers check comprehension using group response techniques. Teachers can use quick comprehension checks during a lesson to gauge how the class is doing. Some group response activities include Thumbs-Up/Thumbs-Down, response boards (all students respond individually on a dry-erase board or sheet of paper and show the teacher), and 3-2-1 for Self-Assessment. Teachers can also use technology options (websites and apps) on handheld devices or tablets.

Teachers gauge individual students' comprehension using digital tools and platforms.
Technology enables teachers to continually check student comprehension, identify areas of difficulty, and provide personalized assistance with lessons and exercises tailored to individual learners' needs. One such tool is Padlet, an online collaboration platform that operates as a virtual bulletin board where one can post text, images, videos, and online links. During a lesson about World War II, for example, a teacher may use Padlet strategically to assess student knowledge. After asking a critical thinking question like "What were the positive and negative effects of World War II?" and having students post responses on Padlet, the teacher can quickly identify gaps or misunderstandings. If many students struggle with a specific concept, the teacher can add further explanations, more examples, and multimedia materials to Padlet for student review or adjust class discussions or activities accordingly. This tool helps multilingual learners of English because its visual and interactive nature enhances language acquisition by integrating different media.

PRACTICE 4B Teachers Adjust Their Talk, the Task, or the Materials According to Learner Responses

As a lesson unfolds, if teachers notice some confusion or misunderstanding, they make adjustments so that all learners can meet the learning goals. They may vary their oral language input to ease the comprehension load or use their speech in other ways to support the lesson objectives. They might adapt a task midstream—add more time, change the product, or pull a small group of students together for reteaching while the rest of the class works on their own. Teachers may help students reexamine the information or the task with supplemental resources such as home language texts, on-topic video clips, and visual aids.

Practice 3b focused on input—namely, what teachers can do to present information or introduce a task in an accessible way for multilingual learners of English. Practice 4b focuses on what teachers can do when, after instruction has happened, students do not understand the material adequately or are not successful with the assigned activity. Many of the strategies and techniques listed in Table 3.1 can be redeployed during a lesson to make adjustments. But if the changes are not sufficient, a teacher may need to reteach the information to the whole class or to a small group on a subsequent day.

Table 3.3 organizes the types of scaffolds and supports teachers may employ when students struggle to understand a concept or complete an assignment. Further discussion of these strategies and techniques is found in the following examples.

Table 3.3	Scaffolding Strategies and Techniques to Adapt Lesson Delivery
Teacher Speech and Verbal Scaffolds	• Restate information in a new way (e.g., simplify, elaborate, embed definitions). • Prompt students with cues (e.g., sentence starters) and clues (*Look back at ...*, *Remember when we ...*). • Use think-alouds. • Provide more wait time. • Model the type of student talk expected. • Provide or ask for interpretation in home languages. • Reduce use of synonyms and pronouns in explanations. • Elicit more ideas and solutions from students.
Instructional Scaffolds and Material Supports	• Use graphic organizers (during and after reading or for prewriting). • Show more visuals (e.g., diagrams, images, videos). • Use props, manipulatives, gestures, or movement. • Provide sentence or paragraph frames. • Provide advance organizers or outlines. • Use structured notes. • Encourage the use of dictionaries (e.g., bilingual, picture) and translation tools. • Provide alternative and leveled texts. • Provide home language texts or summaries. • Incorporate educational technology tools.
Procedural Scaffolds	• Model the directions step by step. • Add illustrations to directions. • Reteach the activity with familiar content. • Show samples of completed student work. • Play audio with samples of speech. • Use the gradual release model of instruction (e.g., *I do, we do, you do*). • Have students use the Turn the Question Around technique. • Bookmark websites.
Social Supports	• Incorporate small-group learning. • Encourage interactive structured conversations (e.g., buddy talk, Think Pair Share). • Use cooperative learning structures (e.g., Numbered Heads Together, jigsaw). • Implement group work with designated roles (e.g., reciprocal teaching, roundtable, round robin). • Offer peer tutoring. • Have students work with study buddies or study groups. • Connect students with home language partners. • Have students work with online groups or partners.

Examples of Practice 4b

Teachers modify their teacher talk as necessary to improve comprehension and scaffold academic language learning. When students do not understand what a teacher has said or a text has presented, teachers often rely on their speech to explain and help students make sense of what they heard or read. Examples of teacher adjustments to speech include restating information in a new way, or perhaps with more visual supports; using think-alouds to orally demonstrate how one considers a problem and sorts through possible solutions or applies a learning strategy; using the home language(s) to explain or summarize; and involving students in a discussion to clear up misunderstandings.

Teachers use additional instructional supports to assist students in processing or applying new information. Tools used to make input comprehensible can also be used when students face a learning challenge. Perhaps a teacher verbally explained the water cycle, but students were confused. Showing a video clip that depicts evaporation, condensation, precipitation, and the like later in the lesson may clear up the confusion. Or perhaps students read through a text but could not respond accurately to comprehension questions afterward. The teacher might give students a graphic organizer, such as a cause-effect chart or sequence map, to complete while they re-read the text.

Teachers turn to procedural scaffolds when students cannot complete a task or perform it well. Many teachers have experienced a situation in which a task that they assumed would be relatively easy for students to complete is not so simple. Students struggle to get started, veer off course, or do not apply their knowledge in the way the teacher anticipated. These challenges sometimes arise because students did not understand the directions for the task. Teachers can remedy this issue by providing written step-by-step instructions, adding illustrations to written directions, modeling the steps, or doing the initial one or two steps or exercises with the students. Showing exemplars of the final product (e.g., a well-written student essay, a Google Slides presentation from another class) may provide just the scaffold the students need to finish their work.

Teachers adapt the task or materials to learners' proficiency levels. As students work on a task (individually or in groups), the teacher may realize that the task is too hard for some and too easy for others. Teachers might change a task to reduce the language load as appropriate to the student (e.g., with a text at a different reading level). Additionally, they may adjust the product of the learning task. Students with developing writing skills, for example, may exhibit content learning in a different way from those writing an essay: presenting their ideas via audio-recording, vlog, sketches, or demonstrations. Students with strong literacy skills may be asked to transform the essay into an op-ed or a newspaper article.

Teachers vary student grouping configurations to aid in comprehension and increase productivity. Adjusting the social organization of the classroom may help students understand the content or the task better. Teachers may regroup students to provide support for beginning learners of English with those who are more advanced learners or with bilingual peers. Teachers may pair a new student with a home language buddy who can informally interpret information. To make group work more productive, a teacher may assign roles and provide sentence frames to help students articulate their roles. For example, if groups are engaged in reciprocal teaching, the teacher may provide the clarifiers with phrases such as *It's similar to …, ___ means ___,* or *Let's read it again and focus on ….*

Teachers prompt students to draw on a range of learning strategies to problem solve breakdowns in comprehension or processing. Effective learners rely on a variety of learning strategies when they need to solve a problem, such as not understanding a text passage, having writer's block, or struggling to complete a task. Learning strategies, therefore, can scaffold student learning. Teachers can encourage multilingual learners of English to apply different learning strategies to help organize their learning, focus on aspects of language, determine the meaning of unfamiliar words, and more. Table 3.4 provides a sampling of such learning strategies. (We separate out vocabulary strategies because of their importance to learners' language acquisition process.)

Table 3.4	Examples of Learning Strategies
Metacognitive and Cognitive Strategies	• Note-taking • Selective listening and reading • Setting a purpose • Summarizing • Organizational planning • Effective memorization • Prediction • Advance organization • Annotating • Monitoring comprehension • Rereading
Vocabulary Strategies	• Making personal dictionaries • Grouping and categorizing words • Defining or translating words in(to) home language • Visualization • Analysis of word parts • Deducing meaning from context and part of speech • Self-assessment • Substituting a known word for an unknown one • Using English and home language glossaries and dictionaries

Principle 5. Monitor and Assess Student Language Development

Mr. Ramirez teaches Grade 4 beginning-level multilingual learners of English in Peru. Because the students have been studying short stories in their Spanish language arts class, he aligned his creative writing unit to that genre. After reading and discussing several stories in English and identifying the main elements (plot, setting, and character), he planned a 2-day lesson for students to generate their own story, which they would tell to the class using expressive language. To motivate the students, he created a magic storyteller's cauldron. Mr. Ramirez formed collaborative groups of four or five students each, then someone from each group drew ingredients for the story—strips from the cauldron with a plot (e.g., a lost item), a setting (e.g., by the sea), and characters (e.g., a parent and child). The groups brainstormed and took notes on a worksheet Mr. Ramirez designed to help them organize the beginning, middle, and end of their original story. Each group then practiced saying their story aloud. Mr. Ramirez listened in and gave feedback on the story and on their expressiveness with comments like "Can you think of a more active verb than goes? How does he move? Does he run or jump or tiptoe?" and "What happens at the end after they find the ring?" and "How does she feel? Okay, say it like she's scared."

The next day, he shared a peer review checklist with the class. Each group took on the role of storyteller and presented the story. The classmates completed the rubric as they listened, noting whether the story elements were present and well developed; whether the story had a clear beginning, middle, and end; and whether the students used their voices in expressive ways. To wrap up, Mr. Ramirez led a discussion on what the students enjoyed about this activity and what they found challenging. Students then conducted a self-assessment on their creativity, collaboration, and language use.

Self-Assessment Corner

Rate yourselves on the following aspects (1–5, with 5 being the highest).

Creativity: ☐1   ☐2   ☐3   ☐4   ☐5

Collaboration: ☐1   ☐2   ☐3   ☐4   ☐5

Language Use: ☐1   ☐2   ☐3   ☐4   ☐5

Thank you for becoming a magical storyteller today! May your words inspire and enchant!

Multilingual learners of English advance to differing levels of language proficiency in varied ways. Certain learners are comfortable with speaking English haltingly and ungrammatically at an early stage of learning. Other students wait until they are sure they will be understood and certain of their grammatical competency. To advance their students' learning efficiently, teachers need to be aware of students' capacities for comprehending and speaking English. Constant monitoring and assessment, built into daily instruction, will provide the best evidence of language growth.

PRACTICE 5A Teachers Monitor Student Errors

By interacting frequently with our students, we can acquire a great deal of information about their progress. Some teachers record the results of their interactions (e.g., sentence patterns, vocabulary knowledge, subject-verb agreement) on a checklist or other note-taking tool. Many of the online learning programs used for language development also keep track of correct and incorrect uses of English, and teachers regularly review these reports. Teachers use the information from these interactions and tools to plan instruction, design mini-lessons, or change student groupings or partners, depending on the learners' developing proficiency.

Teachers take diagnostic notes when students make errors to provide appropriate scaffolding and modeling. Sometimes learners' errors are simply mistakes caused by lack of attention or lack of competence. Some other errors involve cross-linguistic differences, such as word order. Other errors are developmental. These errors indicate that the learner has misconceptions about the features of the target language. Teachers do not have to directly address developmental errors related to language features students have not yet learned, but they can model language usage and teach effective learning strategies.

Teachers reteach when errors indicate that students misunderstood or learned the material incorrectly. When errors are not part of the language development process, teachers plan for reteaching or additional practice. They may present a mini-lesson on the topic for the whole class or work with a small group of learners who need support. Teachers can use certain online programs that target specific skills and can personalize lessons.

PRACTICE 5B Teachers Strategically Provide Ongoing, Effective Feedback

As students develop their skills in a new language, they need feedback to check whether what they say or write is understandable and correct, as well as whether their interpretation of what they heard or read is accurate. The effectiveness of feedback depends on various factors, such as students' proficiency levels, curriculum design, specific linguistic features being taught, and the dynamics of the classroom environment, so teachers play a pivotal role in delivering appropriate feedback.

To be constructive, a teacher's feedback in response to a learner's error is best modulated in delivery and tone, depending on the age of the learner, the proficiency level, and the classroom situation. It is important to remember that not all errors need to be corrected; ones that interfere with comprehension or are related to the lesson objective are prime candidates for attention. When teachers determine that feedback is needed based on their observations of students' behavior, they can intervene with targeted support and strategies to help students understand their strengths and areas of growth (Nassaji & Kartchava, 2017). Effective feedback boosts student language development and motivation.

Examples for Practice 5b

Teachers use specific feedback. Specific feedback that highlights the error in some way leads to better performance than does general feedback. Teacher modeling is one form of specific feedback. Products and presentations can be modeled prior to learning and used for comparison afterward. Demonstrations can help show students how to perform at a high level. For project work and writing assessments, rubrics are effective for identifying specifically how students can achieve success, as long as teachers have explained the rating criteria to students in advance.

Teachers give timely and actionable feedback. Students may be more able to use feedback if they receive it while they work on a task or engage in conversation. Timeliness is more important for oral feedback than for written feedback. Teachers sometimes determine a feedback focus for a particular time period. For example, for 2 weeks, the teacher will provide feedback on the student's proper use of conventions in written work, or, for a project, the teacher will provide feedback at designated intervals along the way, not just when the project is completed.

Teachers harness technology tools to provide personalized feedback for learners. Technology has markedly increased the options for providing timely and relevant feedback. Using advanced data analysis, education technology tools can assess student performance, identify growth areas, indicate improvement opportunities, and generate tasks and assignments to act on the problems noted. This strategic feedback process ensures that students receive tailored assistance when needed, effectively promoting their language development.

Some of Ms. Falamoun's students use Khan Academy (www.khanacademy.org), a free, online learning resource, during study time at school. She knows the platform can monitor students' language development in reading and language arts courses and it can strategically provide continuous feedback through data analytics and customized learning plans. On occasion, she has checked in with the students and found that the platform can track their progress by analyzing their interactions with language-based activities, such as reading comprehension and writing tasks. She noticed that for one student who struggled with complex phrases and vocabulary in reading assignments, the tool identified this pattern and recommended customized vocabulary-building exercises. It also provided explanations to address his specific challenge. For another student, the system detected a pattern of sentence structure errors in her written responses and provided targeted grammar exercises and other suggestions for improvement.

Teachers deliver feedback according to the learner's age and proficiency level. All students appreciate positive feedback, no matter their age. Young children may struggle with processing large amounts of feedback, especially if they consider the feedback to be negative. They tend to be receptive to positive feedback, particularly when it explicitly points out what they are doing correctly and encourages them to continue the beneficial behavior. Older learners can share their feedback preferences (e.g., one-on-one instead of in front of the class) with the teacher. They can also handle more feedback overall and more feedback topics at a time than younger students can.

It is crucial for feedback to align with a student's proficiency level. Imagine a beginning student who has just learned to use the simple present tense. Feedback suggesting that they use an irregular past tense verb form instead is inappropriate and would likely be confusing. In a similar manner, when teachers ask a question, they should accept simple responses and approximations from beginners but expect more complete and accurate responses from those with more proficiency.

Teachers use various types of oral corrective feedback. Oral corrective feedback allows learners an opportunity to notice the differences between their language and the teacher's language. Research indicates that oral feedback in teacher–student interactions can effectively help students develop their language skills (Li & Vuono, 2019). Feedback can be categorized into two main types: reformulations and prompts. Prompts are more likely than reformulations to lead to uptake by the student because they must produce the corrected language, unless the feedback is above their proficiency level or involves something not yet studied. Then it is unlikely to be remembered.

Here are descriptions of these types of oral feedback:

1. **Reformulations** are a teacher's efforts to correct errors in speech—sometimes to clarify what a student has said or model correct speech for others in the class, sometimes to remind students of a word's pronunciation or a language structure that they have studied, and sometimes to move the lesson along. Teachers can make reformulations without drawing attention to the student's error.

   • **Explicit corrections** occur when the teacher indicates to students that they have made an error and supplies a correction.

   Student: The wood … the wood go down in the water.

> *Teacher:* Do you mean the wood went down? We say the wood **sank** in the water.

- **Recasts** occur after students' utterances when the teacher reformulates all or part of an utterance to make it fit the target language.

    > *Student:* The wood no float.
    >
    > *Teacher:* The wood doesn't float.

2. **Prompts for self-repair** signal students to attempt to repair an utterance on their own. Such prompts include repetitions, direct elicitations, clarification requests, metalinguistic clues, open-ended questions, and nonverbal cues (Lyster et al., 2013).

    - **Repetition.** The teacher repeats the learner's utterance, often with exaggeration or inflection to indicate a problem. (Student: *The wood go down.* Teacher: *The wood go down?*)

    - **Elicitation.** The teacher elicits the correct form by asking specific questions, pausing, or asking for a reformulation. (*How do we say that in English?*)

    - **Clarification request.** The teacher uses a phrase to indicate that the learner's utterance was not understood. (*Excuse me? I don't understand. Can you tell me again?*)

    - **Metalinguistic clues.** The teacher asks questions about or states that the form of the utterance is not correct (e.g., verb form, plurality). *(Is there more than one person doing it? You need to use the past tense.)*

    - **Open-ended questions.** The teacher asks general questions that allow the learner to select the information that they will discuss. (*Tell me what you know about …? What did you discover about …? What can you tell me about …?*)

    - **Nonverbal cues.** The teacher's quizzical facial expressions and/or gestures may serve as prompts for self-repair.

Teachers use written feedback when appropriate. Teachers share their insights, opinions, recommendations, and suggestions, with the goal of helping students improve their writing skills. Written corrective feedback provides students with a record they can refer to, and the feedback can foster deep reflection and self-regulation in their learning. With the writing process, teachers often use a collaborative approach to revision, helping students reflect on their strengths and weaknesses in each draft and make improvements. Teachers can achieve this goal through the use of teacher–student memos, portfolios, and learning journals (Andrade & Evans, 2013). Additionally, older students can learn procedures for peer editing to enhance their writing skills. The increased use of collaborative online writing tools (e.g., Google Docs) offers a convenient means for teachers and peers to annotate texts.

PRACTICE 5C Teachers Design Varied and Valid Assessments and Supports to Assess Student Learning

The K–12 educational community in the United States is awash in testing. The amount of testing—ranging from benchmark assessments during the year to state standardized tests in the spring—cuts into instructional time. Although the results of benchmark tests often inform instruction, scores from state tests arrive too late in the school year (often in the summer) to do so. Moreover, assessment specialists have noted that many tests, other than those that specifically measure English language proficiency, are not normed on multilingual learners of English (Abedi & Linquanti, 2012). Furthermore, some required assessments do not align with the curricula students have studied. As a result, some teachers feel that required testing does not accurately reveal what students have learned in their classrooms. This perspective is especially true when considering beginning and intermediate learners who have not yet reached the level of English proficiency necessary for standardized testing. Teachers of multilingual learners of English recognize the value of assessing students through classroom-based assessment instruments that mirror instruction and are discrete enough to show the progress students make.

Although methods for assessing students with traditional paper-based tests have some advantages, technology offers convenience and a variety of platforms with engaging features to help teachers determine what students know and what progress they are making. Nonetheless, it is essential to remember that pedagogical goals should drive technological integration, not vice versa (Sankey, 2020). Teachers should select a tool that aligns with the learning objectives. The assessment results can inform decisions that teachers make about instruction.

Examples of Practice 5c

Teachers use classroom-based assessment to inform teaching and improve learning. The purpose of classroom-based assessment is to gather information regarding learning over a period of time. Teachers are careful to assess language growth separately from content learning. This type of assessment can inform our teaching by helping us become better acquainted with our students' growth in specific skill areas as they work to meet English language proficiency standards, ultimately leading to improvement in students' learning experiences.

Examples of assessments include teacher observations, teacher-developed tests, comprehension checks, and rubrics for student products (e.g., writing projects, presentations, multimedia products), checklists, surveys and questionnaires, and anecdotal records (Farnsworth & Malone, 2014). Classroom-based assessment is integrated into instruction. It not only helps students see how they progress in both language and content but also facilitates effective communication between teachers, parents, and other school personnel (Levine & McCloskey, 2013).

One additional thought is that as we adjust our instruction to focus on the assets that our multilingual learners of English bring to the classroom, we also adjust some of our assessment practices and allow for translanguaging and responses in languages other than English. This shift in practice may lead to a deeper demonstration of student knowledge, as students can interact in the language they choose with their peers for group projects or presentations, which can reduce anxiety during classroom assessment (Gottlieb, 2021). The processes of preparing assessments in other languages and evaluating an assessment written in another language take time but can be worth the effort, particularly for assessments and graded assignments in content-area classes. Online tools can provide some support for these efforts.

Teachers use testing procedures based on principles of assessment. Basic evaluation principles are that assessments should be fair, reliable, and valid.

- **Fairness** requires that all students have an equal chance to show what they know and can do. Fairness does not require teachers to treat all students in the same way, though. Most tests are written in English and have a high language demand. Consequently, multilingual learners of English may not understand test questions or directions, so their performance may not accurately reflect their content knowledge. That type of assessment often contributes to misleading results. To achieve some degree of fairness in classroom-based testing, teachers provide scaffolds and other accommodations. They may scaffold a math assessment, for example, by providing models of problem-solving. They allow students to work in buddy pairs to negotiate the meaning of the questions. They provide oral language practice in describing word problems before moving on to the writing phase of the lesson. They provide a glossary of terms unrelated to the math content.

Consider the following questions to determine whether your classroom assessments are fair:

> » Did the student sufficiently understand the questions asked?
> » Am I evaluating the student's content understanding or language development?
> » Does my assessment reflect my instructional practices?
> » Did I provide appropriate scaffolding?
> » Have I told students what I am evaluating and modeled a desired product?
> » Have I clearly specified the criteria on which the evaluation is based?
> » Am I evaluating the process, the product, or both?

- **Reliability** indicates that the results of an assessment are consistent over a period of time when scored by different raters. Holistic or analytic scoring of writing samples is reliable when raters are trained in the same techniques and achieve similar scores. Oral language scoring can be more reliable when raters use an observational matrix that is specific enough to provide dependable results.

- **Validity** is achieved when instruments measure what they are intended to measure. It is difficult to achieve valid results with multilingual learners of English on standardized tests, particularly those written in English. Testing products may exhibit cultural or experiential bias toward students with different life experiences. Moreover, the test results are often influenced by a learner's limited academic language knowledge. Thus, teachers should collect multiple sources of information about a student. Classroom-based, informal assessment that is varied and reflects the classroom teaching style is the best option for gathering a broad and valid picture of a learner's skills and knowledge (Levine & McCloskey, 2013).

Teachers rely on a variety of assessment types to determine student achievement. Formal assessments are mandated by district and state educational authorities for shaping educational policies and decision-making processes such as resource allocation, instructional strategies, and curriculum development. Nevertheless, standardized testing is not sufficient for presenting a picture of a learner's achievement, particularly at lower levels of English proficiency. A package that includes multiple ongoing and purposeful assessments can provide a more complete picture of a student's achievement. Teachers can use these assessments to determine how well students are making progress toward meeting state standards. Furthermore, if a student is allowed accommodations during the formal test, the teacher needs to use the same accommodations in the classroom. Common types of assessment include the following:

- **Formative assessment** occurs as teachers gather information about student learning during the instructional process. Formative assessment is ongoing, occurs during instruction, and guides the teaching process. Much formative assessment is informal and occurs on the spot (Echevarría et al., 2024). Teachers rely on other formative assessments to evaluate whether students have achieved teaching and learning objectives. These assessments may be graded; marked on a checklist; written as anecdotal notes; recorded as oral speech; or collected through short quizzes, essays, and presentations.

- **Summative assessment**, in contrast to formative assessment, is usually conducted at the end of a long period of learning (a semester or year) and is more formal in tone. Standardized testing and district end-of-year testing are examples of summative assessment. Nowadays, students take most of these assessments online. Although multilingual learners of English must take part in summative assessment, most states and districts permit some learners to have accommodations. Accommodations represent changes in the testing situation or in the test itself that make the assessment process fair and equitable. They increase a student's access to the content of the test or reduce the language demand of the test while preserving test validity (Abedi, 2017). Accommodations may include (but are not limited to) the following (Levine & McCloskey, 2013):
  » extended time for testing
  » use of a glossary or dictionary (English, bilingual, or customized), except with English language arts or English language proficiency tests
  » a separate setting with an ELD or bilingual teacher as proctor
  » translated or extended explanations of the test directions
  » test directions and/or questions read aloud
- **Performance-based portfolios** give teachers access to multiple pieces of student work collected over a period of time. A portfolio may contain different genres of writing and reflect the editing and rewriting process. It may be structured around a particular topic or project. Consequently, a portfolio can provide a comprehensive view of how a student's language skill has grown over time and demonstrate what the student has learned (Maier et al., 2020).
- **Criterion-based rubrics** are useful tools for assessment and learning. They list the specific criteria used to evaluate a performance or a product and indicate performance levels on a scoring scale that uses numbers, letters, or other descriptive labels. Teachers provide these rubrics before students start a project, giving clear explanations and examples so that all students understand the criteria. Rubrics are often accompanied by models of excellent, acceptable, and unacceptable work to clarify expectations (Levine & McCloskey, 2013).

Teachers blend pedagogy and technology in their assessment practices. Today's education practices combine pedagogy and technology and reflect the normalization of the use of digital tools in daily life. We want classroom assessments to be similar to the tasks and activities performed during lessons; this enhances validity. So, if technology is used during instruction, it makes sense to use technology in some way during assessment. Teachers can create online quizzes, using Google Forms and Socrative, for example, to measure knowledge with multiple-choice, true/false, and short-answer question formats. In addition, teachers can tap available online assessments, such as those on Quizalize and Kahoot! These tools also allow teachers to make their own assessments. These online assessments enable teachers to collect real-time statistics on each student's progress and automatically distribute different materials to students based on their results.

PRACTICE 5D Teachers Analyze and Interpret Assessment Data for Multilingual Learners of English

English language teachers know that acquiring a new language takes time and extensive practice. Proficiency levels and educational backgrounds play a role in how well a student may perform on an assessment. In the language classroom, teachers may differentiate the assessments or provide language support to accommodate skill differences. A successful oral presentation for an advanced learner would be different from one presented by a newcomer. In reviewing student work, test scores, and other assessment data, English language teachers determine whether progress has been made or whether reteaching or simply more practice and application are needed. Thus, the close interpretation of assessment data informs instruction.

Many assessments in schools have not been designed for those learning English as a new language. Most tests are—at least in part—tests of language ability (e.g., one has to read the instructions, read the test questions, write responses). As a result, students new to English and who are less proficient may not perform as well as their peers who are proficient in English. Additionally, some students may lack the necessary test-taking skills (e.g., transferring answers, completing fill-in-the-blank sections), which can hinder their ability to demonstrate their content knowledge. English language teachers can help grade-level and subject-area teachers understand what scores and results mean.

> How do you help colleagues interpret the results of multilingual learners' performance on classroom-based and standardized assessments?

Examples of Practice 5d

Teachers use what they know about a student's language development process and educational background to interpret assessment results. Knowing one's learners can help set appropriate expectations and understand student performance on assessments. A standardized Grade 6 reading exam that all students take might result in 20% of the multilingual learners of English scoring at a below-proficient benchmark. Disaggregation of the data by English proficiency level might in turn reveal that all of the students in the below-proficient category are at an English language proficiency Level 1 or Level 2. This finding is consistent with what we know about language development and should not cause alarm. If, however, all Level 4 students score below proficient, a review of the instructional practices or program design might be needed.

Teachers share their data analyses and interpretations with colleagues. In many schools, grade-level or department teams meet to review assessment data. English language teachers are important partners in the data review process. They share what they know about their students' language skills and educational backgrounds. They can examine an assessment and point out unknown vocabulary, cultural biases, assumptions of prior knowledge, and other factors that might affect their students' performance. They can help colleagues determine whether students struggled because they did not know the material being tested or because they did not know the language of the test questions or the directions for particular items.

Consider a high school student who spent several years in a refugee camp with no formal schooling. Placed in an algebra class but having only limited English literacy and no math instruction beyond arithmetic, that student is unlikely to perform well on diagnostic assessments at the beginning of the school year. The interpretation should not be that the student is unable to "do" algebra, but rather that they need targeted math instruction to close the knowledge gap, as well as content-based language instruction to understand math vocabulary and syntax.

Teachers use assessment results to improve assessment practices. English language teachers can assist their students by introducing them to test-like tasks, common phrases in directions, multiple-choice formats, short constructed response writing, and other assessment-related material. They can re-create testing conditions, such as using a computer or speaking into a microphone. Teachers can help colleagues design assessments that are simplified linguistically (e.g., each question begins with a question word; use of synonyms is reduced), include bilingual or oral directions, and avoid U.S. cultural or historical referents (unless relevant to the learning objective). They can also remind colleagues that any accommodation allowed on a state standardized test can be used in the classroom. English language teachers can help colleagues select appropriate accommodations for the students. By familiarizing students with the accommodations in class, teachers can in turn help students be more successful on standardized tests.

Principle 6. Engage and Collaborate Within a Community of Practice

Andres and Marina both teach in a middle school program for multilingual learners of English. During their planning period, they get together and reflect on their latest teaching experiments. They describe to each other the techniques that they have just tried and the results. Their conversations invigorate their teaching, and they are constantly learning tips from each other that they are eager to test in their own classes. After 3 years in the classroom, both teachers have acquired a large set of techniques and have embarked on the road to critical reflection on their teaching.

A community of practice is a group of people who share a profession and engage with one another in learning more about that profession. These communities are widespread throughout K–12 education. No one can know all there is to know about educating diverse learners, and all of us are smarter together than we are as individuals (Lave & Wenger, 1991). We often begin our journey to professionalism by looking outside of our own skill set and exploring the knowledge base of other educators in our schools. In this way, we can add to our repertoire of teaching techniques. For example, our school's special education teacher can show us ways to help learners focus on their work and apply study skills. The dual language teacher can help us understand the structures of our students' home languages and cultures. The reading teacher has wide knowledge of readability levels and text types. The science and math teachers know the vocabulary that is essential to understanding the content they teach. By sharing with one another, we expand and grow together.

PRACTICE 6A Teachers Are Fully Engaged in Their Profession

Although teachers aspire to be fully prepared from Day 1 of their teaching careers, reality is a different story. Effective teachers recognize the need to engage in ongoing professional learning to deliver optimal instruction for their students. What does it mean to be fully engaged in the TESOL profession? (See Chapter 4 for additional discussion on this topic.)

Examples of Practice 6a

Teachers engage in reflective practice to grow professionally. Dewey (1933) discussed reflective practice in his exploration of experience, interaction, and reflection; in today's educational landscape, with increasing diversity in classrooms, the scope of reflective practice regarding instruction for multilingual learners of English has expanded to encompass all teachers, not just those specializing in TESOL. To support these learners effectively, teachers may need to take an initial step to reflect on their understandings of pedagogical practices and be willing to adapt their teaching methods accordingly (Valdés et al., 2014). This adaptation involves dialogues and collaboration among colleagues, as well as a commitment to professional development. It means considering how language and cultural factors impact students' academic development and adjusting teaching strategies to better meet their learners' needs. In this context, reflective practice is not a one-time effort, but rather an ongoing learning process that becomes a crucial aspect of the teaching profession.

The process can be distilled into three essential questions:

- What did I do?
- How did it go?
- What did I learn?

Reflective practice, or critical reflection, can bolster professional growth. As Larrivee (2000, p. 293) explains, "Unless teachers develop the practice of critical reflection, they stay trapped in unexamined judgments, interpretations, assumptions, and expectations. Approaching teaching as a reflective practitioner involves fusing personal beliefs and values into a professional identity." Engaging in cyclical critical reflection enables teachers to continuously test and experiment with teaching and learning hypotheses within the context of their students' needs, leading to increased professional competence.

Teachers participate in continuous learning and ongoing professional development. We face challenges in teaching our students every day. Our response to these challenges is to continually work toward professional involvement and lifelong learning. At times, individual interests will guide our engagement in learning—for instance, a need for more literacy training or classroom management techniques or a desire to learn about student cultures or home languages (Toppel et al., 2021).

At other times, school circumstances give rise to professional learning. Through personal networks and collaborative teacher teams, we can ask questions, share successes, examine student work, develop study groups, pursue online training, write curriculum units, and talk about our classroom experiences: *This is what I did today, and here's what I learned as a result.* These conversations lead to the reflection and development that are so necessary in our teaching lives.

Through participation in professional development associations, we can stay abreast of best practices. We can join a professional English teaching organization such as TESOL or the National Association for Bilingual Education or a content-specific organization like the National Council of Teachers of Mathematics, the National Science Teaching Association, or the National Council for the Social Studies, then get involved with an organization's specialized groups or local affiliates. We can attend or present, virtually or in person, at local, state, or national conferences or sponsored academies and symposia. We can join online webinars and chats. We can also read and write for the publications of these organizations to get new insights and exchange ideas.

In addition, we can pursue learning options in specific skill areas related to teaching—technology, curriculum development, or assessment, for example. We can do online courses and webinars or apply for a grant, fellowship, or award to do language research or pursue a graduate degree. The list is long, but lifelong learning takes time. We need to invest our personal time to become dynamic and effective teachers for our multilingual learners of English.

Teachers embrace technology to stay up to date, access world-class resources, and engage in interactive learning experiences. New approaches, technological developments, and student demands constantly shape the context for teaching and learning. Educators must keep up with the latest trends, research, and innovations to provide their students with the most effective learning experiences. In this digital age, technology has made it easier to become informed and access existing knowledge. Technology connects teachers to a global network of resources, knowledge, and insights that used to be limited by geography. Professional learning networks on social media platforms and educational forums allow teachers to collaborate with peers worldwide, engage in lively discussions, and share experiences. Digital newsletters and subscriptions, delivered straight to their inbox, provide teachers with information on programs, practices, and evolving trends from research papers and other sources.

PRACTICE 6B Teachers Collaborate With Colleagues

Many school districts are moving toward an inclusion-based model of instruction in which collaboration and coteaching play a large role (Staehr Fenner, 2016). Language and content learning are increasingly interconnected in classrooms in K–12 schools across the United States. As a result,

ELD teachers, special education teachers, bilingual and dual language teachers, reading teachers, and content-area teachers must collaborate and coteach effectively (Echevarría et al., 2024; Valdés et al., 2014). Moreover, sharing varied perspectives, thoughts, and experiences improves teachers' skill sets and fosters a culture of ongoing development, eventually improving education for all students.

Examples of Practice 6b

Teachers meet with colleagues regularly to coplan for future learning. Time is the most valuable commodity during the school day. It is challenging for English language teachers to find opportunities for mutual planning on a grade level, within a team or department of content teachers, or even with other English language teaching colleagues. In spite of the challenge, English language teachers need to become coplanners to ensure their students' success in developing English language and content proficiency. These planning opportunities permit teachers to become aware of the extent of the content learning required for students. They also allow English language teachers to share information about students' language proficiency with content teachers.

Some schools are able to schedule joint planning time for English language and content teachers. When shared time is not possible, teachers often exchange information during breaks, at lunchtime, or before or after school. They may use technology platforms like Microsoft Teams and online tools like Google Docs to plan lessons together. Teachers may also utilize applications like Flip to capture and share ideas about their teaching experiences via video and gather comments and reactions from colleagues. School administrators can help by making certain that scheduling allows teachers to collaborate with colleagues for planning.

Teachers develop and strengthen relationships with school colleagues that facilitate coteaching. Teaching in the classroom of another teacher can cause anxiety. Coteaching requires a level of trust on the part of both teachers. Coteachers need to assure each other that they appreciate the collegiality and support that coteaching can offer. The personal relationships that English language teachers develop with colleagues are imperative to a collegial partnership. Coteachers are not in the classroom to "fix each other," but rather to share skills and knowledge that will help all learners achieve at a high level (Dove & Honigsfeld, 2017). Coteaching is a skill that develops over time and requires a level of expertise to be successful. Some school districts provide support for coteaching models, and this support should be applauded. In addition, preservice teaching preparation programs need to include more instruction on effective coteaching skills and models.

PRACTICE 6C Teachers Develop Leadership Skills That Enable Them to Become a Resource in Their Schools

In school districts across the United States, English language teachers have seen a change in their role in K–12 schools. They are increasingly called upon to provide professional development or act as coaches to peers in their school buildings (Staehr Fenner, 2016). Some become teachers on special assignment in the district office (e.g., multilingual coordinators, instructional coaches). The skills required for working with adults are different from those needed for working with children, so it cannot be assumed that all English language teachers are prepared for this changing role. Nevertheless, we need to develop the professional leadership skills necessary to take on this new role. *Standards for Initial TESOL Pre-K–12 Teacher Preparation Programs* (TESOL International Association, 2019) is an excellent source for learning about professionalism in our field.

Teachers build a repertoire of professional development topics on English language education and hone their presenting skills. Some teachers begin by sharing an effective technique with a grade-level team and then at a faculty meeting. They then organize several techniques or guidelines on a topic (e.g., how to build background schema, ways to promote academic conversations) into a workshop for a districtwide staff development day or a local conference. They learn effective delivery methods from others who provide professional development and gradually expand the set of topics they can competently cover in presentations to others. They also reflect on the best ways to transfer their knowledge to participants so the participants can in turn apply new learning in their classrooms.

Teachers develop coaching skills. In studying to become a teacher, one learns pedagogy—the methods of instruction and assessment commensurate with the age of the learners and the curriculum and standards being taught. Coaching requires knowledge, sensitivity, and skills for collaborating with adults, essentially peers, to modify their instruction to serve multilingual learners of English in their classes. It often involves goal setting, classroom observation, lesson planning, lesson modeling, and sometimes coteaching. English language coaches have knowledge of second language learning, ELD methodologies, and cross-cultural communication, but they also need to develop some basic understanding of the content curriculum that the teachers they work with will teach. One option for developing these skills is the Teacher Leadership for School-Wide English Learning (SWEL) certificate workshop series offered by TESOL to prepare English language teachers to share their expertise with colleagues in their school in coaching contexts (Benegas & Stolpestad, 2020).

A Look Back and a Look Ahead

The 6 Principles described in Chapter 3 are the basic tenets that guide our profession. Some of these principles may overlap with the guidelines for other professionals in K–12 schools. Taken as a whole, however, they outline the distinctive responsibilities and skills of all professionals who teach English learners. They concisely state what exemplary teaching of multilingual learners of English requires teachers to do:

- **Principle 1. Know your learners.** Teachers gather information about each student's background, particularly those aspects that are consequential for the student's language development. These aspects include learners' home languages and cultures, their levels of English proficiency, and all the factors that can support or hinder their ELD.

- **Principle 2. Create conditions for language learning.** Teachers make their classrooms into spaces where students are academically and emotionally motivated to learn, practice, and take risks with language. Teachers work to secure all the essential conditions of English language acquisition, draw on beneficial conditions, and set high expectations for their learners.

- **Principle 3. Design high-quality lessons for language development.** Teachers know what students can do at their current level of language development and what they need to learn next. Teachers then determine lesson objectives, plan how they will convey content information, promote rich classroom conversations, decide on tasks that are meaningful and encourage authentic language practice, and explicitly teach learning strategies and critical-thinking skills.

- **Principle 4. Adapt lesson delivery as needed.** Teachers monitor their students' comprehension, adjust teacher talk or materials, differentiate instruction, and scaffold tasks according to students' English language proficiency levels. In short, effective teaching of multilingual learners of English requires making decisions during the lesson delivery on the basis of student responses and actions and a solid understanding of the second language development process.

- **Principle 5. Monitor and assess student language development.** Teachers gauge how well students are making progress in ELD, note and evaluate the types of errors that students make, and offer strategic feedback. They use a variety of assessment types to measure student achievement and carefully interpret results of assessments with second language learning in mind.

- **Principle 6. Engage and collaborate within a community of practice.** Teachers understand that they can serve learners better when they work with their colleagues. Teaching multilingual learners of English requires that teachers be part of a community of practice within their school and the broader education community that affords them access to ongoing professional development. Teachers should coplan with colleagues so they understand the language and content demands of each subject that a learner studies. Coteaching is another way professional learning takes place for language and content-area teachers. English language teachers also take on leadership roles in their schools and districts.

All 6 Principles challenge teachers of multilingual learners of English to develop professionally. Appendix B provides a self-assessment checklist for teachers to use to evaluate their own implementation of The 6 Principles and supporting practices. Our school systems are changing rapidly, our student populations are increasingly diverse, and, as professionals, we must change and grow while holding fast to those principles that we know will lead to excellence and achievement for our learners.

Chapter 4 builds on the practices described in Principle 6 and highlights the ways in which English language teachers can be resources for other educators in their schools and districts. The chapter moves beyond this particular function to explain how English language teachers can be agents of change, advocating for their students and acting as liaisons among families, school personnel, and the community.

Additional resources pertaining to this chapter are available at www.the6principles.org/K-12.

4 ADDITIONAL ROLES FOR TEACHERS OF MULTILINGUAL LEARNERS OF ENGLISH

I graduated from college as a Spanish major and taught high school Spanish for several years. During that time, many families from different countries moved into the neighborhood where I was teaching. We didn't have English as a second language classes at the time, but the principal asked me to form a class with the 10 English learners in the school. "You teach language, so you should be able to figure out how to teach them," he said. Well, I didn't know very much about teaching these students, but I loved trying! This experience inspired me to go back to school to get my TESOL degree. It seemed like a simple transition from teaching Spanish to teaching English; I didn't realize at the time that teaching these learners was much more than teaching a content area. On the contrary, it involved a whole slew of other responsibilities, each more demanding, yet also more rewarding, than the next.

English language development (ELD), bilingual, and dual language teachers (subsequently *English language teachers* for brevity) come to the profession via many different pathways. Some were multilingual learners of English themselves and want to help others learn English. Some have an interest in other cultures or languages and want to work with immigrant communities. Still others, like the teacher in the opening vignette, originally taught other academic subjects but developed an interest in working with multilingual learners of English. Today, many teachers choose to become English language (EL) teachers and study courses in undergraduate or graduate programs. They receive an ELD or bilingual endorsement or certification and are hired specifically as the ELD or bilingual teacher at their school. Once on the job, they are often struck by the many and varied roles that English language teachers assume outside the classroom.

But even if elementary grade–level, secondary content, and special education teachers are not certified ELD teachers, they are in fact teachers of multilingual learners of English when they have these learners in their classrooms. These learners succeed academically when all staff in the school community take responsibility for educating, assisting, mentoring, and guiding them in various ways (National Education Association, 2015). Therefore, this chapter applies to *all teachers* who have these learners in their classrooms.

Being an English language teacher often involves being an adviser to these students and a resource or even coach to other staff who may have recently received these learners in their classrooms. English language teachers are also an important link to parents or guardians of these students, so they serve as advocates for the students and their families. They play a vital role on school leadership teams and committees, and they often become involved in curriculum writing and textbook decisions. Even though these extra roles increase their workload several times over, many teachers take them on with passion and commitment so they can provide a successful educational experience for their learners.

When they assume these varied roles, English language teachers often become agents of change in their school districts. As they interact with colleagues and administrators by participating in meetings, on committees, and through informal dialogue, they communicate information about their students and share effective strategies for teaching them. They point out that the label *multilingual learner of English* is, for most, a temporary designation. Their collaborative efforts extend to advocating for the resources and support services that students need to succeed in school and graduate. They guide and facilitate students' development of linguistic competence, cultural awareness, and the skills needed to navigate school and life.

With the emergence of high-stakes testing and accountability measures since the 1990s, the knowledge and skills that English language teachers possess have become more vital as schools search for strategies to increase their effectiveness with students (Farrell, 2015; Staehr Fenner, n.d.). This chapter describes the various roles that teachers of these learners take on to promote the academic success of their students, and it details these roles within the framework of The 6 Principles for Exemplary Teaching of English Learners®.

We do not mean to imply that English language teachers are the only ones responsible for helping multilingual learners of English succeed and providing language access and ancillary services to the learners' families. Indeed, states, districts, and schools have federal obligations to make these services accessible, and all staff are capable of supporting the learners. Chapter 5 provides more suggestions in this regard.

Adviser

Supporting Principle 1. *Know Your Learners*

Find out what concerns your learners have and how you can help.

At some point in their careers, effective teachers of all grades and subjects play the role of adviser to particular students. For teachers of multilingual learners of English, however, these roles are customary. Many families of our learners arrive in the United States with minimal knowledge of U.S. educational practices and the way schools function. Teachers often become the "go to" staff person that the student and parents or guardians communicate with, trust, and rely on for information and advice. Because teachers of these learners are experienced in working with them and their families, they can often anticipate their questions and needs, and students find it easy to approach them with issues and concerns. EL teachers can find ways to communicate, even if they do not speak their students' home languages, and they increasingly use technology-based translation tools to send and receive messages.

Some learners have come to the United States to escape violence, civil unrest, or a natural disaster. For instance, in the wake of the conflict in Ukraine and the crisis in Afghanistan, many school districts have received students who have experienced upheaval and displacement. Many of these students left behind family members or witnessed difficult situations in their home countries and arrived in the United States having experienced significant trauma and loss. Other learners have accompanied their families in immigrating to the United States, leaving behind close friends and relatives to start a new educational path in this country. Still others join parents or relatives they may not have seen for years.

For these new arrivals, the school environment is unfamiliar, and it takes time to adapt to school routines and social norms. The learning curve varies from person to person, but students usually benefit from asking for guidance from an English language teacher.

Shen immigrated from Taiwan to the United States with his parents when he was a freshman in high school. However, he started his junior year in a new school district after his family moved to a new town. In Ms. Martin's English language arts class, he remained virtually silent and minimally engaged in partner activities. Twice a month, Ms. Martin played movies in class and had students write an essay to respond to the prompts after they watched the movies. Shen never turned in these essays on time, as he did not understand the movies. This isolation extended to his classmates, as he remained largely unknown within groups, and other students hardly felt connected with him as well. But a different narrative unfolded when Shen entered Mr. Castillo's ELD class. Shen's demeanor shifted as he became more interactive, speaking a few English words with other classmates who also spoke languages other than English at home. Shen seemed to find his footing. In Mr. Castillo's class, students felt at ease discussing their ideas in English or by incorporating phrases in their home languages during class presentations. Although he did not always understand the various languages spoken, Mr. Castillo encouraged students to include their home language on presentation slides along with an English translation.

In such sensitive cases, learners may see their English language teacher or any of their other teachers as an anchor in an otherwise chaotic and frightening transition to a new life. The stability and guidance offered by schools in general, and the caring presence of a dedicated teacher in particular, are critical as students struggle through transition and adjustment.

Advocate

Supporting Principle 2. *Create Conditions for Language Learning*

Promote appropriate academic programs and services and a safe and welcoming environment for students and families.

As advocates, EL teachers strive to ensure that students receive an "equitable and excellent education by taking appropriate actions on their behalf" (Staehr Fenner, 2014, p. 8). Both the National Board for Professional Teaching Standards (2016) and TESOL International Association (2019), in its *Standards for Initial TESOL Pre-K–12 Teacher Preparation Programs*, see advocacy as a central role of English language teachers. The need for advocacy remains urgent, given the myriad barriers that many of our students face—barriers that may impede their success in school.

One such barrier is the underpreparation of teachers at preservice institutions. Some grade-level and content teachers, though well intentioned, may lack knowledge about second language acquisition and the academic needs of multilingual learners of English and, consequently, may not be adequately prepared to teach these students. As we mentioned in Chapter 1, national standards for teacher education do not mandate that all preservice teachers complete significant coursework related to teaching multilingual learners of English, yet many of these teachers have these students in their classrooms. As a result, some teachers may not know which strategies and materials work best with multilingual learners of English, and some may not have the same high expectations for these students that they have for other students, potentially hindering their educational progress.

Another barrier these students can face is discrimination in the school and in the wider community, which can affect them and their families in direct and subtle ways as they strive to succeed academically, socially, emotionally, and financially in their new country. Teachers can help by providing advocacy for students and their families who have not yet developed their own strong voice to advocate for themselves (Staehr Fenner, 2014). In light of the rapid growth in numbers of multilingual learners of English in many locations in the United States (National Center for Education Statistics, 2022) and the persistent achievement gap, serving our students effectively and equitably requires that all their teachers take specific steps to advocate for them. Advocates can provide a voice in five key areas.

Areas for Advocacy

- Academics
- Social-emotional needs
- Access to programs and opportunities
- Support for families
- Societal and legal issues

Academics

Supporting Principle 3. *Design High-Quality Lessons for Language Development*

Encourage all teachers to learn appropriate techniques for educating multilingual learners of English.

Before the No Child Left Behind Act of 2001 became law, many districts across the country viewed the education of English learners as mainly the responsibility of the English language teacher. This legislation put the academic progress of these learners on the national radar, and this higher visibility was sustained in a subsequent federal education law, the Every Student Succeeds Act of 2015. Districts have to disaggregate and report the high-stakes testing scores of English learners annually. In many cases, district leaders have turned to English language teachers and administrators for help in improving the quality of education for English learners, with the goal of reducing achievement disparities between English learners and non-English learners. This demonstrates the evolving role of these EL educators in supporting multilingual learners of English and underscores the importance of implementing effective programs and instructional strategies to address learners' specific language needs.

In most education settings, multilingual learners of English spend only part of their day with their English language teacher and spend many hours with grade-level teachers (for students at the elementary level) or content teachers (for students at the secondary level). Although these learners benefit from interacting with students who are proficient in English in these classes, the grade-level and content teachers may need support and training to acquire the tools necessary to deliver appropriate instruction to them. As expressed in the vision outlined in Chapter 1, an important part of the work of English language teachers is to advocate for making their school a place where all teachers recognize that the education of multilingual learners of English is a shared responsibility. In schools that recognize this responsibility, all staff members learn approaches and best practices to make academic content accessible to all students and work together to promote the development of academic English (DelliCarpini & Alonso, 2013; Staehr Fenner, 2014). At the secondary level, English language teachers also advocate for these students to have appropriate courses and pathways that lead to graduation.

Even in districts where multilingual learners of English do spend most of their day with their English language teachers, as in some newcomer programs, educators must recognize that this is a short-term model, in place only until the students have some knowledge of English. Just as with any student in the district, these learners are entitled to be educated by teachers who are qualified and certified in their respective subjects—but these teachers must have the skills necessary to educate these students effectively.

English language teachers can encourage all staff in their schools to be aware of and sensitive to the various cultures and backgrounds of their students so that they use this information to interact with students and their families more effectively and with greater understanding. In addition, they can help colleagues understand the importance of students' maintaining and even improving their home languages, because facility with the home language helps promote English proficiency (Genesee, n.d.). The ability to use the home language can also be an asset in the future as students go on to college and careers (Commission on Language Learning, 2017).

All teachers can advocate for programs in their districts, such as dual language and bilingual programs, that help multilingual learners of English maintain and improve proficiency in their home language (Collier & Thomas, 2017) . They can encourage school libraries to have an adequate supply of books in students' home languages. Recognition of home language skills, a valued asset for 21st-century careers, is growing. Since 2011, many states have approved the Seal of Biliteracy program (www.sealofbiliteracy.org). Students can have a seal embossed on their high school diplomas, which indicates to universities and employers that they are proficient in English and another language.

Social-Emotional Needs

Supporting Principle 1. *Know Your Learners*

Mario, age 16, left Honduras in a hurry, taking his little sister with him. He had stopped going to school after third grade because gangs were kidnapping students and threatening to kill them if they didn't join. But the situation had recently gotten worse, and Mario feared for his sister's life and his own. They crossed the U.S. border in Texas, and after 3 months in a detention center, they ended up living with their brother, whom they had not seen for many years and hardly knew. Mario and his sister now go to school. Mario's classes are very hard for him; his sister is doing a little better. After school, Mario rushes off to his dishwashing job to earn money that he and his sister can live on. He wants to stay in school and graduate, but he is only in ninth grade and is having trouble trying to work long hours and pass his subjects in school.

Help learners get the assistance they need to overcome difficult circumstances.

As teachers of multilingual learners of English know, many of our students come to school with social, emotional, and financial issues that are beyond those of a child's typical experience or development. These learners may have left a war-torn country or experienced violence or extreme poverty. Some have been victims of religious persecution or have witnessed a relative being arrested or killed. Others have arrived in the United States to live with a parent or relative whom they hardly know (Custodio & O'Loughlin, 2017). Addressing the social-emotional needs of multilingual learners of English is paramount to their holistic development.

A promising program developed to address the emotional needs of students who come to school in the United States having experienced trauma is Cognitive Behavioral Intervention for Trauma in Schools. Staff members with counseling backgrounds or clinicians from outside agencies are trained to run group sessions with students who need support in order to function in the school setting despite their difficult backgrounds. (For more information, see www.traumaawareschools.org/index.php/learn-more-cbits.)

Even if students have arrived in the United States with an intact family or were born in this country, they may experience challenges stemming from cultural differences, such as when their American peers adhere to different norms than their immigrant parents. These circumstances can cause turmoil in children and adolescents as they grow up, and they may need culturally sensitive counseling services to work through these issues. English language teachers can advocate for appropriate counseling services to be made available, both in the school setting and outside of school, and in the student's home language, if needed. Teachers can stay informed about developments around the country and the world that can affect the educational, social, and emotional well-being of these learners.

By recognizing and addressing the social-emotional needs of multilingual learners of English, teachers can provide them with a supportive educational environment that nurtures not only their language development but also their emotional well-being (Lau & Shea, 2022; Pentón Herrera & Martinez-Alba, 2021). Creating such an environment promotes students' overall success in school and beyond. When teachers explicitly and intentionally integrate social-emotional learning into their teaching practices alongside academic content, they can strengthen students' sense of belonging within the school community and help them develop essential coping skills for addressing academic challenges (Frey et al., 2019; Rimm-Kaufman, 2021). (For more ideas about how to support the social-emotional needs of multilingual learners of English in secondary school, see www.colorincolorado.org/article/social-and-emotional-needs-middle-and-high-school-ells.)

Access to Programs and Opportunities

Supporting Principle 6. *Engage and Collaborate Within a Community of Practice*

Work with your colleagues to ensure that all programs and opportunities are accessible to multilingual learners of English.

Most school districts meet their students' needs by offering distinct programs such as special education and gifted and talented services. English language teachers work with colleagues, school leaders, and other professionals at school to ensure students have access to the programs they may need for academic success or those they may want for enrichment or enjoyment. These services are especially critical in the area of special education. In some districts, students could be denied services for years because districts wait until students learn enough English to be tested with common testing instruments. This practice is impermissible according to federal guidance and educational laws (U.S. Department of Education [USED], Office of English Language Acquisition [OELA], 2017; USED, Office for Civil Rights [OCR] & U.S. Department of Justice [USDOJ], Civil Rights Division [CRD], 2015a).

Even if students are not yet fluent in English, there are other ways to determine whether they have special needs that should be addressed through school-based services. By the same token, it is equally important to ensure that multilingual learners of English are not referred for special education simply because they have difficulty with English—they may have a language difference, not a language disability (USED, OELA, 2017; USED, OCR & USDOJ, CRD, 2015a). Making this distinction is where the English language teacher's expertise is essential.

English language teachers stay well informed about the referral processes for special education and may initiate the process if a teacher believes a student has a disability. The English language teacher is often the one who explains the referral process to parents (perhaps with the assistance of a bilingual family liaison) and advocates for the student to receive necessary support. Additionally, an English language teacher should be an active member of the student support team and participate in all Individualized Education Program (IEP) meetings involving multilingual learners of English. English language teachers know the students' language development needs and understand the second language acquisition process, so their input on the IEP goals is vital. They may also remind administrators that federal law states that parents have the right to a qualified interpreter as well as translated documents so they understand the proceedings of the IEP meeting and resulting documents. English language teachers therefore play a pivotal role in making sure that dually identified multilingual learners of English receive their legally mandated services—both special education and English language assistance services—and that their parents understand and are engaged in the process. (The federal government and several states have published guidance documents in the area. See, for example, USED, OELA, 2017; USED, 2022; and the resources available at www2.ed.gov/about/offices/list/ocr/ellresources.html.)

In some districts, multilingual learners of English might be denied the opportunity to participate in programs for students who are considered academically talented. Sometimes this happens because staff do not notice that these learners have the ability or interest in participating in these programs. Sometimes there is a false assumption that a student needs a high level of English proficiency. English language teachers can help bridge these gaps in perception. When screening for these programs is conducted totally in English, multilingual learners of English may have difficulty performing well, even if they possess the required knowledge or ability. As in the case with screening for gifted and talented programs, English language teachers can advocate for school districts to use alternative methods, such as the Naglieri Nonverbal Ability Test, for determining whether a student who is not yet fluent in English is capable of participating in such programs (USED, OCR & USDOJ, CRD, 2015a).

Some districts have other academic programs, specialty schools, and extracurricular activities focused on the arts, sciences, languages, or sports. Unfortunately, multilingual learners of English (and their parents or guardians) may not be aware that these opportunities exist or know how to gain access. Because of the language barrier, students may not hear an announcement at school, or their parents may not understand a notice that was sent home with the student. As they often do with regard to gifted and talented programs, school staff may not consider these learners as potential candidates for these other programs, or they may have created obstacles to enrollment, such as requiring an application essay written in English. Many multilingual learners of English, however, are talented in these areas. Participating in these programs affords these learners valuable opportunities to interact and develop friendships with English-proficient students, so teachers of multilingual learners of English should encourage students' involvement in such offerings. These programs and activities provide an excellent opportunity for students to improve their language skills, expand their interests, and enjoy school.

> It is essential to emphasize that language proficiency should not be a barrier that prevents students from accessing valuable educational opportunities. In fact, federal guidance states, "[Local education agencies] must also provide [English learners] with equal access to Advanced Placement (AP), honors, and International Baccalaureate (IB) courses, and gifted and talented education (GATE) programs" (USED, OELA, 2017, p. 2).

Support for Families

Supporting Principle 6. *Engage and Collaborate Within a Community of Practice*

In one school district in Connecticut, potential English learners and their families new to the district are directed to the English Learner Welcome Center, where interpreters are available to welcome families and explain district procedures. At the center, students are screened for English language services and also assessed in home language literacy (when possible) and math. Parents or guardians are interviewed so that the district can obtain a full educational history of the students to help with program placement. The families then receive help with filling out registration and free or reduced-price lunch forms (if desired) and obtaining health services. Before they leave the center, families receive a welcome gift, which consists of a welcome letter, a city and bus map, a public library card application, a list of city services, and a gift for the student. Depending on the student's grade level, this gift could be a bilingual dictionary, a book, a set of alphabet flash cards, or a vocabulary game. The goal is for families to leave the center with their questions answered and a sense that the school district is happy to meet them and ready to welcome them into their new community.

> Encourage the school district to have supports and services in place for families.

When families move to a new town or city, they usually go through an adjustment period during which they must locate and establish access to many places and services such as schools, doctors, and child care. However, when the family does not yet speak English and comes from a different culture, the task of becoming familiar with their new surroundings can be daunting. In some locations, school districts may have established structures to assist families (e.g., welcome centers, parent liaisons), but in other places, the teachers who receive the students may hear about difficulties the students or families encounter as they try to navigate the school district's procedures, forms, and requirements. These teachers can advocate for structures and services to be in place and easily accessible to new families.

Teachers of multilingual learners of English can ensure that when families arrive in the district, they are treated with respect and enter a welcoming atmosphere. If the school personnel who receive families can assist them in their home language, or if an interpreter can be available, either in person or through technology, families will feel more at ease. English language teachers can explain to administrators the advantages of having such personnel at the school. In addition, teachers can work with district or building staff to put procedures in place to help families gain access to needed school and community support services for themselves and their children. Teachers can develop contacts at local agencies that they may call on to help families in need. They can also encourage the district to offer English language classes (and GED or citizenship classes, if appropriate) for adults so that family members can start on the road to empowerment and independence and demonstrate to their children that they are learning English, too. Family literacy nights are another way to engage and empower parents. (See Loop, n.d.; TESOL International Association, 2018b; and USED, OELA, 2023a for helpful ideas.)

> What protocols are in place when families of multilingual learners arrive at your school? Are changes needed?

Once a family becomes part of the school community, teachers of English learners can advocate for interpreters at school functions, and especially at parent–teacher conferences, so that parents can understand information about their children's progress and learn strategies for helping them at home.

Because members of some families have multiple jobs and many responsibilities, teachers often text parents (with translation assistance, if available) to remind them of upcoming events at school and encourage them to attend. They can plan special functions, especially at the beginning of the school year, to explain the expectations and responsibilities of the family (e.g., providing children with a quiet place to study) and the services and assistance that the school can provide (e.g., special education, social services, interpreters at meetings, access to technology tools). At these functions, teachers can also provide activities to help new families meet and get to know other families so they can form their own support systems. (For more ideas about getting families involved, see Haynes, 2021.)

Teachers of multilingual learners of English also advocate for the translation of school–home communication, report cards, district websites, and robocall scripts into the major languages of the school community. School and district handbooks, course selection guides, and other major district publications may also need to be translated. Districts have an obligation to meaningfully communicate with parents and provide language assistance if families do not speak or read in English. (For federal regulations regarding the obligations of school districts to provide interpretation and translations, see USED, OELA, 2017; USED, OCR & USDOJ, CRD, 2015b).

Societal and Legal Issues

Supporting Principle 1. *Know Your Learners*

Three years ago, at a local high school in the Northeast, the valedictorian was a former English learner. He had come to the United States from Mexico when he was 8 years old, and he entered fourth grade in the district not knowing any English. After a rough start and an adjustment period, it became evident that he was a bright and highly motivated student. By eighth grade, he had exited the English as a second language (ESL)/bilingual program, and by the time he graduated from high school, he had taken numerous Advanced Placement and other challenging courses, and he ended up with the highest grade point average in the school. In his speech at graduation, he acknowledged the important role that his first ESL teacher had played in his education while she sat in the audience beaming as his special guest.

The student had been accepted at an Ivy League university, and he very much wanted to attend. However, because of his undocumented noncitizen status, he could not receive federal financial aid, and, without substantial financial help, he could not attend such an expensive university. He had also been accepted at the highest ranked state university in the area. However, in keeping with state policy, that university did not offer financial aid to undocumented students. The state university gave him the option to attend, but only as an international student, meaning he would pay costly out-of-state tuition. In the end, he decided to attend the local community college for his first year. Fortunately, after that year, the state changed its university tuition policy for undocumented students, and he was able to enroll at the state university and pay the in-state tuition. He graduated with honors and is now pursuing a career in business.

> If your students are undocumented noncitizens, educate your colleagues about the sensitive nature of this issue and the right of all students to obtain an education.

This vignette illustrates the financial and political challenges that some of our multilingual learners of English face as they attempt to continue their education after high school. Many are denied opportunities for furthering their education because they cannot obtain the necessary funds from either educational or financial institutions as a result of their immigration status. In some cases, students who arrived in the United States as children are not even aware of their undocumented noncitizen status until they start to apply for college and financial aid. These students are often devastated to learn that they face major obstacles to pursuing the career and life goals that they had worked so hard for and had hoped to accomplish.

English language teachers can ensure that all staff know that even if students are undocumented noncitizens, they have the same right to a K–12 education as all other students. Staff must be informed that when new families arrive at school, asking about immigration status or documentation of that status is, in fact, a violation of a student's civil rights (USED, OCR & USDOJ, CRD, 2014). It is also important to realize that even if a multilingual learner of English was born in this country, one or both parents may be undocumented noncitizens, and the family may be living in fear of deportation and separation. Teachers should watch for signs of anxiety and distress and seek support for the student and family as needed. (For more resources about student and family rights, see the online companion site for this book at www.the6principles.org/k-12.)

Supporting Principle 6. *Engage and Collaborate Within a Community of Practice*

> Become informed, and actively support better educational opportunities for your students.

English language teachers can get involved in advocating for these students through various channels outside the classroom. They can support the passage of legislation and policies, such as an in-state college tuition policy, to help students extend their education beyond high school and allow them to work and be responsible, contributing members of society. (For more updates about legislation and policies related to multilingual learners of English, see TESOL's Advocacy Action Center at www.tesol.org/advocacy/advocacy-action-center.) Teachers can also invite legislators into their classrooms to see the "face" of these learners, with the hope that policymakers will become more sensitive to issues regarding our students and the need for funding to support various programs.

As noted in Chapter 3, teachers of multilingual learners of English can join professional organizations to stay informed about issues concerning their students. At the local level, they can attend school board meetings in their district to appeal for adequate funding for staffing, courses, and programs to help multilingual learners of English succeed.

Resource for Colleagues

Despite the high percentage of multilingual learners of English in U.S. schools and the rising number of former English learners, the preservice training of grade-level and content teachers who will have these learners in their classrooms lags behind where it should be (National Center for Education Statistics, 2021). Experienced teachers of these learners thus have a major role to play in helping their colleagues work with students more effectively in their classrooms. The teachers who can serve in this way as resources to their colleagues are often the English language teachers who have specialized training in appropriate methods and second language acquisition theory. Other teachers who have developed skills and expertise in teaching multilingual learners of English may take on this role as well. For example, a science teacher who has learned strategies for teaching these learners and has successfully taught a sheltered science class such as ESL biology for several years will have much guidance to offer new science teachers who have these students in their classrooms.

Research studies that examine factors that lead to improvements in student achievement repeatedly find that quality instruction makes the biggest difference (Visible Learning, n.d.). For that reason, collaborating, coaching, and coteaching with grade-level and content teachers are the most important roles English language teachers have besides their own classroom instruction. English language teachers can help their colleagues gain the knowledge and skills necessary to feel confident and be successful with the learners in their classrooms by providing professional development, formally and informally, in the general areas found in Table 4.1.

Table 4.1	Professional Development Suggestions
Topics	Examples of Focus Areas
Language Acquisition Theory	The process of second language acquisition (see Chapter 2) and ways that all teachers can promote it
Cultural Competence	Cross-cultural communication and diversity sensitivity, as well as specific cultural information about the ethnolinguistic groups served by the school district
Differentiated Instruction	Collaboration and coteaching approaches that maximize the impact of language support and differentiated instruction for learners to feel more engaged with content material
The 6 Principles	Strategies and techniques that integrate content and language instruction and allow learners at all levels of English proficiency to have access to and participate in grade-level, standards-based instruction (see Chapter 3)
Content Integration	Information about how to design or adapt lessons to set language objectives and embed language development activities
Overview of Language Proficiency Standards	Information about their learners, including their educational backgrounds and English proficiency level scores by language domains to explain the students' reading, writing, listening, and speaking abilities
Advocacy and Assessment Support	Accommodations recommended for multilingual learners of English on classroom, district, and state assessments, as well as information about additional state-mandated assessments that these learners take to measure language proficiency
Social-Emotional Learning (SEL)	Relevant activities such as daily check-ins, discussion prompts, role-plays, and reflective journals that teachers can employ to incorporate SEL topics into literacy instruction

English language teachers assume several roles to assist their colleagues and strengthen their teaching practices.

Resource for Colleagues

- Peer coach
- Coteacher
- Member of a teacher team or professional learning committee
- Professional development provider

We do want to point out that this support and collaboration should be a two-way street. Just as English language teachers can help their colleagues understand students' needs, so too can grade-level and content teachers assist them in understanding the tasks and assignments required of the students in their classrooms. Mutual respect and good listening skills are critical. All teachers bring their strengths to the process and learn from one another.

Peer Coach

Supporting Principle 3. *Design High-Quality Lessons for Language Development*

Help your colleagues use effective strategies for teaching multilingual learners of English in their classrooms.

A peer coach can be a formal or informal role. It involves sharing one's expertise with colleagues to help improve their instruction—often through observation, discussion of students, strategies, and techniques—and providing feedback and resources. A coach is a facilitator, not an evaluator, and builds trust with colleagues. The relationship between coach and teacher is fruitful when they have a commitment to professional growth and are willing to sustain the partnership.

In the formal practice of peer coaching, a common collaborative approach involves (1) a preobservation planning conference to set a purpose for the observation and for the coach to learn about the students in class and the lesson to be delivered; (2) the observation; and (3) a postobservation reflective conference to debrief, ask questions, learn about the teacher's decision-making process during the lesson, and provide feedback. Given teachers' busy schedules at school, the pre- and postobservation discussions may take place online or by phone. No matter the medium, the coach and teacher want to take the opportunity to look over lesson plans, discuss scaffolds and differentiation techniques, gather supplemental resources, and examine student work.

Besides jointly planning or adapting lessons and observing in classrooms, peer coaches may also demonstrate a technique or teach a model lesson in the teacher's class. The teacher observes the coach and they discuss it afterward. Sometimes, the coach might invite another teacher or two into the room as well or videotape the model lesson for use in future professional learning.

Becoming a successful peer coach takes sensitivity, knowledge, time, and effort. It involves developing strong communication and leadership skills. Many resources are available to help coaches not only get started but also hone their skills. (See, for example, Aguilar, 2024; Benegas & Stolpestad, 2020; Hodge, 2023; Honigsfeld & Dove, 2019.)

Coteacher

Supporting Principle 3. *Design High-Quality Lessons for Language Development*

Effective coteaching involves coequal collaboration, clear communication, and mutual support.

Coteaching is used increasingly in U.S. schools to support student learning. This model of collaborative practice originated in the special education field and has expanded to classes with multilingual learners of English to bolster their language development, literacy skills, and content attainment. It takes time and effort to establish an effective coteaching partnership, and all teachers benefit from professional development specific to this topic. English language teachers unfortunately sometimes shoulder a heavy coteaching load, working with multiple teachers, sometimes across grade levels and in different subjects. Advocating for limits on the number of colleagues an English language teacher is partnered with is a reasonable endeavor.

> If you are a coteacher, how do you share The 6 Principles with your partner(s)?

Many coteachers use the collaborative instructional cycle developed by Dove and Honigsfeld (2017), which has four main steps: coplan, coinstruct, coassess, and reflect. Effective implementation requires, among other things, shared goals, knowledge of ways to integrate content and language instruction, an openness to different perspectives and methods, and, crucially, time for planning. This cycle has been aligned to instructional frameworks such as the SIOP Model (Echevarría et al., 2024). As they move through this cycle, English language teachers can provide direct, targeted professional development to their partners on many of the topics listed earlier (e.g., information about the learners, strategies and techniques to bolster oral language).

Coteachers are coequals; they share in decision-making, mutually support one another, and communicate effectively (Honigsfeld & LaChance, 2023). They may apply the cycle through several structures; here are three of the more common structures:

- **Team teaching.** Both teachers take turns delivering the lesson. The content teacher may introduce the topic, share the content objective, and guide the disciplinary-specific activities. The language teacher may explain the language objective, teach vocabulary, and help with reading and writing tasks.

- **Parallel teaching.** The teachers divide the class into two groups. They teach the same lesson separately, providing comprehensible input, scaffolding, and differentiation according to the needs of the students in their group.

- **Station teaching.** The classroom is organized to include three or four learning centers that focus on different skills or concepts. Small groups of students rotate through these stations. The coteachers each teach at one of the stations. Students may do independent or partner work at the other stations.

Tips for Successful Coteaching

- Establish designated, regular time to coplan.
- Maximize preparation before coplanning.
- Consider the best coteaching models for the upcoming lessons.
- Divvy up the responsibilities for each teacher in each lesson beforehand.
- Use digital planning tools such as online lesson planning templates.
- Establish designated reflection time.
- Apply feedback from one lesson to the next.

Member of School Teams and Professional Learning Committees

Supporting Principle 6. *Engage and Collaborate Within a Community of Practice*

Many schools have professional learning communities, grade-level planning teams, or departmental teams (or a combination of these groups). English language teachers have much to offer these teams by explaining or demonstrating effective practices that colleagues can begin to implement on their own. They could suggest the following actions to their colleagues:

> You can enrich professional teams by sharing and demonstrating effective practices.

- Co-construct lesson plans by suggesting effective language development techniques.
- Identify key language forms and functions in written, audio, and online materials that need to be explained to students (Cloud et al., 2009; Short & Echevarría, 2016; Zwiers, 2019).
- Recommend supplemental text materials at various reading levels or in the home language (Baker et al., 2014; Short et al., 2017).
- Help colleagues understand the value of learners' use of their home language to understand content and how to accommodate translanguaging in class.
- Modify classroom assessments to reduce the unnecessary complexity of language.
- Identify suitable instructional supports and testing accommodations, such as using bilingual glossaries, reading test questions aloud, and allowing extended time on assessments.
- Help colleagues interpret and apply the results of English language proficiency assessments.
- Help colleagues interpret state and local assessments in light of a learner's proficiency status.

Professional Development Provider

Supporting Principle 6. *Engage and Collaborate Within a Community of Practice*

Ms. Mussal teaches Grades 10 through 12 at a school in New England. During the 2020–2021 school year, she organized a series of Lunch and Learn professional development sessions for her colleagues. At each session, she crafted informative slideshows, each centered around one of The 6 Principles, drawing inspiration from the quotes found in The 6 Principles book. With the focus on practical implementation, she provided concrete examples of how to apply those ideas to support multilingual learners of English in content-area classrooms. She also made herself available to fellow teachers who wanted to make their lessons more accessible for these students. They worked together to review the lesson plans and materials. (See accompanying slides from the Lunch and Learn session for Principle 4.)

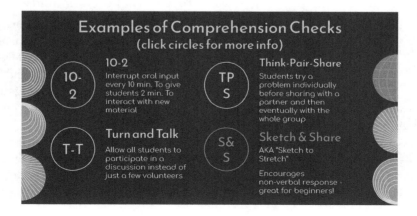

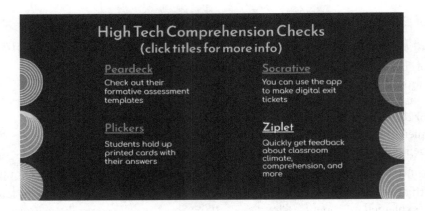

High Tech Comprehension Checks
(click titles for more info)

Peardeck
Check out their formative assessment templates

Socrative
You can use the app to make digital exit tickets

Plickers
Students hold up printed cards with their answers

Ziplet
Quickly get feedback about classroom climate, comprehension, and more

Images used with permission.

Use various means to provide professional development for your colleagues.

In this vignette, the ELD teacher demonstrated some effective practices to support multilingual learners of English through coteaching. Demonstrating practices is one strategy among many that teachers who have experience teaching these learners can use to impart ideas to, and discuss those ideas with, their colleagues. In so doing, they embody the belief that educating multilingual learners of English is a shared responsibility, and teachers can learn from one another (Staehr Fenner, 2014).

English language teachers are commonly asked to present workshops and other types of professional development sessions to colleagues in their school or district. Although it is certainly true that when they coach or coteach, they are providing professional development, the ideas listed here represent other options. Professional development approaches vary by school or district, depending on goals, time availability, and individual preferences. Professional development opportunities include

- presenting a workshop, a series of workshops, or a summer institute;
- presenting a "technique of the month" at faculty meetings;
- organizing Lunch and Learn sessions;
- guiding a summer curriculum development project; and
- establishing online communities for sharing ideas, techniques, and lesson plans.

Other Collaborations

Supporting Principle 6. *Engage and Collaborate Within a Community of Practice*

You can assist colleagues in other ways as an English language specialist.

English language teachers can collaborate in important ways outside the classroom, too. They might help school librarians organize book collections by English proficiency levels. They could meet with guidance counselors in middle and high schools to assist in determining the most appropriate programming and class schedules for multilingual learners of English. They might join administrators on home visits and at community-based meetings.

To be a successful resource for colleagues and serve students well, all teachers of multilingual learners of English should keep abreast of the latest research and developments in the field of English language teaching by pursuing their own professional development. They can read professional articles and journals, attend conferences and workshops, and take online courses, among other ways to strengthen their knowledge and skills. One resource is OASIS, an online platform that provides summaries of language education research articles (see www.oasis-database.org).

Developer and Reviewer of Curricula, Materials, and Assessments

Supporting Principle 3. *Design High-Quality Lessons for Language Development*

Assist in the development of curricula, materials, and assessments, which are the backbone of high-quality language lessons.

Even with the consistent high numbers of multilingual learners of English across the United States, curricula, materials, and assessments are often designed without substantial consideration for these learners' unique language needs. Although some publishers do consider these learners and consult with experts in the field when writing materials, not all do. Moreover, most state English language arts and mathematics standards address foundational literacy and numeracy skills in the standards for primary grades, but these skills are not mentioned in the secondary school standards. Beginning multilingual learners of English of all ages need to acquire basic literacy skills, and our adolescent students with interrupted or limited formal education may need to begin their math education with numeracy lessons. Language arts and math specialists often turn to English language teachers to help develop curriculum frameworks to deliver these foundational skills to these learners.

Educational technology tools in K–12 schools (e.g., interactive reading programs, online learning platforms, and apps) provide linguistic supports and other accommodations (e.g., visuals) to assist students, multilingual learners of English included, in comprehending the content being taught. Those programs for the general education classroom may not have been specifically designed to teach English as a new language, but they can offer, in some cases, targeted exercises related to reading, vocabulary, and writing skills based on data tracked and analyzed by the program and teacher. Nonetheless, having an English language teacher test run these programs and tools with the perspective of a multilingual learner of English is valuable because unexpected road blocks can crop up, such as the heavy use of idioms, assumed background schema, or unclear directions.

English language teachers can help improve curricula, materials, and assessments in several ways:

- **State-level involvement.** At the state level, these teachers can
    - serve on curriculum development or review committees, helping to develop, review, or revise English language frameworks or standards;
    - participate in state-level efforts to infuse language development and teaching techniques that are appropriate for multilingual learners of English into content-area frameworks; and
    - serve on textbook selection committees, especially those for core content areas.
- **District-level collaboration.** At the district level, English language teachers can
    - collaborate with staff to write ELD curricula and infuse best practices for English learning into other district curriculum frameworks;
    - design or modify district formative and summative assessments or create rubrics for measuring student progress, taking into consideration the different English proficiency levels that students exhibit;

- review textbooks and other content programs, technology tools, or other teaching materials, print and digital, to ensure they are responsive to the needs of multilingual learners of English; and
- enable all teachers to engage these learners in appropriate instruction in the core content areas.

Participant on School and District Committees for Programming and Policy

Supporting Principle 6. *Engage and Collaborate Within a Community of Practice*

About 3 years ago, our school district began to get many unaccompanied minors who crossed the U.S. border in Arizona and ended up in our community. Because most of them were students with limited or interrupted formal education, it became apparent quickly that we were not meeting their needs with our regular English language sheltered high school courses. Our administrator called together a group of English language teachers, principals, and counselors to design an "International Academy" for these students, with new courses in basic literacy and basic math, as well as counseling services offered by a bilingual social worker. After about 2 years, however, we realized that we needed to do more. Most of these students were older than others in their grades and needed to make money after school to support themselves and their families. Some of them were showing up late for school after arriving home after midnight from their jobs, and others skipped school altogether. They didn't see a direct connection between staying in school and their futures, and they had more immediate financial concerns. But we strongly believed that staying in school would help them in the long term, and we needed a hook to motivate them to keep up their attendance. We decided to build a career tech program so students could train for productive careers while they pursued their high school education. A group of us established a committee to work on this new component, and we have sent out requests to local businesses to form partnerships.

> Work together with your colleagues to develop or adjust programming and policies.

School districts across the United States have become more interested in ensuring that the needs of multilingual learners of English are taken into consideration during the development of district policies and programs. These learners' performance on high-stakes assessments and their graduation rates significantly impact school and district performance ratings, so superintendents and other high-ranking officials are looking to English language teachers and administrators for guidance as they review existing programs and policies or design new ones.

English language teachers can serve on leadership teams to ensure that these students' needs are considered in district and school improvement efforts. They may help design or refine academic programs for these learners as the population increases or student performance changes. For example, they may help design a newcomer program for older arrivals with limited formal schooling or a new writing intervention course for long-term multilingual learners of English. They may encourage the establishment of a tutoring center or an after-school program in which these students can receive academic support. They may advocate for a welcome center that offers assessment services for these students and provides families with information about various district policies regarding student behavior, homework, school buses, community services, and so forth.

English language teachers may also serve on policy committees of a more general nature so that the learners' voices and needs are heard with regard to the range of district issues. One example is the addition of social-emotional learning (SEL) practices in many schools postpandemic. Embedded within the daily classroom instruction, these SEL practices aim to enhance students' interpersonal skills and overall well-being, thus improving their learning experience. EL teachers, with their expertise in understanding how cultural and linguistic diversity shapes their students' learning experiences, are well positioned to advocate for the inclusion of SEL strategies tailored to the needs of multilingual learners of English. Their insights can help ensure that SEL practices are culturally responsive.

A Look Back and a Look Ahead

Chapter 4 has examined the various roles and responsibilities of all teachers of multilingual learners of English: ELD, bilingual, and dual language teachers; grade-level teachers at the elementary level; content teachers at the secondary level; special education teachers; and more. As detailed in the chapter, teachers of these learners serve as

- advisers for the students and their families to help them become familiar with the school system and their new community;
- advocates for the learners in several key areas, including by promoting learners' academic achievement, meeting their social-emotional needs, ensuring their access to programs and opportunities, supporting their families, and addressing societal and legal issues that they face;
- resources for colleagues through peer coaching, coteaching, providing professional development, collaborating on lesson planning, identifying instructional supports and testing accommodations, helping select appropriate and supplemental materials, interpreting assessment results, and advising on programming for learners; and
- participants on development teams for curricula, technology, materials, and locally designed assessments, as well as on leadership teams for school, district, or state programming and policy.

As teachers take on these various roles, they become agents for change who can have many positive effects on the education of multilingual learners of English. Although these extra responsibilities are considerable and time-consuming, teachers find great satisfaction in knowing that they are making a difference in the lives of their students.

English language teachers cannot meet all the needs of these learners on their own. In sharing their expertise with colleagues, they help build capacity within their school, but offering a truly exemplary education to multilingual learners of English requires the engagement of *all educators* in the design and implementation of successful programs. Chapter 5 discusses the responsibilities of other professionals, both site based and district based, who also play vital roles in educating these learners.

Additional resources pertaining to this chapter are available at www.the6principles.org/K-12.

5 ESTABLISHING A CULTURE OF SHARED RESPONSIBILITY

One stone does not support a cooking pot. —African proverb

Schools that successfully educate and support multilingual learners of English have a shared sense of community and responsibility. Many school-based professionals support these learners' education, not just classroom-based personnel. Reading specialists, instructional coaches, paraeducators, guidance counselors, and school and district administrators contribute to the overall success of programs and services designed for these students. Together with the teachers, these professionals form a *community of practice*—that is, a group of individuals who engage in a process of collective learning as they practice their profession (Lave & Wenger, 1991). These practitioners, each with their own skill set, join together to actively share knowledge, resources, experiences, and orientations to their work. They also build relationships that enhance their collaborative efforts.

When they share responsibility for all learners in the school, school staff can collectively move their school forward to ensure an equitable, high-quality education for multilingual learners of English and create a responsive school for parents and guardians (Cooper, 2020). Because key school-based professionals closely support the type of exemplary teaching that this book describes, they are the focus of this chapter, which extends the discussion of The 6 Principles to outline how those not providing direct instruction can nonetheless further the implementation of exemplary programs in very meaningful ways.

Chapter 5 provides recommendations for the following groups:

- principals and assistant principals
- district curriculum directors
- special education directors and gifted and talented program directors
- reading specialists and instructional coaches
- paraeducators
- technology coordinators
- librarians and media specialists
- guidance counselors, family liaisons, social workers, and school psychologists

To form a successful community of practice that serves multilingual learners of English and their families, all members of the community must fulfill their respective roles effectively. Not every principle is relevant for every group of educators, so this chapter examines only those principles that directly apply. The guidance in this chapter can also support district- or site-based teams as they review their current programs and services for learners and their families with an eye to school and program improvement (Cooper, 2020; Zacharian, 2023).

These roles provide a full picture of a culture of shared responsibility for multilingual learners of English in K–12 schools. If you are an English language teacher, you can share appropriate sections of this chapter with your colleagues, perhaps in one-to-one settings or in smaller learning communities. You might also organize a book study group to foster the growth and development of all of the professionals who make up your community of practice. (See Appendix C for questions to guide discussion and reflection about this book.) If you are a member of one of these groups, you can focus on your own section and examine the recommendations for your role. If you find that you lack information or skills pertaining to any of the points presented, you can work to build those competencies and strengthen your practice so that you can fully contribute to the education of multilingual learners of English. Many resources in this book and on the companion website can help you do so. You can make learning about multilingual learners of English a professional goal. Reach out to local colleges and universities, attend TESOL conferences or TESOL affiliate conferences, join the interest sections of TESOL and online communities focused on English language education, participate in online courses, or explore relevant websites, such as Colorín Colorado (www.colorincolorado.org).

School Principals and Assistant Principals

Making the School a Welcoming Place

As a principal in an urban elementary school, Mrs. McArthur believed in the power of home visits to build strong relationships between teachers and families, so she encouraged teachers to visit all new families prior to the start of the school year. The preference was for in-person visits, but if those were not possible, teachers would conduct the visits virtually using WhatsApp, Microsoft Teams, or Zoom. Because many of the families spoke languages other than English at home, she had to provide the support her teachers would need for these meetings. She first reviewed the registration forms—the home language surveys and section on parents' preferred means of communication. Next, she worked with support staff to identify speakers of those languages among her teachers, staff, and parent volunteers. For the one language they couldn't cover, she made sure that Language Line, a telephonic interpretation service the district subscribed to, would be available. The staff then planned the visits, forming teams and discussing the welcoming message they wanted to give their families. They also discussed how they would handle the two languages when visiting to make sure teachers and parents were at the center of the conversations. Finally, they reviewed important cultural differences in communication styles and culturally appropriate ways of interacting when visiting homes of families from each cultural community. Mrs. McArthur joined in several of the visits. As a result of this effort, staff reported that the new students became part of the classroom community more quickly and that their parents began participating in school activities.

School principals and assistant principals play a critical role as instructional leaders for their schools, especially when it comes to the delivery of a high-quality education to multilingual learners of English. If you are a principal or assistant principal, you need substantial knowledge about these learners, effective instructional programs, and research-based practices to serve them. You supervise and support classroom teachers serving these students and need to be able to judge the quality of instruction occurring in your school. In addition, you help guide the work of ancillary personnel, such as guidance staff, librarians, reading specialists, and instructional coaches, and you need to ensure that they interact effectively with learners and their families. You can turn to English language development (ELD), bilingual, and dual language teachers or program administrators for assistance and to help make your school a welcoming place for families from the cultural communities that make up your school's population. Certainly, you will want to seek the advice of experts as you make decisions about improvements needed at your school in any aspect of program delivery.

This section is designed to guide you as you perform your critical role as an instructional leader. Without your active involvement, your school is far less likely to fully realize The 6 Principles for Exemplary Teaching of English Learners®. We consider The 6 Principles in relation to your essential leadership role and detail actions you can take.

Supporting Principle 1. *Know Your Learners*

- Get to know your school's families through home visits in their homes or community centers. (Virtual meetings should be considered as well, as they can accommodate the busy schedules of parents and guardians.) Ensure that all staff who attend home visits are sensitive toward and skilled in interacting with families from the cultural communities represented in your school. "Conducting Home Visits" (on the following page) offers guidance to school-based personnel who aim to learn about the languages, cultures, educational backgrounds, and life experiences of their school's families. By gathering this information, staff can assemble the resources—both material and human—they need to serve their families well. This action creates truly responsive schools, leading to enhanced professional and parental satisfaction and student success (Gonzalez et al., 2005; Louie & Knuth, 2016).

- Make sure that all staff members who interact with multilingual learners of English and their families learn about, acknowledge, respect, and affirm the strengths, capabilities, and contributions these students and families bring to your school. Ensure that students and families are not viewed from a deficit perspective (because "they don't know English yet"). Instead, affirm the value they add to the teaching–learning community because of their linguistic and cultural resources. Consistently highlight the positive contributions and enrichment opportunities that these learners and their families bring to your school community.

- If your school has access to family liaisons who have been hired to support the students and families participating in English language programs, take full advantage of the special knowledge and skills that they bring to strengthen interactions between school and home. But if they are not trained, competent interpreters or translators, they must not translate official documents or essential other information or interpret at essential meetings, such as Individualized Education Program (IEP), Section 504, and student disciplinary meetings.

- Make sure that all school personnel know the languages in which families would like to receive information from the school and whether they prefer to receive information orally or in writing. Find out the families' preferred communication modes (e.g., print materials, phone, text message, email), and share this information with key personnel. Enter this information in student profiles in the school database so all may access it.

Conducting Home Visits

- Learn all you can about the cultures of your families and the communities in which they live. Be sensitive to the cultural norms and behavioral expectations that make home–school interactions successful and comfortable. Family liaisons who work in your school's or district's English language programs are an invaluable resource for this purpose.

- Conduct interviews or surveys in your families' home languages when the families first enroll their child in your school. Ask questions carefully so you get accurate and detailed information about your families. Be mindful of the fact that norms of disclosure vary across cultures, making some questions feel inappropriate or too personal to some groups but not to others. Avoid asking questions that families will view as intrusive, and before you begin, make sure that parents know the purpose of your questions and what you intend to do with the information.

- Inquire about the language or languages in which families would like to receive information from the school and whether they would prefer to receive information orally or in writing. Find out their preferred communication mode (e.g., print materials, phone, text message, email). This information should be collected as part of the registration process.

- Learn the names of family members and how to pronounce them accurately.

- Learn about parents' expectations for their child's schooling, the expectations that parents have for teachers and the school, and the culturally determined roles that parents typically play in their child's education. Share this information so that all school personnel understand the many traditional roles that parents play in the education of their children from a cross-cultural perspective.

- Ask the parents to list or orally identify some strengths and interests that their child has, and pass this information on to the child's teacher(s).

- Find out ways in which the school can support families, and vice versa, as well as the types of community resources that parents may find valuable.

Source: Gonzalez et al. (2005); Louie & Knuth (2016).

Supporting Principle 2. *Create Conditions for Language Learning*

Too Many Multilingual Learners of English Are Targeted for Intervention

In a rural elementary school, Mr. Simoes, the principal, noticed that a high percentage of kindergarten and first-grade multilingual learners of English were receiving intensive interventions in reading. When he checked into the situation, he was told that these students weren't meeting benchmarks, so they were all placed in the intervention program. Despite these efforts, however, their progress was limited. He learned that the students were being taught with a stand-alone program created for students whose home language is English. He suspected something was wrong.

He called a meeting of his school improvement team, which included the ELD teacher, and invited a specialist in multiliteracy from the local university to participate. The specialist and the ELD teacher explained that the benchmarks set were not appropriate for beginning multilingual learners of English. Thereafter, the team modified their assessment and intervention systems to respond more appropriately to the learning characteristics and needs of these students. Their first priority was to work together to make instruction in the regular classroom more responsive to the students, but they also worked to establish more appropriate assessment guidelines so that these learners would not be overidentified as needing intensive intervention.

- Create a welcoming environment for families and children at your school so they feel a sense of belonging that supports learning. Make multilingualism the norm in signage in the halls, language abilities of front office staff, design of the school website, and all correspondence and communication with families. You may want to use multilingual communication text messaging technology such as Talking Points (talkingpts.org) to facilitate cross-lingual communication among your staff and families.

- Support the use and development of students' home languages to help them develop bilingualism and biliteracy. Promote the Seal of Biliteracy (sealofbiliteracy.org) program if it is offered by your state. If your state does not yet offer the Seal of Biliteracy, advocate for it to do so.

- Ensure that intake and enrollment procedures are easy to implement across the languages used by members of the school community. Create accessible information for parents, such as booklets or short videos in the home languages of families to explain programmatic options and choices parents can make for their children.

- Hire teachers who have an ELD or bilingual certificate or endorsement and staff who are multilingual and culturally sensitive. Provide professional development to teachers and support staff who do not have such endorsements, and encourage teachers without an endorsement to pursue one.

- Provide trained and competent bilingual translators and interpreters for all parent meetings. Remember that these professionals are required by law for IEP and Section 504 meetings. "Resources for Working With Translators and Interpreters" offers further information on this topic.

- Encourage parents to take leadership or governance roles in the school and to work with school personnel to advocate for the needs of multilingual learners of English with decision makers such as the school board, city council members, or state legislators.

- Protect the rights of multilingual learners of English and their families. Ensure that you are well versed about the legal rights and relevant legislation governing the education of these students so you can protect the rights and fulfill your responsibilities to them and their families.

- Become familiar with the educational challenges of your multilingual learners of English. As needed, work with others to develop additional programs to support subgroups, such as students with limited or interrupted formal education, long-term multilingual learners of English, new arrivals, and those students with identified disabilities.

- As you visit classrooms, evaluate the teaching and learning environments with respect to the cultural responsiveness, specifically focusing on the use of time, space, instructional materials, student grouping arrangements, and conditions for testing.

Resources for Working With Translators and Interpreters

American Speech-Language-Hearing Association. (n.d.). *Collaborating with interpreters, transliterators, and translators.* www.asha.org/practice-portal/professional-issues/collaborating-with-interpreters

Lep.gov. (n.d.). *Tips on building an effective staff language service program.* www.lep.gov/sites/lep/files/media/document/2020-03/TIPS_Effective_Language_Program.pdf

Minnesota Department of Education. (2009). *Working with interpreters and translators.* education.state.mn.us/mdeprod/idcplg?IdcService=GET_FILE&dDocName=055113&RevisionSelectionMethod=latestReleased&Rendition=primary

Supporting Principle 3. *Design High-Quality Lessons for Language Development*

- To fully embrace your position as the educational leader of your school, review all of the chapters in this book so that you are well versed in what constitutes a high-quality instructional program for multilingual learners of English. You should also review the *English Learner Toolkit for State and Local Education Agencies* (U.S. Department of Education [USED], Office of English Language Acquisition, 2017). Many chapters have relevant information for school administrators.

- Learn what good instruction for multilingual learners of English looks like in a variety of classrooms—both stand-alone language development classes and sheltered content-area classes (Short et al., 2017). (These classes have names such as ELD 1, content-based ELD, integrated ELD, sheltered biology, and structured English immersion.) Ensure that lessons are differentiated for students of varied language proficiency levels.

- Provide teachers with budgets to purchase materials that help meet the needs of diverse student populations, such as materials for grade-level curriculum units at accessible reading levels and technology tools that support the needs of multilingual learners of English.

- Ensure that teachers who coteach or push in are well prepared for their roles, have joint planning time, and have the administrative support required to help them succeed (Honigsfeld & Dove, 2019).

- Promote interdisciplinary collaboration among teacher teams so that lessons are content rich and provide the conditions needed for language learning.

- Set up workshops and other professional development opportunities to build staff competence in designing differentiated lessons for multilingual learners of English—lessons that teach content *and* help students progress to the next level of language proficiency.

Supporting Principle 5. *Monitor and Assess Student Language Development*

Data Analysis for Program Improvement and Student Success

Ms. Rodriguez, the principal of a large urban middle school; Mr. Sanchez, the assistant principal for curriculum and instruction; and the school's department chairs meet quarterly to review student achievement data, looking for patterns and chances to make improvements. For their multilingual learners of English, these leaders disaggregate the data in many ways: by English proficiency level, by ethnolinguistic background, by length of time in the program, by amount of previous schooling, and so forth. At the end of the prior school year, when they looked at the available data, they clearly saw that a large group of students who had been enrolled in English language programs for 6 years or more had not yet exited the program and had not reached the proficient level of achievement on statewide assessments.

They took this as a call to action. Over the summer, they met with the School Improvement Team, which was composed of school administrators, English language and reading specialists, the family liaison, instructional coaches, and the district directors of the Curriculum and the Multilingual Learner Departments. They also invited lead ELD teachers and administrators from the feeder elementary schools. Together, they analyzed the data and saw a pattern in the language proficiency measures: Academic listening and writing had the lowest performance, and speaking and reading had much higher scores.

They considered whether their curricula and instructional practices were meeting these learners' needs. They reflected on the skills emphasized in their classrooms and instructional materials and determined that the curricula were weak in the same areas in which students were experiencing difficulty. That was their "Aha!" moment. They then planned a two-prong approach. First, that summer, a team of ELD and language arts specialists developed a Language Bridge course for these long-term English learners to focus on academic listening and writing. The students would take the course in the next school year, and the administrators would check in with the teachers and look at the new data at the end of the school year to make sure the course was building the needed skills and leading to increased student success. Second, they drew up a 3-year plan with two goals: (1) Provide professional development to the elementary teachers, and (2) revise their curricular frameworks and materials to ensure more emphasis on academic listening and writing.

Because of federal legislation such as the Every Student Succeeds Act (2015), which makes growth in English language proficiency a required indicator in state accountability systems, school-based leaders need to actively monitor student language development to make sure students are progressing. School-based leaders can take a number of actions to ensure the effectiveness of their English language programs:

- Make sure all staff members understand the importance of growth in English language learning as part of the school's accountability targets.

- Make sure all staff members are familiar with the state English language proficiency tests and understand how to interpret and use the scores for planning instruction and assessment by considering students' proficiency levels in skill areas (i.e., listening, speaking, reading, writing) and their length of time in the language support program.

- Ensure that all staff members who are responsible for the English language proficiency assessments have the preparation that they need to administer and interpret them. Provide sufficient time to administer the assessments, with as little interruption to the instructional program as possible.

- Plan for teachers to use interim language proficiency assessments that are tied to the state's system to monitor student progress in listening, speaking, reading, and writing periodically during the school year.

- Use data generated from your English language programs to improve their effectiveness. Disaggregate language proficiency and achievement data by subgroup, using achievement data known to be valid and reliable for multilingual learners of English. Subgroups might include recent arrivals, long-term learners, students with limited or interrupted formal education, or learners with disabilities. Looking at subgroups' data can help you identify unmet needs of particular groups of learners and generate solutions to improve educational services and schooling conditions for them.

- If statewide or district assessments are required to be administered in English, exercise caution in interpreting scores for learners who have only recently arrived in the United States or who are at beginning levels of English proficiency to ensure scores are interpreted fairly. Consider documenting growth in student performance with alternative measures.

- Ensure that instructional benchmarks and classroom assessments are appropriate for multilingual learners of English, and consult specialists as needed when you detect a pattern of under- or overrepresentation of these learners receiving intensive interventions, special education, or gifted services.

- Ensure that all teachers know which accommodations their multilingual learners of English are entitled to have on district and state assessments, and offer them to students on district, statewide, and classroom-based assessments.

Supporting Principle 6. *Engage and Collaborate Within a Community of Practice*

- Consult TESOL experts—such as English language program administrators and teacher leaders from your district, teacher educators from local universities with TESOL and bilingual programs, and educational consultants with English language expertise—in the decision-making process for policies, curricula, and program development in your school.

- Develop your community of practice by creating a climate of respect for all staff, especially valuing the role of the ELD and bilingual specialists in the school.

- Build joint planning time into the school schedule for teachers who have the same multilingual learners of English in their classes to develop lessons and align their instruction.

- Create access to community services for your learners and their families.

- Engage parents in meaningful ways by reducing barriers to their involvement and providing opportunities for families to contribute to the life and direction of the school. Make virtual meetings an option to accommodate the busy schedules of parents and guardians.

- Consult the English language teachers at all stages of the student referral process for a multilingual learner of English who may have special learning needs. Make sure that at least one of these teachers is on the eligibility and IEP teams.

District Curriculum Directors

District curriculum directors make many curricular and instructional decisions that affect learners every day in classrooms, most often in conjunction with dedicated and knowledgeable teachers and subject-matter specialists. However, although some instructional or supervisory personnel may be content experts, they may be less familiar with the language development and background schema needs of your learners.

If you are a curriculum director, you have an important role to play in ensuring that all curricula adopted by your district are truly accessible by multilingual learners of English of all proficiency levels and support their educational success. The following sections describe some of the actions you can take to support The 6 Principles.

Supporting Principle 1. *Know Your Learners*

- Make sure that comprehensible input techniques, scaffolds, and ideas for differentiation are evident in all district curricula so that linguistically and culturally diverse students of all proficiency levels have access. Include suggestions of materials and online resources designed to serve your beginning to advanced learners.

- Look closely at the curricula taught in the district to make sure that they are culturally responsive to multilingual learners of English, empowering them through the use of themes and materials that connect well with their background knowledge, cultures, and life experiences.

- If the district has a considerable number of students with interrupted or limited formal schooling, work with English language specialists to develop or adapt curricula to help them catch up academically with grade-level peers while building needed literacy skills.

- Make sure that mandated curricular materials are available in the high-incidence home languages of your district, thus supporting delivery of the curricula in dual language and bilingual education programs, as well as providing readily accessible materials for students who are literate in their home languages. These materials will allow students to learn valued content in their home or target language in addition to English.

Supporting Principle 2. *Create Conditions for Language Learning*

- Work with school librarians and media specialists to build classroom and school library collections that are meaningful and relevant to multilingual learners of English and list these in district curriculum guides. Find materials that match students' English proficiency levels.

- Build dual language and home language resource collections to support learning related to grade-level curricula for use at school and at home.

- Work with technology coordinators to select digital tools that will meet the needs of multilingual learners of English. Set policies regarding devices, internet access, and other supports learners might need in situations when remote learning is required.

Supporting Principle 3. *Design High-Quality Lessons for Language Development*

- Make sure that all content-area curricula identify not only content objectives but also a range of language objectives that teachers can draw from when implementing the curriculum with learners of various English proficiency levels. Be sure to include language forms and functions, not just vocabulary and reading skills, as language targets.

- Review all curricula to identify cultural or linguistic barriers that can impede the performance of multilingual learners of English. Suggest ways to modify the curricula for your learners so that teachers take these into account in lesson delivery.

- Make sure that district curricula are aligned with and cross-reference the state English language proficiency standards.

Supporting Principle 4. *Adapt Lesson Delivery as Needed*

- Inspect all curriculum guides to evaluate their appropriateness for students of varied language proficiency levels and literacy levels. Add or modify suggested teaching activities and include model lessons that show teachers how to include multilingual learners of English when delivering instruction.

- In all curriculum guides, suggest foundational background information that multilingual learners of English may need before studying common U.S. curricular topics, particularly if they have lived or been educated outside the United States. For example, they may need an orientation to U.S. geography before studying U.S. history to understand the locations where historic events took place. Or they may need an orientation to the English measurement system for math or science tasks.

- Periodically revisit existing curricula to ensure they meet the needs of current multilingual learners of English, particularly if backgrounds or learning needs change as new learners arrive. For example, if students arrive speaking languages new to the district, find materials in these home languages for the curricular units and make them available.

Supporting Principle 5. *Monitor and Assess Student Language Development*

- Provide clear instructions about when assessments must be conducted in English and when they can be administered in students' home languages. If unit assessments are to be conducted in English, specify the testing accommodations that should be used in the classroom and provided to students to make the assessments as fair and valid as possible.

- Recognize cultural and experiential bias in test items, test content, and test format (e.g., timed tests) on both statewide and local assessments.

- Ensure that district-developed tests
  - measure what is being taught in the most valid and fair way possible;
  - measure all learning objectives established for multilingual learners of English (language and content);
  - do not discriminate against certain linguistic or cultural groups (see Educational Testing Service, 2009, for guidelines); and
  - are designed for students of all language proficiency levels.
- Revisit and modify existing curricula if assessment results determine that changes are needed to improve learners' performance because as a group they are not performing to expectations.

Special Education Directors and Gifted and Talented Program Directors

Multilingual learners of English may have learning disabilities or special gifts and talents just as students in the general student population do. There should be straightforward procedures in place to determine these disabilities or gifts, and language proficiency should not be a barrier to identification for or participation in special education or gifted and talented programs. However, it is important to note that those who qualify for these programs do not cease to be multilingual learners of English. On the contrary, their language learning needs must be respected just as much as their identified disability or their special gifts or talents.

If you are a director of special education or of the gifted and talented program in your district, you play a vital role in recognizing students' unique learning characteristics and meeting both types of their learning needs. Actions that you can take to help these learners succeed will support the implementation of The 6 Principles within a culture of shared professional responsibility.

Supporting Principle 1. *Know Your Learners*

- To comply with legal guidelines, take special care to ensure students' linguistic and cultural differences are never mistaken for disabilities and that students with limited formal schooling are not being placed in special education for lack of appropriate general education alternatives (USED, Office for Civil Rights [OCR] & U.S. Department of Justice [USDOJ], Civil Rights Division [CRD], 2015a; USED, 2011).
- If a teacher or parent suspects a learning disability is interfering with a student's ability to succeed in the classroom, and the teacher's in-class adjustments are not improving the situation, the student should be referred to a student support or intervention team within a reasonable time frame (e.g., 2 or 3 months). Schools should not wait a year or longer before trying interventions or moving to the full referral process (USED, 2011).
- Make sure that students' lack of proficiency in English is not a barrier to their participation in gifted and talented programs. Use assessments with low or no language demands, such as the Naglieri Nonverbal Ability Test, to determine whether multilingual learners of English are eligible for gifted and talented opportunities. Provide training to teachers to enable them to identify learners' gifts and talents.
- Ensure that Multi-Tiered System of Supports (MTSS) and special education procedures account for learners' linguistic and cultural characteristics, and make sure that instruction offered at each tier is built on research-based teaching approaches known to be effective with multilingual learners of English (Burr et al., 2015; Echevarría et al., 2024).

- Take a hard look at benchmarks set at each grade level and benchmarking tools used by your district to identify learners in need of more intensive support. Examine the benchmarks and tools to determine whether they are valid and reliable for students learning English as a new language, especially for those at beginning levels of proficiency.

- Make sure that an English language teacher is present during all meetings for their learners who are going through the referral process or being considered for participation in gifted and talented programs.

- Maintain and review student data to see whether particular subgroups of students are being over- or underidentified for special education or gifted and talented programs under current procedures, and make changes as needed.

Supporting Principle 2. *Create Conditions for Language Learning*

- Make sure that all communication with parents is provided in the language they prefer and that only trained, competent interpreters are present during eligibility and IEP meetings. These steps can empower parents to advocate for their children's educational needs. (See "Resources for Working With Translators and Interpreters" earlier in this chapter.)

- Ensure that multilingual learners of English who have disabilities are afforded all of the instructional accommodations to which they are entitled.

- Make sure that special educators understand how to shape instruction for students of various English proficiency levels and that they know their learners' current levels in listening, speaking, reading, and writing. Remember that, by law, dually identified students must receive both ELD and special education services (USED, OCR & USDOJ, CRD, 2015a).

- Provide teachers with funds from program budgets to purchase materials (instructional and supplemental) that can help them meet the needs of diverse student populations.

- Make sure that all programs are open and responsive to multilingual learners of English, including programs for students with special gifts and talents.

- Ensure that students are placed in the least restrictive, most supportive environments possible for their identified learning needs.

Supporting Principle 3. *Design High-Quality Lessons for Language Development*

- Ensure that the curricula implemented in special education or gifted and talented program settings (both inclusion and stand-alone classrooms) are linguistically and culturally responsive for dually identified multilingual learners of English.

- Appreciate the role of the home language in learning English and help teachers connect instruction delivered in English at school with students' homes by using their home language. This practice may require having some dual language or home language–only materials available to send home for parents to work on with their children.

- Foster collaboration between English language teachers and special educators to ensure the delivery of high-quality instruction to multilingual learners of English with disabilities. Likewise, foster collaboration between English language teachers and teachers working in gifted and talented programs to make instruction truly responsive to learners defined by both characteristics.

Supporting Principle 4. *Adapt Lesson Delivery as Needed*

- Become familiar with the recommended instructional practices for multilingual learners of English that were discussed in Chapter 3. Work with staff to ensure these practices are applied in Tier 1 classrooms and Tier 2 interventions within the MTSS process.

- When evaluating special educators or teachers working in gifted and talented programs, give feedback about how well they adapt their curriculum and instruction for learners with diverse cultural backgrounds and varied proficiency levels.

Supporting Principle 5. *Monitor and Assess Student Language Development*

- Ensure that personnel involved in administering and interpreting assessments conducted to determine students' eligibility for special education or gifted and talented programs are bilingual and bicultural. As needed, hire special education assessors who are bilingual or, at a minimum, trained to assess linguistically and culturally diverse students.

- In cases where interpreters are used during the administration of eligibility assessments, maintain all best practice guidelines. (See "Resources for Working With Translators and Interpreters" earlier in this chapter.)

- Make sure that assessment measures used with multilingual learners of English who have identified disabilities take into account all primary characteristics of the learners—language, culture, and disability—in both their delivery and their interpretation. Exercise caution in interpreting the results of tests conducted in English, accounting for the possible effects of language and culture on the student's performance.

Reading Specialists and Instructional Coaches

Reading specialists and instructional coaches are key players in advancing classroom practices to promote student achievement. They may work directly with students, model best practices in classrooms, or push in or coteach in the classroom to deliver more responsive instruction. Reading specialists and instructional coaches should be well versed in all of the teaching practices outlined in Chapter 3 to support effective instruction for multilingual learners of English. In addition, if you are a reading special or instructional coach, you will want to take the actions recommended in this section to ensure that all of the teachers you support implement The 6 Principles and the research-based practices.

Supporting Principle 1. *Know Your Learners*

Seeking Data Where Data Are Needed

As a result of a steep increase in the enrollment of multilingual learners of English in the middle and high school, content teachers were offered targeted professional development. They received information about the languages and cultures of the students as well as about the district's English language proficiency assessment and how to interpret and use the scores. Special attention was given to ways of using the data to differentiate instruction in classrooms. However, as the workshop progressed, the teachers became frustrated when they learned that the district's electronic data management system did not include detailed language proficiency data. It listed only the students' overall proficiency level—not their abilities in listening, speaking, reading, and writing. Teachers were told to ask the ELD teachers in their schools for this information if they wanted it for guidance in differentiating instruction. The teachers were visibly upset. Given the importance of this information to their lesson planning, why wasn't it easily accessible in the online data management system?

- As you work with teachers, emphasize meaning-based teaching approaches over rote or discrete-skill teaching approaches. Multilingual learners of English need to learn foundational skills like phonics within a meaningful, whole-text framework so that the emphasis is on comprehension over rote decoding.

- If possible, help your school assess students' home language literacy abilities to facilitate instructional decisions as the students begin to learn to read and write in English. Locate literacy tests that are available in the major languages other than English that make up your school community.

- Make sure that all of the teachers with whom you work have access to information about their students' home languages, cultural backgrounds, current levels of language proficiency in each domain (listening, speaking, reading, and writing), and current literacy levels. Help your school make this information readily available in its electronic data systems so that teachers can easily find details about their students as they plan lessons and provide additional instructional and assessment supports.

Supporting Principle 2. *Create Conditions for Language Learning*

- Take every opportunity to honor and affirm children's cultural and linguistic identities. Working with others, create schoolwide literacy events that highlight your students' multilingualism by inviting authors, poets, or journalists from their cultures or home language groups. Consider partnering with the local library for some of these events.

- Help identify materials written by authors who represent the cultural communities of your learners. Choose materials that have won respected awards or prizes (e.g., Pura Belpré Award, New Voices Award) and that represent the cultural worlds and life experiences of your learners. Share these materials with the teachers and families that you support.

- Help teachers set up their classrooms in ways that are comfortable for learners from diverse cultural backgrounds. Consider, for example, grouping arrangements, the amount of talking permitted, use of the home language, and expectations regarding wait time.

Supporting Principle 3. *Design High-Quality Lessons for Language Development*

Creating Lessons That Engage All Learners

An instructional coach spent the day observing content-area classes at one of the high schools in her district. As she sat in a U.S. history class, she watched the two multilingual learners of English sitting by the window toward the back of the room. While the teacher was speaking to the class and pointing to terms on the board, the two students alternated between gazing out the window and sneaking glances at their cell phones. After a few minutes, a class discussion ensued, with the teacher calling on students who raised their hands. The two multilingual learners of English didn't participate. The teacher focused on other learners for the entire class period. When the instructional coach discussed her observations with the teacher after the lesson, the teacher said that she knew that the students didn't understand much of the lesson, but she was unsure what to do. She asked the coach for assistance, and they set up a schedule to meet regularly.

As the vignette illustrates, teachers need to design lessons that are differentiated, relevant, and engaging for all students—not just deliver lessons that are suitable for some but leave others to get what they can. To create and deliver high-quality lessons, teachers may need support. As a reading specialist or instructional coach, you can aid teachers in fully understanding the characteristics of lessons that promote maximum language growth for students learning English while imparting valuable content-area knowledge and skills. Consider taking the following actions to support teachers in designing high-quality lessons for language development:

- Guide teachers as they work to make their instruction linguistically and culturally responsive. In particular, make sure teachers understand the cultural dimensions present in classrooms and how they can shape instructional and social interactions to create positive learning conditions for learners with diverse backgrounds.

- Make sure that the teachers with whom you work know how to shape listening and speaking activities, as well as reading and writing activities, depending on their students' current proficiency levels in English. Providing scaffolds (e.g., language frames) for speaking and writing activities is a good place to begin. (See details on scaffolds in Chapter 3.)

- Help the teachers you support understand the role that oral language and culturally determined background knowledge play in English language reading comprehension and writing performance. Show teachers how to front-load essential language and background information before engaging students in reading or writing activities.

- Show all teachers of reading how to make connections with the knowledge that multilingual learners of English bring to the act of reading or writing from their home language. Give examples of language transfer (e.g., finding the main idea, noticing English words that look like words in the home language), and help teachers learn how to enhance the transfer process during instruction. Investigate the orthographies of the language groups you serve to know what may or may not transfer to reading and writing in English; share this information with the teachers with whom you work.

- Offer teachers selected materials to enhance learning for multilingual learners of English and guide them in selecting or adapting instructional materials for students of varied proficiency levels. This guidance applies to print and online textbooks and programs. Help teachers understand the types of scaffolds to look for as they choose materials (e.g., bolded words, illustrations and graphics that match the text, embedded definitions, glossaries, audio versions of texts, video clips). Provide materials in the home language that can be used with learners who are literate in their home languages to support content learning.

- When you provide direct services to students, coordinate your work with the English language teachers; make sure you both use the same research-based methods. Where possible, maintain the themes being used in the classroom to deepen and enrich students' language and literacy development. Work collaboratively to develop high-quality lessons that simultaneously develop language and content.

- Help extend the high-quality language and literacy lessons delivered at school to students' homes and communities. Help the teachers you support send home dual language or home language books on the same theme to link family literacy activities to those going on at school.

- As an instructional coach, demonstrate how to promote academic language learning (Echevarría et al., 2024; Staehr Fenner & Snyder, 2017). Model lessons that promote language development and critical thinking across listening, speaking, reading, and writing for students of all proficiency levels.

Supporting Principle 4. *Adapt Lesson Delivery as Needed*

- If your school or district uses a reading program not designed for multilingual learners of English and your students are struggling, augment or find alternative programs. Phonics programs that use nonsense words, for example, will not be recognized as non-English terms by beginning learners of English. Sounding out words that students do not know is ineffectual.

- If your secondary schools have multilingual learners of English with limited or interrupted formal schooling and who are preliterate in their home language, ensure that the teachers you work with know how to begin literacy instruction at later ages than is typical.

- If you are an instructional coach, revisit the methods and materials that all teachers use to determine whether any changes are needed to respond well to new populations' language and literacy levels.

Supporting Principle 5. *Monitor and Assess Student Language Development*

Interpreting Statewide Assessment Data for Learners New to English

At the Grade 4 team meeting, the math instructional coach and the ELD teacher carefully explained current testing policies requiring students learning English to take the state mathematics test in English no matter when they arrived in the country, unless a home language test was available and a student was literate in that language. They also explained that scores obtained in English on the math test were not reliable for new arrivals or learners at the beginning level of proficiency.

As the Grade 4 teachers reviewed the scores from the most recent statewide assessment, they were asked to put an asterisk next to the name of any learner whom they knew was a new arrival when the test was taken or had language proficiency scores at the two lowest levels. If the teachers were unsure of a student's proficiency level, the English language teacher added that information. The math coach and the classroom teachers then reviewed all of the names marked with asterisks and used their knowledge of the child in each case to determine which of the new arrivals or students at beginning proficiency levels would now receive additional support from the math coach. In cases where there was any doubt, the math coach scheduled the student for diagnostic testing with the aid of an interpreter to be sure that all students needing support received it. The ELD teacher and the math coach also determined which students would be placed in a team-teaching intervention group offered by the math coach, with support from a bilingual assistant.

As noted earlier in the chapter, the Every Student Succeeds Act (2015) has made growth in English language proficiency a required indicator in every state's accountability system. All schools attend to the education of their students who are learning English because they must demonstrate that they are improving students' English language proficiency and helping them reach academic parity with their grade-level peers. As a reading specialist or instructional coach, you will also want to interpret scores on statewide or district assessments fairly for your learners who only recently arrived or are at beginning and intermediate levels of English proficiency when tests are administered in English. You can take the following actions to help monitor learners' progress and support their performance on assessments:

- Help teachers with whom you work design classroom assessments on which multilingual learners of English can demonstrate their knowledge, making adjustments for language proficiency levels and cultural backgrounds.

- Make sure that all reading assessments are appropriate for students learning English as a new language and accurately assess the reading abilities of students in the process of learning English. Consider cultural bias, task bias, unknown vocabulary, use of nonsense words, and other language barriers.

- Help incorporate test-like tasks in ongoing classroom assessments to familiarize students with test formats and tasks they will encounter when taking district and state assessments. Many assessments are now online, so make sure teachers give students practice with the computers, tablets, and/or microphones they will use.

- Ensure that all assessments (e.g., running records, diagnostic reading tests, math tests, science tests) are appropriately administered to multilingual learners of English and are interpreted with consideration of issues typically faced by students in the process of learning English (e.g., not being able to answer a question because of cultural bias or unknown vocabulary in the prompt).

- In cases where students are not making adequate progress, help teachers look for instructional or program weaknesses before attributing underperformance to deficiencies in students. Work to correct instructional or program weaknesses so that students can be more successful.

Supporting Principle 6. *Engage and Collaborate Within a Community of Practice*

When Student Needs Change

As a result of an influx of recent refugees from war-torn countries, teachers in an urban school district in the Midwest noticed that among the district's newcomers were many students who had either not been to school consistently or never attended school. These students were placed in middle school classes with other students who were beginners in English, but the ELD teacher, Ms. Manning, believed that their needs were not being adequately addressed. She didn't know how to provide the foundational literacy instruction that they needed while also responding to the needs of the other beginners, who had strong or at least adequate literacy and educational backgrounds. She reached out to her reading specialist for assistance, but the specialist didn't know what materials might be suitable for the students. The teachers saw that their state TESOL affiliate was sponsoring a preconference session on exactly this topic. They quickly registered, hoping they would get ideas about how to adapt their instruction for this special group of students and learn about methods and materials that they could use for basic literacy instruction.

It is not uncommon for districts to see changes in their population of multilingual learners of English from one year to the next. The languages and cultures of their students might change, or instead of learners with strong educational backgrounds arriving, more refugees and asylum seekers with limited formal education are now enrolling. Instruction that was effective for a certain population may need to be revisited for a new population. As a reading specialist or an instructional coach, you can work with classroom teachers as they adapt to these significant changes. The vignette provides an example of the benefits that come from these types of collaboration. You can also take these actions to engage with the instructional personnel in your district:

- Bring all instructional personnel together in making decisions about students; respect the knowledge and skills of each person, and use their expertise when formulating instructional plans for multilingual learners of English.

- Continue your own personal, professional, and role-specific growth so you can enhance service delivery to multilingual learners of English.

- Help form school-based study groups to promote growth for teams of professionals in the use of best practices for multilingual learners of English.

Paraeducators

Paraeducators, also known as instructional assistants, play important roles in most K–12 educational settings. They provide additional support during classroom lessons and teach small groups of students, during time set aside for math intervention or reading rotations, for example. They support both language development and content learning. Many speak one of the learners' home languages or share a common cultural background, which helps them develop relationships with the students and create a welcoming and responsive learning environment.

Paraeducators who work with multilingual learners of English are effective when they utilize The 6 Principles. Knowing their students and what conditions help them learn a new language, paraeducators support the delivery of high-quality lessons. When students struggle with a task, paraeducators draw from a bank of strategies to adapt instruction. They are also well placed to assist teachers in monitoring and assessing students' language development due to their direct contact and frequent interactions with the learners. (See Amaral, 2019, for sample practices.) If you are a paraeducator, you can take the actions described in the following sections to support students' growth.

Supporting Principle 1. *Know Your Learners*

- Build relationships with and get to know your multilingual learners of English. Share relevant information you learn (e.g., interests, challenges, family life) with classroom teachers.
- Advocate for your students if you learn of needs or concerns related to their family circumstances.
- Request access to information on students' backgrounds and language proficiency levels to better tailor the instruction you provide.

Supporting Principle 2. *Create Conditions for Language Learning*

- Help learners become familiar with school policies and procedures, classroom routines, and instructional activities—especially if they enroll after the start of the year.

Supporting Principle 3. *Design High-Quality Lessons for Language Development*

- Integrate reading, writing, listening, and speaking activities because these skills are mutually supportive for language development. In small groups, multilingual learners of English can often be more active participants.
- Collaborate with teachers to provide visuals, on-page glossaries, annotations, and home-language summaries to support content learning.
- Encourage students to use their home language to figure out a word, activate background knowledge, or draft a written response. Explain that these translanguaging practices can be effective learning strategies.

Supporting Principle 4. *Adapt Lesson Delivery as Needed*

- When students struggle with a classroom task, encourage them to keep trying. Provide a range of supports and feedback to promote student thinking and learning. Simplify your oral language. If struggles persist, discuss ways to differentiate, modify the language, or reteach a concept with the teacher.

Supporting Principle 5. *Monitor and Assess Student Language Development*

- Monitor students' language errors and share this information with the English language teachers. Be sensitive to error correction and base it on a student's proficiency level.
- Consult with the teachers to set up a system to record student progress through checklists or anecdotal notes of observations. Online tools can assist with this effort.

Supporting Principle 6. *Engage and Collaborate Within a Community of Practice*

- Participate in professional development opportunities to learn more about effective instruction for multilingual learners of English. Many resources are available online.
- Meet regularly or collaborate online with the teachers you support to coplan.
- Participate in meetings about your students, when possible, such as student data reviews or parent–teacher conferences.

Technology Coordinators

The use of instructional technology in K–12 schools skyrocketed during the global pandemic and made the role of the technology coordinator more visible. Schools continue to use a wide range of digital tools in the classroom, as well as remote and hybrid learning on occasion. Teachers may need not only technical support and training but also advice when choosing online programs and digital resources that will provide comprehensible input, promote language learning, and be culturally responsive. As an instructional technology coordinator, your collaboration with English language teachers is crucial to ensure technology is integrated in ways that improve students' education. (See Hellman, 2021, for sample practices.) Through the following actions, you can help teachers incorporate technology as they implement The 6 Principles.

Supporting Principle 2. *Create Conditions for Language Learning*

- Assess whether multilingual learners of English who are new to the school are familiar with the technology used in their classrooms, including computers and tablets, the learning management system, commonly used programs and apps, and digital textbooks. If not, offer these students one-to-one or small-group tutorials to demonstrate use and answer specific questions and issues.

- Beware of digital inequities and work with administrators and English language teachers to provide equipment, software, internet access, and other digital tools, if needed, to ensure that multilingual learners of English can participate in remote learning. Offer user support to students and their families.

Supporting Principle 3. *Design High-Quality Lessons for Language Development*

- Create virtual language laboratories and digital language resources specific for learning English. These labs can take various forms, from web-based platforms to mobile applications. Collaborate with language teachers to provide engaging tools with interactive language exercises that offer ample opportunities for speaking, listening, reading, and writing practice.

- Provide professional development to teachers on existing and emerging digital tools and resources to maximize technology integration in lessons.

- Assist English language teachers in creating technology-enhanced curriculum projects, such as digital stories that can highlight learners' cultural backgrounds and experiences.

Supporting Principle 6. *Engage and Collaborate Within a Community of Practice*

- Periodically collect community feedback and suggestions about the use of educational technology in the school system. For instance, design a Google Forms survey to gather information you can use to improve services and identify additional necessary resources.

- Assist teachers in showcasing student work to parents and the broader community. You might video-record presentations and post them on the school's website or organize online exhibits (e.g., using Padlet) where students post their projects and creative work.

- Set up and maintain online platforms, such as school-specific social media groups or forums, where teachers, students, parents, and community members may talk about language learning, share resources, and ask questions.

- Work with the family liaison or social worker to develop an online repository of community resources for families to access.

Librarians and Media Specialists

School librarians and media specialists serve their schools in an essential capacity. They build and maintain rich instructional collections of print and multimedia resources that serve teachers, students, and families. Librarians and media specialists also promote literacy and content learning through their interactions with students. If you are a school librarian or media specialist, you are in a perfect position to support teachers as they seek culturally and linguistically responsive materials for their students. You can contribute to the learning that goes on in school and at home by adding resources to your collections for teachers, students, and parents. In these ways, you support the full implementation of The 6 Principles. The following sections describe key actions you can take.

Supporting Principle 1. *Know Your Learners*

Developing Parents' and Children's Literacy Skills

Taking a page from the local library's playbook, Beaumont Elementary School's librarian decided to offer a bilingual story time once a month. She scheduled this event to start 10 minutes after the school day ended so that parents who came to pick up their children could bring them to the library for a snack and a story. Younger siblings were welcome. The librarian, who was studying Spanish as a second language herself, read two books aloud each month—one fiction and one nonfiction, on related topics. Sometimes a parent helped her with the pronunciation of unfamiliar words! She modeled how parents could read such books at home, by doing a picture walk before reading, asking high-level questions about the text while reading, and making connections to other stories that they knew. At the end of the reading time, parents could use their children's school ID cards to check out books to bring home.

- Educate yourself about the levels of English proficiency through which learners progress so you can identify materials that support learners at each level.
- Ensure that the resource collection you manage is responsive to multilingual learners of English at all proficiency levels and that materials connect with the students' life experiences and diverse cultural backgrounds.
- Affirm the identities of multilingual learners of English by mounting displays that show the richness of their cultural worlds (e.g., exhibits of books from students' countries of origin; collections of materials about artists, authors, musicians, scientists, or historical figures from students' cultural and geographic backgrounds).
- Create online and print collections in the home languages of your students and families to support learning at school or at home. Encourage younger learners to bring texts or online resources home to involve their parents in literacy activities and content learning. These collections can include fiction and nonfiction texts; graphic novels; manga; picture books; audiobooks; high-interest, low-Lexile reading materials; and reference materials.
- Make sure that the library has bilingual dictionaries in the major home languages.

Supporting Principle 3. *Design High-Quality Lessons for Language Development*

- Cultivate collections of resources, including multimedia resources, in both English and the home languages of your students, to support teachers in their work with multilingual learners of English at all proficiency and literacy levels.
- Locate parallel materials in the students' home languages for the main curriculum units at each grade level, and make that material available to classroom teachers and reading and learning specialists.

- Bookmark key websites for translations, home language readings, home language newspapers, and sources of texts at different reading levels, such as Newsela, Epic!, Reading A-Z, and Raz-Kids.
- Help multilingual learners of English reinforce the reading skills they have been taught in the classroom, such as decoding unknown words, identifying parts of book, and summarizing main ideas from a text.
- Organize a reading club for older students to encourage a habit of reading.
- Teach critical media literacy skills to multilingual learners of English so they can browse and evaluate web material strategically. Because the students are still developing proficiency in English, they may be unable to determine reliable sources.

Supporting Principle 6. *Engage and Collaborate Within a Community of Practice*

- Work with classroom teachers and language specialists to design lessons that orient multilingual learners of English to the school library and teach them how to use it effectively, including how to access helpful materials online.
- Coordinate with teachers regarding upcoming research projects to preselect print and online materials that may assist their students who are learning English.
- Reach out to public librarians and help multilingual learners of English and their families become members of their local libraries. Help them understand how to use their local library's services that may be offered to adults (e.g., English, citizenship, or technology classes) or children (e.g., book clubs, story hour). Let them know that the library staff cannot ask them about their immigration status as a condition for library membership, but they may need to show evidence of local residency.
- Welcome parents to the school library, and hold outreach events so parents know the resources and services you can provide. Encourage parents to take out books in the home language and in English to read at home with their children. Make sure parents know the importance of continuing to develop the home language and how doing so contributes to children's English learning and academic success.

Guidance Counselors, Family Liaisons, Social Workers, and School Psychologists

School guidance counselors, family liaisons, social workers, and school psychologists bring special expertise to the team of practitioners working to meet the needs of multilingual learners of English and their families. If you are a guidance counselor, family liaison, social worker, or school psychologist, you likely have a rich background in, and a strong understanding of, cultural diversity and all of the implications for providing responsive services to students and families. However, you may not be as well versed in second language development or know how to deliver counseling services to learners who are in the process of learning English—unless you speak the home language. If you receive students from new ethnolinguistic groups in your school, you may need to learn about the home languages and cultures of families that you are new to serving. This section outlines actions you can take to help your school as it works to implement The 6 Principles in its efforts to provide a high-quality education for students who are in the process of learning English.

Making Multilingualism the Norm

Mr. Lakin, a bilingual social studies teacher, and Ms. Leininger, an ELD teacher, noticed that the parents of their students who were learning English were not participating at open houses or other school functions at their suburban high school. They decided to take action to see whether they could change the situation. They contacted the bilingual guidance counselor to develop a plan of action. First, they made signs for every classroom in the school, listing the name of the teacher and the language(s) that the teacher spoke. Next, they created a student club called Language Ambassadors. To participate in the club, students had to speak English and another language of the school community well. Before each school event, with the guidance counselor's supervision, the Language Ambassadors personally invited parents by phone, explaining the purpose of the function, mentioning that they would be there to greet them, and answering any questions the parents had about the event. They followed up with a reminder via the school's text communication program. The night of the first school event, the Language Ambassadors wore nametags with their names and the languages they spoke, and they greeted parents at the door. Each Language Ambassador then met with parents who spoke a given language in a separate orientation room to give an overview of the evening's event. The two teachers were astonished. In less than 6 months, and with only these two strategies in place, they went from a school with less than 10% of language minority parents participating on average to one where 70% of their students' parents came to school events designed for families.

Supporting Principle 1. *Know Your Learners*

- Share information with all instructional personnel about the cultures of your multilingual learners of English and the communities in which they live, including cultural norms that make home-school interactions successful and comfortable. Inform teachers about any sensitive or taboo topics and how to handle these in the classroom.

- Learn about parents' expectations for their child's schooling and the culturally determined roles that parents typically play in their child's education. Share this information so that all school personnel understand the many traditional roles that parents play in their children's education from a cross-cultural perspective.

- Help all school personnel learn to appreciate and respond to the personal, academic, and career needs of multilingual learners of English. Provide culturally responsive support to facilitate their academic success and personal growth.

- Share information with teachers about the social-emotional status of your multilingual learners of English so they can make lessons responsive to the personal and social needs of students.

- Be sensitive to and ensure that all school personnel are aware of issues relating to the possible undocumented status of students or their family members. Consult organizations such as the American Civil Liberties Union and Informed Immigrant to be clear about the rights of students and families who are undocumented. Learn about ways of supporting undocumented students in your school. (See "Resources to Support Undocumented Families and Deferred Action for Childhood Arrivals [DACA] Youth" on the following page.) You should also be aware that the threat of deportation (either for themselves or for a family member) may create great stress for some learners and affect their performance and behavior in school.

- Recognize that planning for postsecondary options may be complicated. Some high schoolers who are undocumented may not eligible for in-state tuition at a state university. None are eligible to receive federal financial aid. Keep these limitations in mind when discussing postsecondary options with them.

Resources to Support Undocumented Families and Deferred Action for Childhood Arrivals (DACA) Youth

American Civil Liberties Union: www.aclu.org/documents/faq-educators-immigrant-students-public-schools

Immigration Legal Resource Center: www.ilrc.org/daca

Informed Immigrant: www.informedimmigrant.com/resources/undocumented-students

National Immigration Law Center: www.nilc.org

United We Dream: unitedwedream.org/resources

- Ensure that multilingual learners of English have access to both special education and gifted and talented services, as appropriate, and that parents understand these programs. Limited language proficiency in English may not be a barrier to their access to these services (Seddon, 2015; USED, OCR & USDOJ, CRD, 2015a).

Supporting Principle 2. *Create Conditions for Language Learning*

- Make sure you account fully for students' previous educational experiences, both to place them in the appropriate grade and courses and to award high school credits fairly.

- Consult students and their parents or guardians to ensure that multilingual learners of English are placed in appropriate programs on the basis of their educational characteristics and their families' expressed goals (e.g., placement in a bilingual, ESL, or dual language program; referrals to gifted and talented programs).

- Add additional information to the learners' profiles in the school database, as appropriate, such as IEP information or prior educational experiences, including high school courses taken elsewhere for which they received credit.

Supporting Principle 3. *Design High-Quality Lessons for Language Development*

- Share information with teachers about community resources that can enrich the lessons that they plan, such as local cultural or art museums, community centers, and individuals who possess special talents and skills and live in the cultural communities around the school.

Supporting Principle 5. *Monitor and Assess Student Language Development*

- Make sure that parental reporting systems are well designed, accessible, and easy to interpret so that parents of multilingual learners of English can easily understand how their children are doing. These systems should be accessible in the parents' preferred language or mode of communication. Provide training for parents on how to access these tools.

- Educate parents about your state's language proficiency measures; make sure they understand the expected amount of growth that students should attain from one year to the next, depending on their starting level.

- Inform parents about the meaning and purpose of district and state assessments.

- If you are involved in special education assessments or the identification of students with special gifts and talents, review resources and recommendations in the section "Special Education Directors and Gifted and Talented Program Directors" earlier in this chapter.

Supporting Principle 6. *Engage and Collaborate Within a Community of Practice*

- Educate parents and students about the local school system; attendance, promotion, and graduation requirements; grade-level learning expectations; grading practices; and postsecondary options for high school students.

- Lead outreach efforts to the school's language and cultural communities; share resources and connections with all school personnel. Serve as a liaison to student homes and the community and help build effective family–school partnerships. (See USED, Office of English Language Acquisition, 2023a, for ideas.)

- Identify local linguistic and cultural resources that the school can tap as needed. Partner with community services that can help families with social, health, housing, and employment concerns. Identify community resources that teachers could use to give their students support outside of school as they adjust to their school and community.

- Ensure that students and parents feel safe and secure and that school personnel maintain families' confidentiality. Use trained, competent interpreters and translators to communicate with families. Help all families feel respected and included in decisions that affect their children's educational futures.

Other Educators and Policymakers

> How might you assist others who routinely come in contact with multilingual learners of English or their families (e.g., school nurses, bus drivers, cafeteria workers)?

This chapter has focused on the key school-based professionals who are best able to implement The 6 Principles, but these individuals are not alone. Many other professionals are involved in the education of multilingual learners of English, including support staff at school. School nurses, cafeteria workers, and security guards all communicate with these learners and can support their development of social language and add to a welcoming climate in the school.

School board members; state policymakers; and curriculum, test, and technology developers, despite their distance from the classroom, affect the education of multilingual learners of English as well, despite their distance from the classroom. Test developers, curriculum writers, and creators of online platforms and apps have a direct impact on students; they can either support or hinder the success of multilingual learners of English, depending on how their products are designed, implemented, or interpreted. School board members and other policymakers affect these students through the educational policies they adopt, the curricula and assessments they approve, and the human and material resources they make available to schools.

State education departments and teacher educators are also critical players in the delivery of programs to multilingual learners of English. The former create the conditions necessary for local schools to succeed through the funding they allocate and the regulations they issue, and the latter prepare future personnel who will work in the schools. Indeed, teacher education institutions and schools are partners in the preparation of future teachers; as such, they will find valuable information in this book as they work together to prepare teachers who will serve multilingual learners of English during their professional careers.

A Look Back and a Look Ahead

Chapter 5 has examined the roles of a range of school-based professionals whose work complements that of teachers in supporting the education of English learners. For each group of practitioners, the chapter has outlined key actions to aid in the full implementation of The 6 Principles. In making these recommendations, the chapter has highlighted the following ideas, based on research and best practice:

- Successful programs depend on establishing a strong culture of shared responsibility among educators for multilingual learners of English and their families.

- Multilingual learners of English and their families bring linguistic and cultural resources to the school and classroom. These assets should be welcomed, promoted, and fully used to strengthen teaching and learning. This goal cannot be accomplished unless we take time to investigate the linguistic and cultural resources possessed by our learners and their families.

- Equity and access can only be achieved if all professionals work together to ensure that multilingual learners of English receive high-quality programs and services designed to support their educational success in a positive, welcoming school climate.

- Many different personnel can aid in the planning and delivery of high-quality lessons that adapt instruction as needed for key learner characteristics and promote both language and content development. They can also play a role in monitoring and assessing students' language learning and academic achievement in ways that are culturally and linguistically appropriate, valid, and fair.

- To ensure the success of our multilingual learners of English, specific actions can be taken by school principals and assistant principals; district curriculum directors; special education directors and gifted and talented program directors; reading specialists and instructional coaches; librarians and media specialists; technology coordinators; and guidance counselors, social workers, and school psychologists. Other educators and policymakers have responsibilities in creating conditions for success as well, from teacher development to state curricula and assessments to funding to academic policies.

Chapter 6 builds on the practices described in this book and demonstrates how The 6 Principles may be implemented. It illustrates how a middle school classroom teacher, a team of university teacher educators, and a professional developer adapt the principles to their contexts to ultimately serve the needs of multilingual learners of English.

Additional resources pertaining to this chapter are available at www.the6principles.org/K-12.

6 IMPLEMENTING THE 6 PRINCIPLES IN DIFFERENT CONTEXTS

The 6 Principles for Exemplary Teaching of English Learners: Grades K–12 are applicable to any elementary or secondary classroom where students are learning English as a new language or learning content through that new language. English language development (ELD), dual language, bilingual, elementary grade-level, secondary content, special education teachers, and others can and do implement The 6 Principles in their classrooms. The principles are a framework for designing or improving instruction, regardless of the setting, drawn from decades of research in language pedagogy and language acquisition theory. It is important, however, that teachers think about the underlying ideas and adapt the practices according to their own teaching situation.

This chapter describes the implementation of The 6 Principles in three different settings:

- an ELD class in a middle school
- an online, graduate-level university foundations course in a TESOL program
- professional development sessions for practicing teachers

The cases described in this chapter are based on real programs and offer a window into the lives of these professionals as they seek to improve educational practices so multilingual learners of English can be successful in school. Whether you are a teacher candidate, a practicing teacher, a teacher educator, a professional developer, or an administrator, you will gain insights and suggestions as to how you can implement—or help others implement—The 6 Principles in your contexts.

It Starts With the Students: Teaching English Language Development With The 6 Principles in Middle School

Katherine (Kathy) Lobo is an experienced teacher of multilingual learners of English. Over the course of 25 years, she has taught Grades 5–12 in international schools in Japan and Australia and in private and public schools in the United States. Since 2015, she has taught in Newton Public Schools in Newton, Massachusetts, located near Boston, most recently at Charles E. Brown Middle School, where she is an English language teacher for Grades 6–8. She speaks Mandarin and Japanese and is an artist, too.

Kathy has implemented TESOL's 6 Principles in her classrooms for years. She finds them applicable to a wide range of contexts:

> No matter what's going on at the school or district level, you can guide your practice with The 6Ps. The guiding principles fit across different grade levels and can be used in different schools, [in] different states, and with different language standards. That's why people internationally can use them, too.

The following case offers a look at Kathy's instructional process, conveying how she thinks about The 6 Principles and embeds them in her classroom and lesson design. She uses The 6 Principles as a framework to engage with colleagues as well.

Principle 1. Know Your Learners

We're encouraged to be lifelong learners. Knowing your learners is part of that.

Like many teachers, Kathy checks the student records at the start of each year to learn basic information about her new students, such as their home countries, home languages, prior schooling, English language proficiency test scores, state achievement test scores if available, and languages their parents prefer for communication. She knows that each year she will have a mix of home languages, English proficiency levels, and educational backgrounds in her classes; students are assigned by grade level, not by proficiency level.

Boston is a metropolitan area that draws academics, business professionals, service and hospitality employees, refugees, and more. Students arrive from Asia, Europe, Central America, South America, the Middle East, the Caribbean, and Africa. Some students have bilingual parents who have graduated from or are attending graduate school programs, and others have parents with an elementary school education who do not speak English proficiently. Some students may have started studying English in their home countries as a second or third language; others may not yet be literate in their home language. In a recent year, across the three grades she teaches, Kathy had close to 30 students from 15 countries outside the United States; her students spoke 13 different languages at home. Her class size varies during the school year because new students can enter at any time and others move away.

Kathy is committed to going beyond the student data to get to know her multilingual learners of English. Early in the school year, she plans "get to know you" activities so students share information about themselves while practicing language skills. One favorite culminating activity of the first unit is a student poster. She shares a sample from a former student (Fig. 6.1) and a template (Fig. 6.2) with the class while also encouraging them to be creative. If they want to draw or write something different in some of the spaces, that is fine with her.

FIGURE 6.1	Student Poster

Image used with permission.

FIGURE 6.2   Student "Get to Know You" Poster Template

Country flag	Favorite food	Picture of someone in your family	Favorite drink
Age	PHOTO OF YOU		Birthday
Length of time in the United States			Favorite animal
Something you like to do at home	Something you like to read	Job you want as an adult	Something you like to do in class

To help students create their posters, Kathy introduces key vocabulary about numbers, days, years, school activities, family members, life at home, countries, and flags. She also teaches language functions so students can express their likes, dislikes, hopes, and wishes (e.g., *I like …, I hope …, I want to …*). While students work on their posters, the multilingual learners of English have the opportunity to use their home languages, translation tools, and web resources to express themselves. Once the students have made their posters, they take turns explaining them to a partner, using key phrases they have already practiced in earlier lessons.

> What do you see as the key roles and responsibilities of an ELD teacher?

As Kathy gets to know her learners, she pays particular attention to those who may be struggling with language development. Her professional training and long experience in working with students learning English as a new language enable her to notice when a student is not making expected progress. If she suspects the student has a learning disability, she takes several steps before starting the referral process for a special education evaluation. She communicates with the student's other teachers to see how the student is progressing in their classes, and she contacts families, when possible, to learn how the child has developed in terms of learning the home language and participating in household life. She considers an important role for an English language teacher is to be an advocate for multilingual learners of English who have disabilities.

Kathy also sets a goal for herself regarding her class each year:

One of my personal goals for each student is to help them to have the language and cultural proficiency to make a friend. If they can make a friend, so many other challenges and problems are avoided. By my learning about the student, I in turn can help them to make connections and learn about another student and the culture of our school.

Principle 2. Create Conditions for Language Learning

We don't adapt to the classroom; the classroom adapts to us.

Kathy is very deliberate in setting up her classroom to make the students feel comfortable and to promote their language learning. She has tables and chairs that she can move to form different groupings as desired. She posts students' home countries' flags and student work on the walls. She maintains a classroom library with books and other supplementary materials. She sets up a system of files and folders to organize lesson tasks for students.

Besides the physical environment, Kathy tries to create a classroom culture in which students feel respected, their languages and cultural backgrounds are appreciated, and their personal assets (e.g., talents, skills, experiences) are valued and made visible. Students may use their home language to express themselves, and Kathy works with them to articulate their ideas in English. An artist herself, Kathy incorporates many crafts and hands-on activities in her lessons. For example, as part of a lesson on the U.S. Constitution, students dressed like "patriots" and practiced writing using ink and a quill pen. She uses certain techniques routinely as well, such as jigsaw, that she introduces to students with easy content (i.e., something they already know) so they can learn the steps; she revisits the technique multiple times in later lessons, ramping up the cognitive load with new content. These types of activities lower the affective filter for many students and allow all to participate despite their varied proficiency levels.

When it comes to motivating students, Kathy speaks to Principle 1:

I try a variety of ways to motivate some students, especially if I can find something they are interested in and can incorporate it in class. I also think about what might be in the way of their participation.

Kathy pairs and groups students strategically, considering the lesson task and students' relationships and abilities. For some research projects, she makes space for them to pursue their own interests using a framework she prepares for gathering information and reporting it back. She adjusts some of her regular lessons each year based on the students in her class.

Principle 3. Design High-Quality Lessons for Language Development

I have freedom to plan lessons as I see fit, and I take advantage of teachable moments as they arise. I think about current events in the world and school and about the mainstream curriculum. What have my students missed, and what background building do they need? What are their peers doing, and what do they need to know next?

As Kathy prepares thematic instructional units, she keeps several things in mind: (1) where the students are in developing their reading, writing, listening, and speaking skills; (2) what topics students are studying in their core classes at their grade level; (3) what academic skills they need to practice (e.g., debating, supporting claims with evidence and reasoning, doing research); and (4) what curriculum materials are available and, in particular, if differentiated texts for the topic can be found. She uses the backward design approach. Accordingly, she determines a final project or task and works backward to figure out what skills to teach, what vocabulary to preteach, what texts and other materials to include in the lessons, and what activities will help students develop the language and content knowledge they need to complete the final task successfully. From there, she can plan the individual lessons, set learning objectives, and design scaffolds and other supports to help her learners. Depending on the final product, she might design an assessment rubric.

Kathy wants to build her students' English knowledge with explicit instruction, practice, and informal assessment. In the lessons, Kathy creates opportunities for collaboration. She frequently relies on the "I do, We do, You do" sequence of teaching and learning through a series of lessons. For "I do," she explains and models. For "We do," students practice in pairs or small groups with teacher guidance. For "You do," they work independently, although some learners who are less proficient may work with a partner or with the teacher. She incorporates technology into the lessons seamlessly. Students use Schoology, an online learning management platform, that dovetails with other online tools, platforms, and resources. For example, students collaborate on writing projects using Google Docs and prepare oral presentations with slides and recordings on Canva.

To deepen her students' knowledge of English, Kathy creates opportunities for repetition and application. For example, if students learn new words for one story or article, they revisit these words when discussing other situations, making predictions about a story or text they will read, and sharing personal experiences. Early in the year, for instance, Kathy introduces terms and expressions associated with maps along with phrases like "head east on Elm, drive north and cross over 95, we travel for 17 miles then …" with her students at lower levels of proficiency; students use this vocabulary again and add more terms in later units. She also revisits grammar points and language functions in later lessons and across the four language skills.

Knowing the importance of academic literacy to success in school, Kathy makes sure her students read a variety of texts. Her units revolve around a text, and she teaches vocabulary and reading comprehension strategies as students progress through the story, article, or biography. Figure 6.3 shows an example where the class learned how to annotate a text to aid in comprehension. Using an electronic document reader, Kathy read the text aloud with the class, asked them questions about it (e.g., What words don't you know? What seems important?), and demonstrated how she would annotate the text. To help students learn to read more independently, Kathy sometimes uses two or three different versions of a text so students can read at their ability levels. One source for such reading materials is Newsela (www.newsela.com).

FIGURE 6.3   Annotated Text

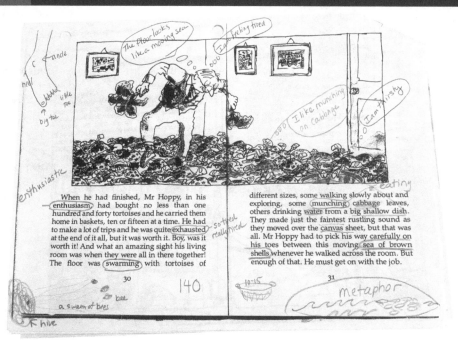

Image used with permission.

Figure 6.4 shows a unit plan that Kathy created about *The Gold Cadillac*, a 1987 novella of realistic fiction by Mildred D. Taylor. This is the story of an African American family from Ohio that buys a new gold Cadillac and drives it to Mississippi in 1950 to visit family. Along the way, they experience racism and discrimination in the southern part of the United States, where segregation was still prevalent. Kathy can introduce several themes with this book, such as the strength of family relationships, dealing with discrimination, and perseverance, and make connections to her students' lives.

As Kathy and her students read the text, Kathy often teaches vocabulary in context, although she preteaches some key terms. Students annotate or define words on their copies, and she sometimes creates Quizlet games to reinforce the words. She also prepares materials to support the students' language learning. She explains:

I made a little zine book for each student to take notes on the video. I slow the speed down a bit. We fill in the map in the book and then watch the video once without stopping. Then we watch it again, and I pause every so often to explain and have students do a listening or note-taking task to fill in the blanks in the mini "green book" zines.

FIGURE 6.4 Unit Plan on *The Gold Cadillac* by Mildred D. Taylor

Lesson and Objectives	Tasks	Materials	Extension
1. Prereading activity Students will be able to (SWBAT) calculate monthly payments related to purchasing a car. SWBAT summarize their math calculations.	Buying a Car game: Students calculate the costs of purchasing a new car with or without a trade-in car, following a teacher model. Students share what they learned and the monthly payments for each car.	Worksheet and car-buying options, used-car options sheet, dice, coins, calculators Paragraph frame handout	Write a summary of the car "purchase" process using a paragraph frame. Print out and post the students' essays. Include a photograph of the car they chose.
2. Pages 9–13 SWBAT read the beginning of the novel. SWBAT discuss characters and their relationships.	Begin reading the novel. Ask comprehension questions. With the class, make a list of the main characters and fill in a family tree for the characters introduced in the novel so far. Have students discuss aunts, uncles, and cousins.	Pictures of the cars from the novel (e.g., 1930 Ford Model A, 1945 Buick, 1945 Chevrolet, 1946 Chevrolet, 1949 Mercury Coup, 1950 Cadillac, 1950 Mississippi police car)	Have students make a family tree or a sketch of people they live with.

Lesson and Objectives	Tasks	Materials	Extension
3. Pages 14–18 SWBAT find locations on a map. SWBAT describe orally and write about families (those in the book and their own).	Have students label the illustration on pages 14–15 with the characters in the novel, then sketch and label their family tree. Using key words, have students orally describe their family and then write 3–5 sentences about them. Read pages 16–18 and teach a mini geography lesson about Ohio, Michigan, and the Mason–Dixon line. Teach the terms *state, province, capital, body of water, border, state line.* Fill in a map of Ohio with places mentioned in the novel (Bowling Green, Cincinnati, Cleveland, Dayton, Toledo).	Map of Ohio Map of the United States to show Ohio, Michigan, and the Mason–Dixon line.	Give students a map of the United States and have them ask and answer questions to practice map skills. Show how U.S. highways that go from north to south have odd numbers and roads that go from east to west have even numbers.
4. Pages 19–22 SWBAT make text-to-self connections about the story's plot, characters, and setting.	Read pages and discuss the plot and characters' actions and feelings. Have students identify any "aha moments" or "tough questions" experienced by the characters. Have students make text-to-self connections, share them with a partner, and discuss as a class.	A sketch of the outside of a home and a floor plan of the home (or room)	Students draw a picture of their neighborhood (e.g., where they buy groceries, go to school, play with friends). Teach a mini-lesson on contractions (e.g., I would = I'd).
5. Pages 23–25 SWBAT create dialogue for characters. SWBAT infer the thoughts of characters based on actions and situations.	Read and discuss the story so far. Model how to complete speech bubbles (i.e., what the character might be saying) and thinking bubbles (i.e., what a character might be thinking). Have students complete the illustration on page 25.	Samples of speech bubbles and thinking bubbles	Look at the U.S. map and discuss the Mason–Dixon line. Introduce the topic of the U.S. Civil War.

Lesson and Objectives	Tasks	Materials	Extension
6. Pages 26–27 SWBAT compare events in the text with personal experiences.	Read and discuss the text. Tap student experiences about picnics or eating outside. Have students draw and label a basket with the things they would take on a picnic. Have students work with partners to compare their drawings with the story.	Images of the foods described	Have students share orally and/or write about a picnic they have had or would like to have, including when, where, with whom, the food, and the weather.
7. Pages 28–32 SWBAT watch a video and make connections to the story. SWBAT listen and take notes to record information from the video.	Read and discuss the text. Show "The Real Story of the Green Book" video clip, and show students images of the books. Pause the video to explain and support student note-taking.	"The Real Story of the Green Book" documentary video clip from YouTube* Images of Green Book pages (Note: Publication of Green Books stopped in the mid-1960s.) Student Green Book zines	Use the U.S. map to trace the family's trip to Mississippi.
8. Pages 33–37 SWBAT infer and then write the thoughts of characters based on actions and situations. SWBAT connect conflicts in the story with conflicts they are aware of.	Read and discuss the text. Make connections to conflicts with which students are familiar. Students complete speech and thinking bubbles for characters in the illustration on page 34. Ask: What are the four characters in the car thinking, dreaming, or saying?	U.S. map (from 1860s if available)	Using the U.S. map, explain some of the events that occurred during the U.S. Civil War. Tailor the discussion to what the students know and are learning on this topic and the topic of civil rights in the grade-level classroom.
9. Pages 38–43 and Culminating Activity SWBAT compare events before and after 1964, with a focus on events in the novel and now. SWBAT write an essay about a theme in the book.	Read and discuss the text while filling in a T-chart. Students discuss and write an essay on either (1) what it means to be rich or (2) what the author meant when she wrote, "We and the family knew the truth. ... So I hold my head high" on page 43.	T-chart of Before 1964 and After 1964 Word bank and sentence frames to help complete the T-chart Sentence starters and paragraph frames to help complete the essay	Read and discuss the Author's Note in the book. Share information about the author and other books she has written. Consider introducing or reading another book by Mildred D. Taylor, such as *Song of the Trees*.

Lesson and Objectives	Tasks	Materials	Extension
10. Introduction to Dr. Martin Luther King Jr. SWBAT read a timeline for specific information. SWBAT use prepositional phrases of time to respond to questions.	Build on the civil rights discussion and share a timeline of the life of Dr. Martin Luther King Jr. Introduce the federal holiday Martin Luther King Jr. Day. Using the timeline, students answer Wh– questions about Dr. King using prepositional phrases about time (e.g., in 2019, on the 23rd, on January 23, 2010).	Timeline about the life of Dr. Martin Luther King Jr.	Have students share information about holidays related to famous people or events from their countries.

*www.youtube.com/watch?v=b33PN2NB2Do

Note. The unit includes approximately 10 lessons for students at advanced beginner and intermediate proficiency levels of English.

The unit also shows how the lessons have a cross-curricular dimension with the inclusion of math activities, map skills, and U.S. history topics. As Kathy explains, "I combine the timeline of history with the timelines of their lives." The class usually studies this unit in January, as a prelude to Martin Luther King Jr. Day.

Principle 4. Adapt Lesson Delivery as Needed

Besides adjusting my lessons, I sometimes help content teachers reduce the language load in their materials and think about the jargon or vocabulary that the students may not know.

As an experienced teacher, Kathy is not a stranger to adapting lessons if students are struggling to understand a concept or complete a task. She differentiates in many ways, such as by drawing pictures, letting students use online translators, having students discuss in their home and target language, annotating texts in a home language, and using peer assistance. For a writing task, she may provide a graphic organizer, a paragraph frame, or word banks. For a speaking task, she may have students use technology options to record, get teacher feedback, then re-record. For English proficiency level–specific supports and scaffolds, she may consult the GO TO Strategies matrix (Levine et al., 2013) and the WIDA Can-Do descriptors (WIDA, 2020a).

Kathy believes in the art of teaching: "I like to create new learning experiences each year." She applies her knowledge of her learners to modify lesson activities and offer flexibility with assignments. Instead of doing a book review for *The Gold Cadillac* unit, for instance, one year a group of boys designed their dream cars, learned how to draw dynamic images using two-point perspective, and presented their sketches to the class.

Principle 5. Monitor and Assess Student Language Development

I monitor and assess all the time. I am interested in the progress, the growth of each student.

Kathy monitors her multilingual learners' use of English for both accuracy and progress. She provides specific feedback on accuracy, aligning her corrections or suggestions to a student's English language proficiency level. One student who is learning to write a simple sentence may benefit from help with subject-verb agreement, while another who can write a paragraph might receive feedback on the clarity of the topic sentence. She monitors language development growth so she can challenge students to do more and learn more. That same student who needs a sentence frame at the start of the year will likely have that scaffold removed over time and be able to write one or more paragraphs on their own by the end.

Kathy offers oral feedback during class to help with pronunciation or clarification of a student's utterance. If Kathy notices that students are unable to produce or recognize certain sounds, she designs a minimal pairs activity, which she views as "exercises for our tongues to make new and more refined sounds." Pronunciation matters, and errors can lead to confusion or even embarrassment for her middle schoolers. She also uses the minimal pairs list as a means to teach or review vocabulary (see Fig. 6.5). For a specific task, like a debate, she gives feedback on the content the learners presented, the evidence they provided, how they used their voice, and how well they listened to others during the debate.

FIGURE 6.5 Minimal Pairs Exercise

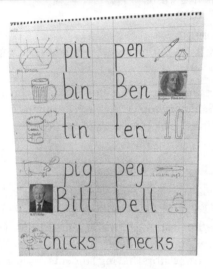

Image used with permission.

Kathy provides one-on-one feedback to students on written texts that will later be graded, and she gives the students opportunities to revise their work:

> *I go through a student's essay on a Google Doc. I'll use different colors to signal changes that are needed, use comment tags, and give choices for revision. Sometimes I might stop halfway through the text and have the student apply my comments from the first half to his second half.*

Effective teachers assess their students daily—most often informally with comprehension checks, exit tickets, observations, and similar approaches. Projects, writing prompts, oral presentations, quizzes, and unit tests are other common in-class assessments. These measures help teachers track students' language development over short intervals and are closely tied to the curriculum. The results allow teachers to adjust their instruction, reteach topics or skills the students have not mastered, offer additional practice for a few students who might need it, or support students in other ways.

Kathy employs a wide range of assessments, including those listed earlier. She often develops a rubric to evaluate student work (e.g., a project, an essay) and turns each into a checklist that she shares with students beforehand. When students have a project in another class, she works with them to understand the assignment and any accompanying rubric. Each year, her students prepare a portfolio of their writings as a summative measure of progress. The compilation includes a variety of genres students have explored during the year. Kathy provides feedback on their drafts before students finalize the pieces. The students must include a reflection on how their writing has evolved over time.

Students take the state standardized tests in Massachusetts[1] in the late winter and spring as a summative assessment of their learning, but teachers and students do not receive the scores until the school year is about to end. As a result, teachers cannot use the information to plan instruction for the students they have in class that year. To gather information in a more timely manner, Kathy's district uses an online reading assessment tool, i-Ready, three times per year to measure student progress and determine reading strengths and weaknesses. This tool offers personalized, online lessons to help students overcome their weaknesses, and students can complete the lessons on their own during scheduled time each week.

Principle 6. Engage and Collaborate Within a Community of Practice

The 6Ps books are wonderful desktop references for teachers. Great support. Accessible for teachers. You can use the framework for any lesson and classroom.

Kathy has been a strong advocate for The 6 Principles since the publication of the first book in 2018. The principles resonated with her and have been a mainstay of her teaching approach. Because Kathy is very active in her professional association, TESOL, and in her local affiliate, MATSOL, she continually expands her professional knowledge. She stays up to date on best practices for teaching multilingual learners of English and findings from new research about second language acquisition. She participates in many district- and state-sponsored professional learning opportunities as well. She shares knowledge that she gains with colleagues and has given presentations on The 6 Principles at several professional conferences around the United States.

As part of her job, Kathy regularly collaborates with fellow teachers at her school, including the core content teachers that her students have, as well as another English language teacher. The content teachers keep her apprised of units and activities in their classes, some of which she can preview or review in her English language class. She, in turn, helps these teachers understand what her students can do language-wise, what types of tasks they might need support with, what supports are helpful according to proficiency level, and more. She answers questions about students' home languages and cultures and does her best to help her colleagues know their learners better and incorporate effective teaching practices.

Kathy also engages with her students' families. Parents are invited to attend school events and participate in the English Learner Parent Advisory Council, a district-based committee. She and the other English language teacher host parent coffees three or four times each year so parents can meet other parents and network. The informal setting not only gives parents a chance to ask questions about the school or particular lessons or even life in Boston, but also gives Kathy the opportunity to learn more about her students' lives and interests at home and about family and cultural traditions.

In summary, Kathy's extensive teaching career of more than 25 years showcases her unwavering dedication to multilingual learners of English. This case offers insights into Kathy's adept integration of The 6 Principles into her teaching practice.

---

[1] The tests for middle school are ACCESS for ELs, which assesses the English skills of multilingual learners of English annually, and the MCAS (Massachusetts Comprehensive Assessment System), which assesses all students in Grades 6–8 each year for mathematics and English language arts and in Grade 8 for science.

Collaboration as Key: Preparing English Language Teacher Candidates in Higher Education

Drs. Gretchen Oliver and Karen Gregory are assistant professors and codirectors of TESOL programs at Clarkson University (Capital Region Campus) in Schenectady, New York. They have been coteaching in the graduate-level TESOL K–12 Teacher Preparation Program since 2019. This online program has a diverse student population: Some students have been multilingual learners of English themselves, with at least 12 different home languages represented among them. The students are studying to become English as a new language (ENL) teachers, a term widely used in New York State.

Gretchen and Karen have been using TESOL's 6 Principles with a group of graduate students in their online, asynchronous Foundations of Teaching TESOL course since summer 2021. They decided to adopt The 6 Principles as a framework for their 5-week course to introduce ideas about teaching ENL in the K–12 settings.

We found that The 6 Principles is very digestible for students in an introductory course. ... In each of the learning modules of our course, TESOL Foundations, students study The 6 Principles under the following guiding questions:

- *Who are multilingual learners of English?*
- *How do people learn a second or new language?*
- *How do we plan for instruction?*
- *How do we create a positive classroom culture for multilingual learners of English?*

This case study provides an overview of the foundation course, a collaborative effort by Gretchen and Karen. Throughout their instructional experience in this course, they have observed The 6 Principles to be a recurring theme in both class discussions and the teacher candidates' work. The box "Foundations of Teaching TESOL Course Outcomes" shares the intended outcomes of the course.

Foundations of Teaching TESOL Course Outcomes

In taking this course, students will

- identify defining characteristics of multilingual learners of English in U.S. schools;
- identify various program models for providing instruction to multilingual learners of English;
- understand aspects of second language learning, including theoretical foundations as well as practical aspects of language functions, academic vocabulary, and modalities;
- develop fundamental lesson planning skills, with a focus on writing objectives and developing an engaging learning sequence;
- create materials to welcome immigrant and refugee students to a learning environment, based on knowledge of the learners;
- collaborate with and provide helpful feedback to colleagues on group projects and presentations around second language teaching and learning issues; and
- reflect on how to continually expand one's understanding and application of content knowledge and pedagogical knowledge/skills.

For every module, Gretchen and Karen divide up the sections and take turns narrating the lectures, which they upload to VoiceThread. (See Fig. 6.6 for examples of VoiceThread lecture slides.) They ask teacher candidates to watch short video clips (e.g., "Interacting With Complex Texts: Jigsaw Project" at learn.teachingchannel.com/video/groups-to-analyze-complex-texts) and have them reflect on and respond to specific prompts (e.g., *What practices did you notice? How does this lesson reflect The 6 Principles?*). Gretchen and Karen try to make this process as interactive as possible. They work together to offer different perspectives when providing feedback on assignments to their students.

FIGURE 6.6   VoiceThread Lecture Slides

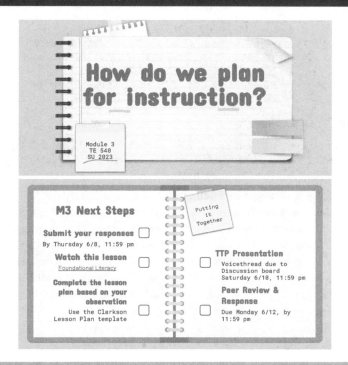

Images used with permission.

The course design follows The 6 Principles book itself. For example, Module 1 addresses Chapter 1 topics and Principle 1; Module 2 addresses Chapter 2's focus on language acquisition and Principles 2 and 3 on language teaching; and Module 3 follows Chapter 3, which includes detailed descriptions of all 6 Principles. Table 6.1 shows how Karen and Gretchen integrate The 6 Principles into their course.

Table 6.1 — Integration of 6 Principles in TESOL Foundation Course

Module	Examples of Theory to Practice Discussion Topics and Assignments	Principles Addressed
1	Go to the Green Card Voices website (www.greencardvoices.org) to learn more about immigrant and refugee students.	1
2	Observe a classroom lesson: "Group Work in the Multilingual Classroom."	2, 3
3	Watch the lesson "Foundational Literacy," then write a lesson plan for this class using the Clarkson MATESOL lesson plan template.	1, 2, 3, 4, 5, 6
4	Create an infographic to welcome students to your classroom.	1, 2, 3, 4, 5, 6
5	Complete the final project, a presentation on conscious competence. Explain your conscious competence through the lens of the TESOL 6 Principles.	1, 2, 3, 4, 5, 6

Principle 1. Know Your Learners

We think about what it means to really know your learners. … What does this look like in a real sense in a classroom? And why do you need to know your learners? And what do you do to make it practical?

For the first module of their course, Gretchen and Karen have designed a series of activities aimed at engaging teacher candidates in creating materials to foster an affirming environment for students in class. Using the website Green Card Voices (www.greencardvoices.org), teacher candidates explore biographies through written transcripts and oral interview clips of students who have immigrated to the United States and are enrolled in K–12 schools. This resource offers a platform for teacher candidates to gain insights into the unique experiences of multilingual learners of English in U.S. schools. As part of these activities, teacher candidates are prompted to identify the distinctive characteristics of these learners within the American educational context. This reflective activity encourages teacher candidates to contemplate effective strategies for welcoming these learners into their classrooms.

Gretchen and Karen incorporate New York State's *Culturally Responsive-Sustaining Education Framework* (CR-S Framework; New York State Education Department, n.d.) into their course. This framework links the overarching 6 Principles to the expectations and standards set forth by New York State. Teacher candidates read the CR-S Framework in Module 1 and are asked to make explicit connections to The 6 Principles in the lectures, "theory to practice" assignments, and peer review. By making this connection explicit, teacher candidates can understand how The 6 Principles align with their state's educational goals.

In addition to doing these practical activities, Gretchen and Karen encourage teacher candidates to discuss theoretical concepts, such as funds of knowledge, after they read assigned texts such as Hammond's (2015) *Culturally Responsive Teaching and the Brain*. *Funds of knowledge* refers to the knowledge and experiences grounded in students' homes and communities and displayed through their cultural practices and daily activities (Gonzalez et al., 2005). These readings provide a theoretical foundation, and Gretchen and Karen take them a step further by challenging teacher candidates to develop actionable strategies that translate these theories into classroom practices. For example, they give a written assignment based on the required text readings and ask teacher candidates to reflect on their personal connection to the text and how they can apply the knowledge gained to their future teaching career.

Principle 2. Create Conditions for Language Learning

We want them [the teacher candidates] to think deeply about what it means to create those conditions. … How does the teacher in the video create that welcoming environment?

For Module 2, titled "How Do People Learn a Second or New Language?", Gretchen and Karen have designed a range of engaging activities to deepen the teacher candidates' understanding of how to create conditions for language learning with the support of language acquisition research and instructional strategies. One prominent feature of this module is the incorporation of video analysis.

For this activity, Gretchen and Karen have teacher candidates watch a video exemplar of an elementary classroom: "Group Work in the Multilingual Classroom" (learn.teachingchannel.com/video/group-work-in-the-multi-language-ell-classroom) from the Teaching Channel website. The primary objective of this activity is to encourage teacher candidates to discern and articulate various facets of language use within the video content. This includes identifying and describing characteristics of academic language by categorizing words as used by both students and teachers into three tiers of vocabulary:

- *Tier 1:* Basic, familiar words
- *Tier 2:* High-frequency academic words used across different content areas and topics
- *Tier 3:* Low-frequency words that are content specific or technical

Additionally, Gretchen and Karen guide teacher candidates to determine possible content and language objectives for the lesson demonstrated in the video. A graphic organizer tool enables teacher candidates to compile their observation notes and insights from the video analysis.

One notable aspect of this module is how Gretchen and Karen integrate Principles 2 and 3 into the activities. By blending these principles, teacher candidates understand the interconnectedness between creating conducive learning conditions and effective instructional planning.

Principle 3. Design High-Quality Lessons for Language Development

Topics related to planning for instruction cover how to design a learning sequence; content-based instruction; differentiated instruction; WIDA and TESOL standards; scaffolding (i.e., Gradual Release of Responsibility); and connections among planning, instruction, and assessment.

In their course, Gretchen and Karen take a practical approach to guide teacher candidates in lesson planning. They introduce the Clarkson University lesson plan template, a tool that enables teacher candidates to begin thinking critically about the process of crafting effective lesson plans.

They then ask teacher candidates to conduct another video analysis. In this analysis, teacher candidates have to write a lesson plan as if they were the teacher who delivered the lesson in the video. Teacher candidates also learn specific strategies for writing plans, such as employing the Gradual Release of Responsibility model, which involves systematically shifting the responsibility for learning from the teacher to the students in a learning sequence.

Principle 4. Adapt Lesson Delivery as Needed

We try to help our students [the teacher candidates] to think about The 6 Principles as the umbrella and to think about what New York State has in terms of expectations because they are getting certified in New York State, then [think about] how these two frameworks are really connected.

Gretchen and Karen emphasize the importance of aligning lesson planning and delivery with The 6 Principles and New York State's guidance. They prompt teacher candidates to seek out relevant evidence in the video analyses that aligns with The 6 Principles, fostering a deeper understanding of how to effectively provide a supportive learning environment for multilingual learners of English.

Regarding Principle 4, Gretchen and Karen introduce topics such as classroom management, engagement, motivation, and four zones of teaching and learning to help teachers create a positive classroom culture for their learners. In their lecture, Gretchen and Karen show a graphic that they adapted from Gibbons (2015, p. 17), "Four Zones of Teaching and Learning." When teachers introduce material with a high cognitive load but no support or scaffolds for students, the students become frustrated. If teachers include scaffolds, learning and engagement can happen. Gretchen and Karen add a piece about scaffolding to the graphic to show how to use scaffolding to move learners toward autonomy and thus keep them in the "learning and engagement zone."

Principle 5. Monitor and Assess Student Language Development

In this foundation course, we discuss monitoring and assessing student language development in terms of the lesson plan, because what we teach in this course is how to plan a good language lesson. The two courses that follow [in this graduate program] are when we delve into details of scaffolding, differentiation, assessment, feedback, and all of that.

In their introductory course, Gretchen and Karen discuss how to write solid language and content objectives with teacher candidates. The teacher candidates learn how to formulate both content and language learning objectives that not only align with the curriculum but also are clear and attainable for learners. Additionally, Gretchen and Karen devote attention to the concept of formative assessment. They guide teacher candidates in how to do formative assessment, including what teacher candidates can do to assess students at various points throughout a lesson. For example, when teacher candidates watch those video lessons on the Teaching Channel, they need to figure out what kinds of formative assessment the teachers employed during those lessons. They also note how the teachers in the videos wrap up the lessons.

Prompts Used for Video Analyses

- What did the teacher do?
- Was there an exit ticket?
- Was there some kind of activity that made sure the teacher met their objectives?
- Did you think they met the objectives of the lesson?

These questions encourage teacher candidates to closely examine the teacher's actions in those videos.

Teacher candidates then refer to The 6 Principles Checklist for Teachers (Appendix B) to make connections between video analyses and the principles. This checklist serves as a structured guide for teacher candidates to correlate The 6 Principles to the instruction in the lessons they observe.

Besides preparing their teacher candidates to implement The 6 Principles in their teaching practices, Gretchen and Karen monitor and assess their students in this course. The three main assessment activities are Theory to Practice Presentations and Discussions, Interactive Lectures, and the final project. Teacher candidates discuss their lesson plans and video analyses in class. They submit Theory to Practice reflections that summarize and apply what they are learning. Each week, Gretchen and Karen post their lecture on VoiceThread and ask the teacher candidates to respond to the prompts on the same platform. The teacher candidates also complete a final project that includes two tasks: (1) Create a VoiceThread presentation to reflect on their preparation and learning, and (2) write a synthesis essay of their learning in response to the essential questions posed in the course. Figures 6.7 and 6.8 show a portion of the rubric for the final presentation and essay.

FIGURE 6.7   Final Project Part 1: Presentation

Criteria	Excellent 9-10	Good 7-8	Satisfactory 5-6	Inadequate 1-4	Unsatisfactory 0
A. Connection to and application of ideas from the texts and readings, class lectures, and/or other materials	Strong evidence of detailed and thorough application of ideas from the lectures and readings to the final project. Key concepts, ideas, research findings clearly synthesized, explained, evaluated, and integrated.	Convincing evidence of application of ideas from the lectures and readings to the final project. . Key concepts, ideas, research findings synthesized, explained, evaluated, and/ or integrated .	Some evidence of application of ideas from the lectures and readings to the final project. Key concepts, ideas, and research findings integrated with some explanation of concepts in relation to work.	Little application of ideas from the lectures and readings to the final project. Vague description, evaluation, and discussion of concepts in relation to work	Almost no application of ideas from the lectures and readings to the final project. Description, evaluation, and discussion of concepts in relation to work are almost non-existent.

Reprinted with permission.

FIGURE 6.8   Final Project Part 2: Essay

Criteria	Excellent 9-10	Good 7-8	Satisfactory 5-6	Inadequate 1-4	Unsatisfactory 0
A. Connection to and application of ideas from the texts and readings, class lectures, and/or other materials	Strong evidence of detailed and thorough application of ideas from the lectures and readings to the final project. Key concepts, ideas, research findings clearly synthesized, explained, evaluated, and integrated.	Convincing evidence of application of ideas from the lectures and readings to the final project. . Key concepts, ideas, research findings synthesized, explained, evaluated, and/ or integrated .	Some evidence of application of ideas from the lectures and readings to the final project. Key concepts, ideas, and research findings integrated with some explanation of concepts in relation to work.	Little application of ideas from the lectures and readings to the final project. Vague description, evaluation, and discussion of concepts in relation to work	Almost no application of ideas from the lectures and readings to the final project. Description, evaluation, and discussion of concepts in relation to work are almost non-existent.

Reprinted with permission.

Principle 6. Engage and Collaborate Within a Community of Practice

We really value sociocultural learning theory and creating a community of practice and having students learn from and with one another. … In the classes that we are coteaching, if you were to ask our students who is your professor, they would say both of us. They would never say one or the other of us because they hear our voices equally. They meet with both of us. They get feedback from both of us.

Gretchen and Karen explicitly try to create a community of practice and promote that engagement in collaboration with one another through their online Foundations course. With each module and the final project, teacher candidates need to complete a peer review of one another's work. Not only do they complete the assignments themselves, but they review at least one other classmate's work. Gretchen and Karen ask them to provide feedback, build on ideas, ask questions, clarify questions, and make connections back to the readings through the peer reviews. In this way, they try to lay the foundation for collaboration and show teacher candidates the value of collaborating with fellow teachers (including classroom teachers and content-area teachers) because developing collegial professional relationships is something that they will do as ENL specialists. They add:

We get them [the teacher candidates] accustomed to doing that from the very start. And then they start to conceptualize what it is going to be like when they are in that classroom, and they have to collaborate and coteach. It [Principle 6] sets the tone for them because it just becomes second nature to them.

In addition, Gretchen and Karen highlight that coteaching between ENL teachers and classroom content teachers is a standard instructional model in New York State, which they demonstrate through the Foundations course for TESOL graduate students. They purposely coteach their Foundations course to provide the model of coteaching in terms of The 6 Principles. Because the course is online, Gretchen and Karen use the learning management system Moodle to post all course materials. Teacher candidates collaborate online mostly via the Moodle course site and through interactions in VoiceThread. They are required to create their own VoiceThread presentations to share ideas with their peers. Through peer review, they provide oral or written feedback directly to their partner's VoiceThread slides. Gretchen and Karen provide direct instruction on how teacher candidates should use discourse moves in online discussions to explore topics and ideas in a deeper way, moving beyond simple comments like "Great idea" or "I love this." Gretchen and Karen suggest the following discourse moves for peer review:

> **What online resources do you use to facilitate class discussion in teacher education programs?**

- Compare or contrast something in their peer's post.
- Affirm or support something in their peer's post by connecting it to an idea from the readings.
- Build on an idea they have presented in their post.
- Respectfully challenge something in their post.
- Ask for clarification or elaboration.

These methods serve as a model for teacher candidates, demonstrating ways they can design instruction to foster collaboration and interaction among students.

Gretchen and Karen also emphasize that collaboration is crucial to the role of being an ENL teacher:

[As an ENL teacher,] you are going to be working with all the different teachers in the building, as well as the administrators, to design the best instructional plans for the multilingual learners of English in your building. So we really try to model that ourselves.

In fall 2023, Gretchen and Karen started offering six 1-hour sessions about The 6 Principles to teacher candidates in the Master of Arts in Teaching Secondary Subjects program. Their next step is to use The 6 Principles framework as part of their program's teacher performance assessment.

Building Bridges in Education: Connecting Teachers With The 6 Principles in Professional Development

Karamjeet Singh is an academic coordinator, mentor teacher, and teacher of English with the Directorate of Education Delhi. He has a diversified experience of 25 years teaching and developing professional development trainings for preservice and in-service teachers who work with multilingual learners of English in the government-run schools located in Delhi, a capital city in India. The classes in those elementary, middle, and high schools are populous, with an average class size of between 45 and 60 students who come from diverse linguistic backgrounds.

Karamjeet conducted the first 6 Principles training for his colleagues in 2018. He brought the book from the TESOL Convention in Chicago to India, then developed and presented the professional development modules. He provided a 6-week training called Be Exemplary that provided practical tools for teachers in Indian classrooms to learn about The 6 Principles (see examples of training slides of the presentation in Fig. 6.9). The training included theories of language learning and a community learning platform for participating teachers of English in India to share, create, and develop resources for each core principle. In discussing The 6 Principles, he said:

I found it to be much beyond just for English teachers. You must have also noticed that they [The 6 Principles] are applicable for almost every teacher because those principles are the crux of any classroom teaching. I called these principles "K.C.D.A.M.E."—K for Know your learners, C for Create conditions, D for Design high-quality lessons, A for Adapt lesson plan delivery, M for Monitor and assess, E for Engage and collaborate—so that teachers could remember them better.

FIGURE 6.9 K.C.D.A.M.E. Training Slides

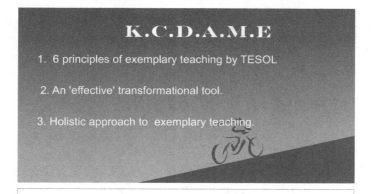

Images used with permission.

The following case shows Karamjeet's repertoire of instructional tools and his efforts at collaborating with teachers in implementing The 6 Principles in multilingual classrooms.

Principle 1. Know Your Learners

Knowing the learner is the first step to developing connections, which is why I find the first principle the most important among these 6 Principles.

With Karamjeet's training, teachers on his team start making portfolios for their students, gathering information that students share about their lives, such as their own language, cultural backgrounds, and interests. To be more specific, students' portfolios include their demographic, biographic, and parental information; memorable anecdotes of childhood; academic performance; hobbies; and habits. He recalled:

The moment when I ran into The 6 Principles, I realized that there is so much more to know about learners, not only their languages but also their interests.

He encourages teachers to leverage large- and small-group activities to better know their students. For example, he shared a board game template called Socratic Hexagon (Fig. 6.10), which helps both teachers and students develop skills of questioning while getting to know each other.

FIGURE 6.10 Socratic Hexagon

Image used with permission.

There are six prompts shown in the hexagon—when, who, where, what, why, and how—with corresponding numbers 1, 2, 3, 4, 5, and 6. Teachers have students write their names on the hexagon board and take turns rolling a number to find out their prompts. In this classroom game, students sit in a group asking questions and sharing their interests. Students frame and ask their own original questions, such as "Who is your role model?" or "How do you respond when someone irritates you?"

Karamjeet is also committed to his school community and has devised ways to connect with students' lived experiences in school, such as celebrating students' birthdays and organizing cultural events and festivals with parents and other schools to engage students in showcasing their cultural dress, dances, and songs.

Principle 2. Create Conditions for Language Learning

We extensively use the building as a learning aid. We had beautiful things drawn and written on the walls, which were not only informative but also indicated a subconscious condition for a better learning environment.

Karamjeet is keen on inculcating active learning in schools where teachers can create a psychologically safe environment for students. Teachers arrange designated learning spaces in classrooms, such as the Reading Corner, where elementary students can find comics, books, and magazines to read. For secondary students, Karamjeet tries to create conditions to make them feel more confident. For example, he has placed podiums in his classroom to encourage students to speak up in front of the class and to participate in debates and formal public speaking activities. He also has created certain areas in schools, such as the Stress Buster Room, where students can go to play board games, usually during their library or games period.

Specifically for English learning, his schools have integrated technology into classroom instruction to enhance digital learning conditions. For instance, the schools he works with have given each teacher a Bluetooth speaker to carry from class to class to provide audio-enhanced lessons. Teachers in those schools may also have a portable device called KYAN, an integrated computer and projector that enables teachers to show PowerPoint presentations and videos. These tech devices provide teachers and students with more opportunities to teach and learn through multimedia platforms. Karamjeet shared one learning activity:

> What we do in our classroom is that we play those silent videos made without sound by Pixar, and we tell students to come up with the dialogues, such as what that character would have been saying.

Regarding language learning conditions, he discusses a range of ideas with teachers that blend technology in classrooms and create purposeful spaces where students can engage in learning activities socially and academically. For example, he suggests the use of applications such as Mentimeter, Padlet, and Wordwall to display assignments that students can access on their phone while they are at home.

Principle 3. Design High-Quality Lessons for Language Development

So the lesson plan has been designed; is it being delivered accordingly?

Karamjeet helps teachers design lesson plans that focus on not only objectives of the subject-area content but also on objectives of the language that students will be learning. During the design process, he wants teachers to think about their rationales for using certain strategies and activities such as icebreakers, brain breaks, and energizers in lessons. He also provides templates for teachers so they already have certain activities they can incorporate into their lessons. For example, he knows teachers in his schools use 2-minute brain breaks frequently when they feel their class is getting boring. He suggests specific tools and strategies such as K-W-L charts, the Frayer model, and jigsaw reading. He also created a mnemonic device for designing a lesson plan, which he calls the 4Ps: First, *prepare* students for the content, then *present* the information, later let students *practice*, and finally ask them to *perform*.

Another model he has used to train teachers in lesson planning is the 5E Instructional Model: Engage, Explore, Explain, Elaborate, and Evaluate. He believes the first step to design lesson plans effectively is to design the right objectives, and the next step is to select the right strategies, not only for teaching but also for ongoing formative assessment to check whether students understand the lesson.

Principle 4. Adapt Lesson Delivery as Needed

When it comes to adapting the lesson plan, the first thing is to have an ongoing comprehension check. While teaching, how can we check whether our students understand or not?

Checking comprehension is an essential component of lesson delivery. Karamjeet shares various strategies to gauge students' understanding. One such technique is the use of nonverbal cues like thumbs-up or thumbs-down to quickly determine whether students comprehend the content. Additionally, he employs the use of exit tickets as an assessment at the end of a lesson to provide insights into students' grasp of the learning material. Another strategy he shares with teachers is called No-Hands Activity in which they instruct students not to raise hands when the teacher asks questions. They cold-call students so that the whole class remains attentive, and everyone gets a fair chance to answer.

Sometimes students become inattentive. Their minds wander, or they engage in off-task behaviors. In these cases, Karamjeet and his colleagues make adjustments and implement other activities such as scavenger hunts, learning stations, brain breaks, and mindfulness practice to bring students' focus back to the lessons.

Principle 5. Monitor and Assess Student Language Development

When we talk about giving feedback, that is one thing that I have really carried forward from The 6 Principles books, and I train teachers to give oral and written feedback to their students.

Karamjeet has noticed that it is new to some teachers that they need to consider how to give specific feedback to support students. As a teacher mentor, he conducted observations in various classrooms and had to give teachers feedback. Regardless of the subject being taught, he always used The 6 Principles to evaluate how teachers supported students' learning. In particular, he asked questions like the following while observing in a classroom: *Is the teacher putting forth some effort to know the learners? Are they trying to create some good conditions? How are they monitoring and evaluating their students? How are they giving feedback? Are they giving timely feedback? Are they giving feedback about the students' actions?*

He suggests that teachers need to plan for formative assessments and also share results with students, colleagues, and families. Teachers in Karamjeet's schools also utilize the practice of peer assessment, usually once a month in certain classes, when teachers have students work with peers to grade their work. In this way, peer assessment gives students a sense of responsibility.

When it comes to student achievement, teachers in Karamjeet's schools adopt a culture of knowledge sharing. They come together to talk about teaching and learning and share feedback on students' academic performance. Teachers in his schools teach from 8 a.m. to 2 p.m., then from 2 p.m. to 2:30 p.m. they sit with the whole school to share success stories and challenges they are facing in class and discuss how they conduct their assessments, including unit tests, written tests, oral tests, and project-based tasks. He regards these daily faculty meetings as culture-building opportunities.

Principle 6. Engage and Collaborate Within a Community of Practice

The principle of engaging and collaborating with all the stakeholders is the most challenging one.

Having teachers collaborate and reflect is important to Karamjeet. His practical approach to collaboration involves actively engaging with fellow teachers and nurturing mutually beneficial relationships between schools and parents. Drawing from his extensive experience, Karamjeet candidly acknowledges occasional challenges. He understands that teachers have their own agenda, goals, and philosophies, which can create complexities. Nevertheless, these challenges serve as valuable lessons, strengthening Karamjeet's resolve to foster collaborative practices and enhance professional development of teachers through a focus on The 6 Principles. This endeavor involved guiding them in areas such as engagement and collaboration.

In 2019, Karamjeet started providing professional development on The 6 Principles for teachers by telling them how to engage, collaborate, and, more practically, create a professional learning community. During the pandemic, he and the teachers formed a WhatsApp group that included teachers of English from nearly 200 schools in Delhi, and, in collaboration with some colleagues, he organized the Communicative English Language Training for teachers via the WhatsApp group and Google Classroom.

Three Objectives of Communicative English Language Training

1. To create a professional learning network or community of practice with teacher participants of mentee schools
2. To make teacher participants comfortable with the digital mode of training
3. To share ideas and information that improve teachers' communicative skills in English

As an outcome of his school-based training efforts, classroom observations, and years of experience in education, Karamjeet has coauthored a book, *Smiling Chalk* (Singh & Bhasin, 2023), with his colleague Aditi Bhasin. The ideas about knowing one's learners in the book are inspired by The 6 Principles.

In his ongoing role as a coordinator, Karamjeet not only oversees various aspects of the curriculum but also invests significant effort into cultivating the skills and knowledge of individuals involved in curriculum development. One of his key initiatives involves organizing comprehensive training programs for those engaged in the creation of curricula, textbooks, and educational content. His rationale is firmly rooted in the belief that a well-structured curriculum needs activities that promote optimal conditions for language learning and include methods to assess and enhance student performance—a belief that is grounded in The 6 Principles.

> What are some reflective practices you have used or intend to implement within your community of educators, and how do you promote collaboration among them?

Furthermore, Karamjeet is deeply committed to fostering a culture of reflection within the teaching community in his local school. In regular faculty meetings, as discussed in the preceding section about Principle 5, he and his colleagues have dedicated time for "reflective sessions." During these sessions, teachers engage in self-examination, both during and after their teaching experiences. The first form of reflection, known as reflection *in* practice, encourages teachers to contemplate their actions and observations during teaching, fostering immediate actions to adapt their lesson delivery. The second form, reflection *on* practice, encourages teachers to revisit their teaching experiences, allowing for deeper analysis of their instructional methods. These reflective sessions thus play a pivotal role in nurturing a community of teachers who are dedicated to continuous growth and the enhancement of their teaching practices.

A Look Back and Final Observations

The 6 Principles is a framework for high-quality instruction that can be used in any teaching context. This chapter describes three different ways to implement The 6 Principles: in an ELD middle school class, in a higher education teacher training course, and in a professional development setting for practicing teachers. These educators use their knowledge of their learners to connect instruction to their learners' goals and needs. They purposefully engage them in relevant lessons with targeted activities that enable them to develop and reflect on their expanding language skills (for K–12 students) or pedagogical skills (for teachers).

As you use The 6 Principles to guide your instruction, consider these takeaways:

- The 6 Principles provide teachers with the knowledge to make informed decisions to improve instruction and assessment, so curricula and courses for multilingual learners of English are rigorous, relevant, and designed and delivered with second language acquisition in mind.
- The heart of exemplary instruction is knowing your learners. From there, high-quality lesson planning and delivery can grow. You create conditions in your classroom that

promote language learning for your students. You choose from an array of strategies and techniques to engage your learners in reading, writing, listening, and speaking tasks. You differentiate or scaffold when student learning hits a roadblock. And you monitor and assess students' progress, giving feedback to move their language development forward.

- Wrapped around the lesson planning process is the support of a wider community. Collaborating in a community of practice—whether with a coteacher or coach, in a grade-level or department team at your school, in a professional association, or with an online group—strengthens your pedagogical knowledge, provides opportunities for reflection, and generates personal growth.

- The 6 Principles will help educators respect, affirm, and promote students' home languages, cultural knowledge, and experiences and incorporate them in classroom practices. Using The 6 Principles as a framework, schools can establish a strong culture of shared responsibility among educators, hold high expectations for multilingual learners of English, and ensure that high-quality programs and instruction are designed to support students' educational success in a positive and welcoming environment.

Additional resources pertaining to this chapter are available at www.the6principles.org/K-12.

APPENDIXES
GLOSSARY
REFERENCES

Appendix A
Common Acronyms in the Field of English Language Teaching

English Language Teaching Term	Acronym
Emergent bilingual	EB
English as a new language	ENL
English as a second language	ESL
English as an additional language	EAL
English language development	ELD
English language proficiency	ELP
English language teaching	ELT
English learner/English language learner	EL/ELL
English speakers of other languages (refers to students)/ English to speakers of other languages (refers to programs)	ESOL
Former English learner	FEL
Fully English proficient	FEP
Limited English proficient (used in some federal and state regulations but not a preferred term)	LEP
Long-term English (language) learner	LTEL/LTELL
Multilingual learner/multilingual learner of English	ML or MLL/MLE
Students with (limited or) interrupted formal education	SIFE/SLIFE

Appendix B
The 6 Principles Checklist for Teachers

Do you know your learners? (Principle 1)

___ **You gain information about your learners.**

For example, you

___ review student records and gather additional information on their backgrounds.

___ gather information about new students' language skills from the registration process.

___ help students construct a personal profile, using digital tools as available.

___ organize and share information about learners.

___ **You embrace and leverage the resources your learners bring to the classroom to enhance learning.**

For example, you

___ collect resources about your students' home cultures and languages.

___ engage with parents or guardians to gain knowledge about students' experiences.

___ guide students in an autobiography project.

___ act as a cultural mediator for students.

Do you create conditions for language learning? (Principle 2)

___ **You promote an emotionally positive and organized classroom.**

For example, you

___ ensure that new students receive a warm welcome from classmates.

___ design appropriate work spaces.

___ organize the physical environment of the classroom to help students learn and use the new language.

___ organize online learning platforms with the students' access to technology and supports in mind.

___ identify a mentor for each student.

___ use clear, patterned, and routine language to communicate with new learners.

___ invite and support students' home languages and cultures as essential to building rich understanding.

___ facilitate social-emotional practices.

___ **You demonstrate expectations of success for all your learners.**

For example, you

___ believe all students will learn language and academic content to a high level.

___ praise effort and persistence in order to communicate how success is achieved.

___ use a wide variety of instructional approaches for diverse learners.

___ promote students' self-efficacy in learning.

___ **You plan instruction to enhance and support student motivation for language learning.**

For example, you

___ prompt students to connect their learning to their own lives.

___ build a repertoire of learning tasks that students enjoy and experience.

___ use technology applications to craft activities that develop a stronger connection to language learning.

___ help students focus on a well-defined project with a future outcome to motivate and structure their behavior.

___ expect student ownership and support students' engagement with learning.

Do you design high-quality lessons for language development? (Principle 3)

___ **You prepare lessons with clear outcomes and convey them to your students.**

For example, you

___ determine content and language objectives for your lessons.

___ communicate learning objectives to students.

___ review learning objectives at the end of the lesson.

___ **You provide and enhance input through varied approaches, techniques, and modalities.**

For example, you

___ use comprehensible input to convey information to students.

___ adjust your language to enhance input to students.

___ use multiple sources of input.

___ utilize technology to personalize input to meet students' needs.

___ communicate clear instructions for lesson tasks.

___ **You engage learners in the use and practice of authentic language.**

For example, you

___ elicit output from students.

___ create opportunities for learners to be active participants.

___ use techniques to promote active language practice throughout the lesson.

___ encourage language learning beyond the classroom.

___ **You integrate language and content learning.**

For example, you

___ become familiar with the language demands of different subject areas.

___ consult with colleagues to support multilingual learners of English in grade-level or content classrooms.

___ introduce common academic tasks and provide practice opportunities.

___ **You design lessons that incorporate culturally responsive teaching practices.**

For example, you

___ plan tasks that are culturally relevant and interesting to your students.

___ uncover the "funds of knowledge" in students' households.

___ select materials that reflect students' backgrounds and interests.

___ integrate social-emotional learning and culturally responsive teaching.

___ create space for translanguaging.

___ **You plan differentiated instruction according to your learners' English language proficiency levels, needs, and goals.**

For example, you

___ build scaffolding into lessons for different purposes.

___ employ grouping patterns designed to promote peer support, engagement, and comprehensibility.

___ provide supplemental materials.

___ plan for appropriate challenge depending on learners' language proficiency levels.

___ **You promote the use of learning strategies and critical thinking among your students.**

For example, you

___ teach a variety of learning strategies for specific purposes.

___ design tasks for students to practice using critical-thinking and learning strategies.

___ **You promote students' self-regulated learning.**

For example, you

___ facilitate students' setting of meaningful goals for themselves and monitoring their own progress.

___ provide self-assessment tools that allow students to evaluate their strengths and weaknesses.

___ help students develop effective study habits.

Do you adapt lesson delivery as needed? (Principle 4)

___ **You check student comprehension frequently and adjust instruction according to learner responses.**

For example, you

___ use teaching practices that ensure better auditory comprehension.

___ check comprehension with group response techniques.

___ gauge individual student comprehension with digital tools and platforms.

___ **You adjust your talk, the task, or the materials according to learner responses.**

For example, you

___ modify your teacher talk as necessary to improve comprehension and scaffold academic language learning.

___ use additional instructional supports to revisit or assist students in processing or applying new information.

___ turn to procedural scaffolds when students cannot complete a task or perform it well.

___ adapt tasks and/or materials to learners' proficiency levels.

___ vary student grouping configurations to aid in comprehension and increase productivity.

___ prompt students to diversity their learning strategies to problem solve breakdowns in comprehension or processing.

Do you monitor and assess student language development? (Principle 5)

___ **You monitor your students' errors.**

For example, you

___ take diagnostic notes when students make errors to provide appropriate scaffolding and modeling.

___ reteach when errors indicate students misunderstood the material or learned it incorrectly.

___ **You strategically provide ongoing, effective feedback.**

For example, you

___ use specific feedback.

___ give timely and actionable feedback.

___ harness technology tools to provide personalized feedback for learners.

___ deliver feedback according to the age and proficiency level of the learner.

___ use various types of oral corrective feedback.

___ use written feedback when appropriate.

___ **You design varied and valid assessments and supports to assess student learning.**

For example, you

___ use classroom-based assessment to inform teaching and improve learning.

___ use testing procedures based on principles of assessment.

___ rely on various assessment types to determine student achievement.

___ blend pedagogy and technology in your assessment practices.

___ **You analyze and interpret assessment data for multilingual learners of English.**

For example, you

___ use what you know about a student's language development process and educational background to interpret assessment results.

___ share your data analyses and interpretations with colleagues.

___ use assessment results to improve assessment practices.

Do you engage and collaborate within a community of practice? (Principle 6)

___ **You are fully engaged in your profession.**

For example, you

___ engage in reflective practice to grow professionally.

___ participate in continuous learning and ongoing professional development.

___ embrace technology to stay up to date, access world-class resources, and engage in interactive learning experiences.

___ **You collaborate with colleagues.**

For example, you

___ meet with colleagues regularly to co-plan for future learning.

___ develop and strengthen relationships with school colleagues that facilitate coteaching.

___ **You develop leadership skills that enable you to become a resource in your school.**

For example, you

___ build a repertoire of professional development topics for educating multilingual learners of English and hone your presentation skills.

___ develop coaching skills.

Appendix C
Book Discussion Questions

Chapter 1

1. Consider the reasons given for establishing The 6 Principles. Which reasons are most relevant to your teaching situation? What are some steps that you and your school have taken locally or regionally to address some of these concerns?

2. We refer to students as multilingual learners of English in this book to reflect an asset orientation to teaching and learning. What does your school or program do to harness the assets these learners bring to the classroom? How do you promote multilingualism and multiculturalism and prepare students to become global citizens?

3. Review all of TESOL International Association's vision statements. Which one resonates with you most deeply? Share your thoughts with colleagues.

Chapter 2

1. All students learn academic English as a new language. In what ways does learning academic English differ for multilingual learners of English compared with those for whom English is a home language?

2. Think about three different students you have and compare their English language performance with the English language development levels in Table 2.3. How well do your students' levels match up with descriptions in the table?

3. Review the section "Asset-Based Literacy Instruction for Multilingual Learners of English" (p. 28). Which considerations do you take into account when planning instruction? How? Which of the considerations listed are new to you? How can you incorporate them in your teaching?

4. How does language play a role in shaping your own and your students' identities?

5. How do you define social-emotional learning? How do you think students' social-emotional needs influence their language learning?

6. Which of the "obstructive beliefs" have you encountered before? What were your reactions? Are there other beliefs you've heard? How do your own reactions compare with the suggested "constructive responses"?

7. What have you learned about second language development in Chapter 2 that may change the way you approach the instruction of multilingual learners of English?

Chapter 3

1. The 6 Principles aim to support classroom practitioners in providing a positive learning environment for multilingual learners of English. Which one of The 6 Principles resonates most with your teaching experience, and what makes this principle meaningful for your approach to teaching?

2. Principle 1 is "Know your learners." Although teachers of students who are proficient in English also consider this a good guiding principle, why is this advice even more significant for teachers of multilingual learners of English?

3. Principle 2 describes ways to create conditions for more effective learning of language and content. What conditions do you or might you create to support multilingual learners of English? How can social-emotional learning and culturally responsive teaching practices help?

4. Principle 3 explains methodology for designing high-quality lessons for language and content learning across the grade levels. Which of the eight practices discussed in this section are most

essential for you in your teaching? Are there any specific practices you would like to learn more about? If so, why?

5. Principle 4 indicates that effective teachers often adjust instruction according to learner responses. Teachers may not always be aware that students do not understand instruction. Discuss how these practices can be used routinely in class for all learners. Which practices appear to be most useful for students who are multilingual learners of English? What other techniques for checking comprehension or adjusting your lesson have you used?

6. Principle 5 refers to monitoring and assessment of student language development. Effective feedback and multiple modes of assessment are important components of this principle. Which feedback techniques do you use, and how effective do they seem to be? What assessments give you the most information about your students' language development? How do you use the results of these assessments?

7. Principle 6 suggests that engagement and collaboration within the profession are necessary for effective teaching. Which practices do you engage in to help colleagues improve their own practice and to sustain your professional learning?

8. Technology plays an increasingly prominent role in language education. What benefits and challenges have you experienced with technology tools in your teaching situation?

Chapter 4

1. Describe some ways in which you informally share strategies and best practices for working with multilingual learners of English. Discuss how you can support your colleagues in implementing these strategies.

2. What professional development does your school, district, or program provide for teachers who work with multilingual learners of English? Is this professional development accessible to all teachers? Do all participate? Is additional professional development needed? If the current professional development is not sufficient, discuss what professional development you and your colleagues can plan in order to share your collective expertise and learn from one another.

3. Describe procedures for determining if a multilingual learner of English has special needs. What works well? What does not? Are there any actions you can take to further explore this issue or develop or improve the protocols currently in place?

4. In which schoolwide or districtwide committees (e.g., curriculum revision, instructional materials selection, assessment development) do you participate? Are the needs of multilingual learners of English addressed during these committee meetings? Give an example. Think of issues or concerns related to these learners that you might want to bring up the next time you participate on one of these committees.

5. Which role(s) discussed in this chapter do you already carry out? How might information in this chapter be helpful to you?

Chapter 5

1. In TESOL International Association's vision of effective education, all teachers take responsibility for teaching multilingual learners of English and helping them succeed in school. Do all educators you work with uphold this responsibility and maintain high expectations for these learners? If not, what steps could be taken to generate a shared sense of responsibility?

2. What specific actions does your school or district most need to take to fully implement The 6 Principles? How might the School Improvement Team use this book to form a 3-year action plan to improve services for multilingual learners of English and their families? Keep the spirit of shared responsibility for these students in mind to ensure that the team draws upon the skills of a range of school- or district-based professionals, according to their specializations and roles.

3. How can English language development and bilingual specialists in your district best support the specific personnel discussed in this chapter to implement The 6 Principles?

4. What other ideas emerged as you read this chapter, in terms of additional ways you can assist in fulfilling The 6 Principles?

Chapter 6

1. Read one vignette that is most similar to your current situation. What did you learn about implementing The 6 Principles? What new ideas do you have?

2. Share your experiences with implementing or learning about The 6 Principles. For example, do you make different instructional decisions for multilingual learners of English now?

3. What are some challenges you face in implementing The 6 Principles? Discuss potential steps to overcome them with others in your group.

Glossary

Academic language: a register of the English language; the formal variety of language used for academic purposes (e.g., in scholarly discussions, lectures, and textbooks) and connected with literacy and academic achievement. Academic language includes reading, writing, listening, and speaking skills used to acquire new knowledge and accomplish academic tasks; it is sometimes referred to as *academic English.*

Accommodation (in testing): a change in an assessment itself or the way in which it is administered, intended to make the test results more accurate by creating conditions that allow test-takers to demonstrate their knowledge or skills. Examples of accommodations include allowing extended time and permitting the use of a bilingual glossary.

Assessment: a systematic process that allows teachers to gather, evaluate, and interpret their students' progress, performance, and understanding of the learning content. Two common types of assessment are *formative assessment* and *summative assessment.* Assessment data are used to inform instruction.

Authentic language: language used in real-life situations that has not been modified or simplified; typically refers to language that is written or spoken for a proficient audience to convey a message.

Autonomy: a learner's ability and willingness to take control and responsibility of their own learning process.

Benchmark assessment: a short assessment administered at regular intervals to give teachers feedback on how well students are meeting the academic standards that have been set; a tool to measure student growth and tailor curriculum or design an intervention to meet individual learning needs.

Bilingual education: a school program using two languages, typically the home language of some students and a target language. The amount of time spent and the subject(s) covered in each language depend on the type of bilingual program, its specific objectives, and students' levels of language proficiency. Transitional bilingual programs in the United States usually last between 2 and 3 years before students move to all English-medium classes. Some schools without a full bilingual program offer bilingual content courses, which typically are content courses taught in students' home language.

Collocations: words or terms that occur together in a language more frequently than chance would predict and that are used as fixed expressions (e.g., *fast food, take a break, go online*).

Community of practice: a group of people who engage in a process of collective learning as they practice their profession; term coined by Lave and Wegner (1991). Each group member brings their own skill set, and the group actively shares knowledge, resources, experiences, and orientations to their work, while strengthening their relationships with one another, to enhance their collaborative efforts.

Comprehensible input: oral or written input, such as new information, structured or presented in a way that is understandable to the learner through visuals, gestures, annotations, and other means. Over time, the input typically increases in complexity of the language structures and vocabulary used or the amount of information shared.

Content-based language instruction: an approach in which teachers use academic content topics as the vehicle for helping students learn a new language (e.g., English). Teachers use a variety of techniques to help students develop language, content knowledge, and study skills. Instruction may be delivered through thematic units and tied to the subject-area texts and instruction that multilingual learners of English receive in grade-level and content-area classrooms.

Content objectives: statements that identify what students should know and be able to do related to subject-area information for a given lesson. Content objectives are typically drawn from state content standards and learning outcomes, and they guide teaching and learning in a lesson.

Cooperative learning: a teaching approach that encourages students to collaborate, share ideas, and use individual strengths to achieve shared tasks and learning goals. Students often work in pairs or small groups and have different roles.

Cultural diversity: the variety of cultures that students have in a classroom or school. Culture includes the customs, lifestyles, traditions, attitudes, norms of behavior, and artifacts of a given people. Students from culturally diverse backgrounds may have different races, ethnicities, languages, religions, and socioeconomic statuses. Classroom goals should include respecting and honoring diverse cultures and building on different ways of knowing or interpreting the world.

Culturally responsive instruction: an approach (also known as *culturally responsive teaching* or *culturally relevant teaching*) to classroom instruction that respects and builds on the different cultural characteristics of all students and ensures that academic discussions are open to different cultural views and perspectives, student ways of knowing are elicited, pedagogical materials are multicultural, and values are shared and affirmed. This approach aims to enrich learning experiences and promote academic success among students from different cultural backgrounds by leveraging their prior knowledge.

Differentiated instruction: an approach to teaching that provides multiple pathways to learning to address students' diverse abilities and language proficiency levels. According to student needs, teachers may adjust their speech, the pace of a lesson, the way they present new information, the texts and materials used, the tasks the students conduct, or the grouping of the learners.

Discourse: a sequence of utterances (i.e., spoken or written sentences) that form a larger unit in a specific social context (e.g., dinner conversation, academic lecture, weather report, kindergarten show-and-tell).

Dual language program: a type of bilingual education (also known as *two-way immersion*) in which the goal is for a student to develop proficiency in two languages, typically the student's home language and the target language (e.g., Spanish and English). The amount of time and academic subject(s) taught in each language may vary. Most dual language programs have both English speakers and speakers of the target language (e.g., Spanish); some have speakers from the same language background. A dual language teacher may teach using both languages, or they may be paired with another teacher and each teacher uses one of the languages for instruction.

Dually identified students: school-age students who are eligible for both special education services and English language development programs. Identified as multilingual learners of English who have various types of disabilities that impact their participation in the learning process, such as learning disabilities, autism, speech impairment, or other special needs.

Dynamic bilingualism: the ability to use more than one language flexibly and strategically, depending on the audience, conversational partners, or the situation.

Emergent bilinguals: students who are in the early stages of language development in their additional language(s) while continuing to use their home language. The term reflects the eventual goal of bilingualism.

English as a foreign language (EFL): refers to programs and classes in which students learn English as a foreign language; the teaching and learning of English in countries where English is not the official language.

English as a medium of instruction (EMI): the use of English as the language of instruction. EMI is an increasingly popular approach for teaching subject-area topics to students whose home language is not English in higher education and secondary school contexts in countries where English is not the dominant language. EMI is sometimes referred to as *English-medium instruction. English-medium education* (EME) is also sometimes used.

English as a new language (ENL): used in some U.S. states to refer to programs and classes in which students learn English as a new (or second or additional) language. (See *ELD, EAL,* and *ESL.*)

English as a second language (ESL): refers to programs and classes in which students learn English as a second (or additional or new) language, usually in English-speaking countries. ESL may refer to the language teaching specialists and their teaching certifications or endorsements, or it may refer to the learners (i.e., ESL students), although this term is no longer commonly used in the context of U.S. schools.

English as an additional language (EAL): used to describe the teaching of English to students who are learning and using English in addition to their first language(s). This term is more inclusive than *ESL*.

English language development (ELD): used in many U.S. states to refer to programs and classes in which students learn English as a second, additional, or new language. ELD may refer to the language teaching specialists and their teaching certifications or endorsements. (See *ESL*.)

English language proficiency (ELP) standards: a set of concise statements identifying the knowledge and skills that multilingual learners of English are expected to know and be capable of doing in English; statement-by-statement articulations of what students are expected to learn and schools are expected to teach. ELP standards may refer to national, state, or district standards. Each state is required by the U.S. government to have ELP standards and related assessments. (See *ELD* and *ESL*.)

English learner: a student who is learning English as a second, additional, or new language, at various levels of proficiency. These learners may also be referred to as *English language learners, multilingual learners of English, emergent bilinguals,* and *nonnative speakers*. The term *limited English proficient student* is outdated.

English speakers of other languages (ESOL): students whose first language is not English and who do not write, speak, or understand the language as well as their classmates. In some regions, ESOL means "English to speakers of other language" and refers to the programs and classes for English learners.

Error: an unintended deviation made by learners as part of the language acquisition process. A learner's lack of knowledge of the accepted rules of the target language results in an error, which can manifest in different uses of language, such as grammar, pronunciation, vocabulary, and spelling.

Every Student Succeeds Act (ESSA): the U.S. education act signed into law in December 2015 and implemented in the 2017–2018 school year. ESSA holds schools accountable for the success of all of their students, including multilingual learners of English and other underserved populations. Each state must have standards and assessments for mathematics, reading, English language development, and science. This law replaced the No Child Left Behind Act of 2001.

Exit tickets: a brief formative assessment technique used by teachers at the end of a lesson, class, or learning activity to quickly assess their students' understanding of the material and gather feedback on instruction.

Family engagement: a mutual partnership among families, communities, and schools built on respect and recognition on all sides of the shared responsibility that families, schools, and communities have to support student learning and success.

Feedback: the response by the teacher (or peer) to a student's output with the intent of helping the student with language learning. Common feedback types include a clarification request, repetition, praise, recast, reformulation, explicit correction, and elicitation of self-repair or self-correction.

First language (L1): a term that refers to the language a student learns first and acquires naturally through interactions at home before they start school. It is also known as a *mother tongue, native language,* or *home language*.

Flipped learning: an instructional method that moves the lecture or presentation of new information outside the classroom and the follow-up activities (in which learners apply the information, such as homework) inside the classroom.

Formative assessment: typically classroom-based assessment of student performance during lessons. Formative assessment takes place frequently and may involve techniques such as verbal checks for understanding, teacher-created assessments, and other nonstandardized procedures. Formative assessments are informal assessments that provide teachers with immediate information on how well a student is progressing and how effective the teacher's instruction is.

Funds of knowledge: knowledge and skills embedded in cultural, experiential, and daily activities that may be learned from family and community members. Funds of knowledge may include knowledge of the natural world, agriculture, food preparation, crafts, customs, personal histories, legends, and occupational skills.

Gradual Release of Responsibility (GRR) model: an instructional model that shifts students' dependency on the teacher to taking more responsibility and becoming independent and self-regulated in the learning process. The GRR model typically involves four stages: modeling by the teacher, guided instruction by the teacher with the students, collaborative practice among students, and independent application by each student.

Higher order thinking: thinking that requires more than memorization, recall, and the basic comprehension of ideas from texts or teacher presentation. Higher order thinking involves using ideas actively: applying, analyzing, evaluating, synthesizing, and creating.

Home language: the language that a learner speaks at home, usually the first language learned. Home language is also known as *primary language, native language,* and *first language (L1).*

Language form: typically refers to aspects of the structure of a language, such as the patterns, rules, and organization of words; comprises parts of speech, sentence formation, usage, punctuation, and so on, sometimes referred to as the *grammar* of a language.

Language frame: a partially complete spoken or written sentence that a teacher can provide to help students express ideas (e.g., *I think _____ is relevant because _____; The reason I agree with _____ is that _____*). A language frame is also known as *sentence frame, sentence starter,* or *academic language frame.*

Language function: typically refers to the specific purpose for which language is being used (e.g., to define, compare, persuade, evaluate).

Language input: oral or written language directed to the student; sources may be teacher speech, texts, videos, websites, or other media.

Language objectives: statements that identify what students should know and be able to do related to a language goal for a given lesson. Language objectives are typically drawn from state English language proficiency standards and learning outcomes, and they guide teaching and learning in a lesson.

Language proficiency: a student's degree of competence in using a language for communicative and academic purposes. In U.S. schools, language proficiency is typically measured by levels or may be categorized as a stage of language acquisition.

Language transfer: a process that occurs when a student applies knowledge of one language to another, often with regard to vocabulary, sentence construction, phonology, and cognitive skills. *Positive transfer* can take place when linguistic features and learned patterns (such as cognates, letter-sound correspondences, or ways to find the main idea in a text) of a known language are similar to those in the new language and a student accurately applies them when learning the new language.

Lesson objectives (e.g., language, content, and learning strategy): statements that represent what students should know and/or be able to do at the end of a lesson.

Limited English proficient (LEP): describes a student who is still developing competence in using English and has limited understanding or use of written and spoken English. This term is outdated because of its deficit lens. The U.S. government used *LEP* in the past, but *English learner (EL)* is used in more recent legislation. *Multilingual learner of English* is also being used across the United States.

Long-term English learner: a student who has been enrolled in U.S. schools usually for more than 5 years but is still designated as an English learner. This designation is typically given to students who do not meet reclassification criteria (which vary by state); at a minimum, they have not reached the proficient-level threshold on the state English language assessment.

Multilingual learners of English: students who are developing proficiency in the English language while knowing one or more other languages. They may be at any level of English proficiency. This term emphasizes the language assets of the students rather than the language they are learning. They are also referred to as *English learners* or *English language learners.*

Multilingualism: the ability of people or groups to use more than one language to communicate effectively in various contexts and for diverse purposes.

Multi-Tiered System of Supports (MTSS): the comprehensive process to identify at-risk learners and provide effective instruction to address students' cognitive, behavioral, social-emotional, and academic issues—first in general education classrooms (Tier 1), followed by targeted intervention if needed. Tier 2 intervention occurs in a small group, Tier 3 typically involves individualized intervention. MTSS involves data-based decision making and documenting of changes in behavior or performance as a result of intervention. A similar process is called *Response to Intervention* (RTI).

Newcomer programs: academic programs specially designed to meet the academic and transitional needs of newly arrived students in U.S. schools who are at low levels of proficiency in English. Newcomers attend these programs for a limited period of time (between 6 months and 2 years) to develop academic English, acculturate to U.S. schools, and build subject-area knowledge. Newcomers may attend these programs before they enter the ELD or bilingual program, or a newcomer level may be part of the progression in these programs. The programs may be located within a school or at a separate site.

Output: oral or written language generated by a student; sometimes called *production*.

Pull-out instruction: when students (e.g., multilingual learners of English) are pulled from their general education class for a separate class of English language development. These classes are most commonly found in elementary schools. Pull-out instruction is a term used for intervention classes as well.

Push-in instruction: when an English language teacher comes into a class for a period of time to provide support to multilingual learners of English, but is not considered a coteacher.

Reclassification: the decision to exit a multilingual learner of English from a language development program because the student has demonstrated that they have met the exit criteria (e.g., achieved the required score on an English language proficiency exam). Reclassified, or former, multilingual learners of English are monitored for several years after they leave the language development program.

Register: a variety of language associated with specific social situations and topic areas. Examples include scientific language, legal language, baby talk, or the language of sportscasting.

Routine: a set of procedures that teachers expect students to regularly follow during the school day or a lesson. Typical examples of classroom routines include morning greetings, warm-up activities, handing in homework, and seeking permission to leave the classroom. Certain instructional techniques that are commonly done in class have routines, too (e.g., cooperative learning activities, setting up lab equipment).

Scaffolding: classroom support given to assist students in learning new information and performing related tasks, often provided by the teacher through demonstration, modeling, verbal prompts (e.g., questioning), feedback, adapted text, graphic organizers, and language frames, among other techniques. Scaffolds are gradually modified over time and then removed in order to transfer more autonomy to the learner, leading to independence.

Sheltered content instruction: an instructional approach that makes academic content comprehensible for multilingual learners of English while they are developing academic English proficiency. Sheltered lessons integrate language and content learning and may include culturally responsive instruction as well. Sheltered classrooms may include a mix of proficient English speakers and English learners, or only English learners. Content and language integrated learning (CLIL) is a type of sheltered instruction that is found outside the United States.

Social-emotional learning (SEL): a systematic approach that supports students in developing essential social-emotional competencies to promote their well-being and learning in school and life. Such competencies include understanding and managing emotions, raising social awareness, establishing and maintaining positive relationships, and making responsible decisions.

Social language: a register of the English language that is also referred to as *conversational language* and is the basic language proficiency associated with fluency and vocabulary in everyday situations. Most multilingual learners of English acquire social language more rapidly than they do academic language.

Students with interrupted formal education (SIFE)/Students with limited or interrupted formal education (SLIFE): students who have significantly less education than their age-level peers. Such students may have missed years of schooling or several months over the course of several years, resulting in broad knowledge gaps that inhibit their ability to perform to grade-level expectations or standards. Many have limited reading and writing skills in their home language. Some states identify these students as being 2 years or more below their peers in academic performance.

Summative assessment: a formal assessment, such as an end-of-course exam or a state standardized test, that is used to measure student knowledge over an extended period of time and may be used to measure growth in a subject area from year to year.

Target language: language a student is learning or wishes to learn; also known as *second language (L2), new language, additional language,* or *foreign language.*

Think-alouds: technique whereby teachers verbalize their thought processes or make their thinking explicit to students while engaging in tasks such as reading, problem solving, and analyzing questions. Think-alouds provide a way for teachers to model thinking patterns and analyses for students.

Translanguaging: a strategic choice to use one's full linguistic repertoire in two or more languages to serve a specific purpose in a communicative situation or to accomplish a task; in classrooms, a pedagogical approach for strategically drawing on student knowledge of two or more languages, and knowledge gained through these languages, to make meaning or complete academic activities.

Utterance: unit of language in spoken or written use. An utterance may be a partial sentence as well.

Utterance control: the ability to produce well-formed, grammatically correct, and coherent language deliberately and purposefully when speaking or writing.

References

Abedi, J. (2017). Utilizing accommodations in assessment. In E. Shohamy, I. Or, & S. May (Eds.), *Language Testing and Assessment*. Springer. https://doi.org/10.1007/978-3-319-02261-1_21

Abedi, J., & Linquanti, R. (2012, January). *Issues and opportunities in improving the quality of large scale assessment systems for English language learners* [Paper presentation]. Understanding Language Conference, Palo Alto, CA, United States. https://ul.stanford.edu/sites/default/files/resource/2021-12/Abedi%20Linquanti_Large%20Scale%20Assessment%20Systems.pdf

Aguilar, E. (2024). *The art of coaching 2.0: How to thrive as a transformational coach* (2nd ed.). Jossey-Bass.

Amaral, E. (2019). *The 6 Principles quick guide for paraeducators*. TESOL Press.

American Speech-Language-Hearing Association. (n.d.). *Language in brief*. https://www.asha.org/Practice-Portal/Clinical-Topics/Spoken-Language-Disorders/Language-In-Brief

Anderson, S. R., & Lightfoot, D. W. (2002). *The language organ: Linguistics as cognitive physiology*. Cambridge University Press.

Andrade, M. S., & Evans, N. W. (2013). *Principles and practices for response in second language writing*. Routledge.

Anstrom, K., DiCerbo, P., Butler, F., Katz, A., Millet, J., & Rivera, C. (2010). *A review of the literature on American English: Implications for K–12 English language learners*. George Washington University Center for Equity and Excellence in Education.

Au, K. (2009). Isn't culturally responsive instruction just good teaching? *Social Education, 73*(4), 179–183. https://www.socialstudies.org/system/files/publications/articles/se_7304179.pdf

August, D., & Shanahan, T. (Eds.). (2006). *Developing literacy in second-language learners: Report of the national literacy panel on language-minority children and youth*. Lawrence Erlbaum.

Baker, C. (2014). *A parents' and teachers' guide to bilingualism* (4th ed.). Multilingual Matters.

Baker, S., Lesaux, N., Jayanthi, M., Dimino, J., Proctor, C. P., Morris, J., Gersten, R., Haymond, K., Kieffer, M. J., Linan-Thompson, S., & Newman-Gonchar, R. (2014). *Teaching academic content and literacy to English learners in elementary and middle school* (NCEE 2014-4012). National Center for Education Evaluation and Regional Assistance Institute of Education Sciences, U.S. Department of Education. https://ies.ed.gov/ncee/wwc/Docs/practiceguide/english_learners_pg_040114.pdf

Benegas, M., & Stolpestad, A. (2020). *Teacher leadership for school-wide English learning*. TESOL Press.

Bialik, K., Scheller, A., & Walker, K. (2018, October 25). *6 facts about English language learners in U.S. public schools*. Pew Research Center. https://pewrsr.ch/2EAPAnV

Biemiller, A. (2010). *Words worth teaching: Closing the vocabulary gap*. SRA/McGraw-Hill.

Birdsong, D., & Vanhove, J. (2016). Age of second language acquisition: Critical periods and social concerns. In E. Nicoladis & S. Montanari (Eds.), *Bilingualism across the lifespan: Factors moderating language proficiency* (pp. 163–182). American Psychological Association. https://psycnet.apa.org/doi/10.1037/14939-010

Borgwaldt, S. R., & Joyce, T. (2013). Typology of writing systems. In S. R. Borgwaldt & T. Joyce (Eds.), *Typology of writing systems* (pp. 1–11). John Benjamins.

Breiseith, L. (n.d.). *Getting to know your ELLs: Six steps for success*. Colorín Colorado. https://www.colorincolorado.org/article/getting-know-your-ells-six-steps-success

Brinks Lockwood, R. (2018). *Flipping the classroom: What every ESL teacher needs to know*. University of Michigan Press.

Burr, E., Haas, E., & Ferriere, K. (2015). *Identifying and supporting English learner students with learning disabilities: Key issues in the literature and state practice* (REL 2015-086). U.S. Department of Education, Institute of Education Sciences, National Center for Education Evaluation and Regional Assistance, Regional Educational Laboratory West. https://ies.ed.gov/ncee/rel/regions/west/pdf/REL_2015086.pdf

California Department of Education (2010). *Improving education for English learners: Research-based approaches*. CDE Press.

Cambridge English. (n.d.). *Cambridge English teaching framework*. Cambridge University Press & Assessment. http://www.cambridgeenglish.org/teaching-framework

Canagarajah, A. S., & Wurr, A. (2011). Multilingual communication and language acquisition: New research directions. *Reading Matrix, 11*(1), 1–15.

Castañeda v. Pickard, 648 F. 2d 989 (5th Cir. 1981).

Chamot, A. U. (2009). *The CALLA handbook: Implementing the cognitive academic language learning approach* (2nd ed.). Pearson.

Çinar, İ., & Arı, A. (2019). The effects of Quizlet on secondary school students' vocabulary learning and attitudes towards English. *Asian Journal of Instruction*, 7(2), 60–73.

Cloud, N., Genesee, F., & Hamayan, E. (2009). *Literacy instruction for English learners: A teacher's guide to research-based practices*. Heinemann.

Coelho, E. (2012). *Language and learning in multilingual classrooms*. Multilingual Matters.

Collaborative for Academic, Social, and Emotional Learning. (n.d.). *The CASEL 5*. https://casel.org/fundamentals-of-sel/what-is-the-casel-framework/#the-casel-5

Collier, V. P., & Thomas, W. P. (2017). Validating the power of bilingual schooling: Thirty-two years of large-scale, longitudinal research. *Annual Review of Applied Linguistics*, 37, 203–217. https://doi.org/10.1017/S0267190517000034

Commission on Language Learning. (2017). *America's languages: Investing in language education for the 21st century*. American Academy of Arts and Sciences.

Conley, D. T., & French, E. M. (2014). Student ownership of learning as a key component of college readiness. *American Behavioral Scientist*, 68(8), 1018–1034. https://doi.org/10.1177/0002764213515232

Cooper, A. (2020). *And justice for all: Creating and sustaining equitable schools with English learners*. Corwin Press.

Council for the Accreditation of Educator Preparation. (2022). *2022 CAEP standards*. https://caepnet.org/standards/2022-itp/introduction

Council of Europe. (2020). *Common European framework of reference for languages: Learning, teaching, assessment—Companion volume*. Council of Europe. https://rm.coe.int/common-european-framework-of-reference-for-languages-learning-teaching/16809ea0d4

Council of the Great City Schools. (2023). *A framework for foundational literacy skills instruction for English learners: Instructional practice and materials considerations*. https://www.cgcs.org/cms/lib/DC00001581/Centricity/domain/35/publication%20docs/CGCS_Foundational%20Literacy%20Skills_Pub_v11.pdf

Coxhead, A. (2000). A new academic word list. *TESOL Quarterly*, 34(2), 213–238. https://doi.org/10.2307/3587951

Cummins, J. (2001). *Negotiating identities: Education for empowerment in a diverse society* (2nd ed.). California Association for Bilingual Education.

Cummins, J. (2015). Affirming identity in multilingual classrooms. *Educational Leadership*, 72(6), 32–38.

Custodio, B., & O'Loughlin, J. B. (2017). *Students with interrupted formal education: Bridging where they are and what they need*. Corwin Press.

Dang, T. N. Y., & Webb, S. (2016). Making an essential word list for beginners. In I. S. P. Nation (Ed.), *Making and using word lists for language learning and testing* (pp. 153–167, 188–195). John Benjamins.

Day, R. R. (2020). *Teaching reading* (Rev. ed.). TESOL Press.

DeKeyser, R. (2010). Practice for second language learning: Don't throw out the baby with the bathwater. *International Journal of English Studies*, 10(1), 155–165.

DeKeyser, R. (2013). Age effects in second language learning: Stepping stones toward better understanding. *Language Learning*, 63(1), 52–67. https://doi.org/10.1111/j.1467-9922.2012.00737.x

DelliCarpini, M., & Alonso, O. B. (2013). *Content-based instruction*. TESOL Press.

Dewey, J. (1933). *How we think: A restatement of the relation of reflective thinking to the educative process*. D. C. Heath.

Dodge, J., & Honigsfeld, A. (2014). *Core instructional routines: Go-to structures for effective literacy teaching, K–5*. Heinemann.

Dörnyei, Z. (2014). Motivation in second language learning. In M. Celce-Murcia, D. M. Brinton, & M. A. Snow (Eds.), *Teaching English as a second or foreign language* (4th ed., pp. 518–531). National Geographic/Cengage Learning.

Dörnyei, Z., & Ushioda, E. (2011). *Teaching and researching motivation* (2nd ed.). Longman.

Douglas Fir Group. (2016). A transdisciplinary framework for SLA in a multilingual world. *Modern Language Journal*, 100(S1), 19–47. https://doi.org/10.1111/modl.12301

Dove, M. G., & Honigsfeld, A. (2017). *Co-teaching for English learners*. Corwin Press.

Duke, N. K., & Cartwright, K. (2021). The science of reading progresses: Communicating advances beyond the simple view of reading. *Reading Research Quarterly*, 56(S1), S25–S44.

Duke, N. K., Ward, E., & Pearson, P. D. (2021). The science of reading comprehension instruction. *The Reading Teacher*, 74(6), 663–672. https://doi.org/10.1002/trtr.1993

Dvorskiy, V., & Gudkova, N. (2023, June 16). Exploring the role of technology in language acquisition. *Proceedings of IV International Scientific and Theoretical Conference*, Athens, Greece (pp. 99–102). https://doi.org/10.36074/scientia-16.06.2023

Dweck, C. S. (2006). *Mindset: The new psychology of success*. Random House.

Ebe, A., Soto, M., Freeman, Y., & Freeman, D. (2021, September). Translanguaging in bilingual and ESL classrooms. *TESOL Connections*. https://tcnewsletter.s3.amazonaws.com/newsmanager.commpartners.com/tesolc/issues/2021-09-01/3.html

Echevarría, J., Vogt, M. E., Short, D. J., & Toppel, K. (2024). *Making content comprehensible for multilingual learners: The SIOP Model* (6th ed.). Pearson.

Educational Testing Service. (2009). *Guidelines for the assessment of English language learners*. Educational Testing Service.

Elias, M. J. (2019). What if the doors of every schoolhouse opened to social–emotional learning tomorrow: Reflections on how to feasibly scale up high-quality SEL. *Educational Psychologist, 54*(3), 233–245. https://doi.org/10.1080/00461520.2019.1636655

Elias, M. J., & Tobias, S. E. (2018). *Boost emotional intelligence in students: 30 flexible research-based activities to build EQ skills (Grades 5–9)*. Free Spirit.

Ellis, R. (2017). Oral corrective feedback in L2 classrooms. In H. Nassaji & E. Kartchava (Eds.), *Corrective feedback in second language teaching and learning: Research, theory, applications, implications* (pp. 3–18). Routledge.

Ellis, R., & Shintani, N. (2014). *Exploring language pedagogy through second language acquisition research*. Routledge.

Every Student Succeeds Act of 2015, Pub. L. No. 114-95 § 114 Stat. 1177 (2015–2016). https://www.congress.gov/114/plaws/publ95/PLAW-114publ95.pdf

Fairbairn, S., & Jones-Vo, S. (2019). *Differentiating instruction and assessment for English language learners: A guide for K–12 teachers* (2nd ed.). Caslon.

Farnsworth, T., & Malone, M. (2014). *Assessing English learners in U.S. schools*. TESOL Press.

Farrell, T. S. C. (2015). *Language teacher professional development*. TESOL Press.

Frey, N., & Fisher, D. (2009). *Productive group work: How to engage students, build teamwork, and promote understanding*. Association for Supervision and Curriculum Development.

Frey, N., Fisher, D., & Smith, D. (2019). *All learning is social and emotional: Helping students develop essential skills for the classroom and beyond*. Association for Supervision and Curriculum Development.

Fromkin, V., Rodman, R., & Hyams, N. (2014). *An introduction to language* (10th ed.). Wadsworth Cengage Learning.

García, O., Ibarra Johnson, S., & Seltzer, K. (2017). *The translanguaging classroom: Leveraging student bilingualism for learning*. Caslon.

García, O., & Kleyn, T. (Eds.). (2016). *Translanguaging with multilingual students*. Routledge.

Gardner, D., & Davies, M. (2014). A new academic vocabulary list. *Applied Linguistics, 35*(3), 305–327. https://doi.org/10.1093/applin/amt015

Gardner, R. C. (1985). *Social psychology and second language learning: The role of attitudes and motivation*. Edward Arnold.

Gay, G. (2018). *Culturally responsive teaching: Theory, research, and practice* (3rd ed.). Teachers College Press.

Genesee, F. (n.d.). *The home language: An English language learner's most valuable resource*. Colorín Colorado. http://www.colorincolorado.org/article/home-language-english-language-learners-most-valuable-resource

Genesee, F., Lindholm-Leary, K., Saunders, W., & Christian, D. (2006). *Educating English language learners: A synthesis of research evidence*. Cambridge University Press.

Gibbons, P. (2015). *Scaffolding language, scaffolding learning: Teaching English learners in the mainstream classroom* (2nd ed.). Heinemann.

Goldenberg, C. (2020). Reading wars, reading science, and English learners. *Reading Research Quarterly, 55*(S1), S131–S144.

Goldenberg, C., & Cárdenas-Hagan, E. (2023, January/February). Literacy research on English learners: Past, present, and future. *Reading League Journal*, pp. 12–21.

Gonzalez, N., Moll, L., & Amanti, C. (Eds.). (2005). *Funds of knowledge: Theorizing practices in households, communities, and classrooms*. Routledge.

Gottlieb, M. (2021). *Classroom assessment in multiple languages: A handbook for teachers*. Corwin Press.

Greenberg Motamedi, J. (2015). *Time to reclassification: How long does it take English learner students in Washington Road Map Districts to develop English proficiency?* (REL 2015-092). U.S. Department of Education, Institute of Education Sciences, National Center for Education Evaluation and Regional Assistance, Regional Educational Laboratory Northwest. https://files.eric.ed.gov/fulltext/ED558159.pdf

Hammond, Z. (2015). *Culturally responsive teaching and the brain: Promoting authentic engagement and rigor among culturally and linguistically diverse students.* Corwin Press.

Harper, D., Bowles, A. R., Amer, L., Pandža , N. B., & Linck, J. A. (2021). Improving outcomes for English learners through technology: A randomized controlled trial. *AERA Open, 7*(1), 1–20. https://doi.org/10.1177/23328584211025528

Hastings, C., & Jacob, L. (Eds.). (2016). *Social justice in English language teaching.* TESOL Press.

Haynes, J. (2021, September 9). *4 more ways to support the families of multilingual learners when school opens.* TESOL International Association. https://www.tesol.org/blog/posts/4-more-ways-to-support-the-families-of-multilingual-learners-when-school-opens

Hazen, K. (2015). *An introduction to language.* Wiley Blackwell.

Hellman, A. (2021). *The 6 Principles quick guide: Remote teaching of K–12 English learners.* TESOL Press.

Helman, L. (Ed.). (2016). *Literacy development with English learners: Research-based instruction in grades K–6.* Guilford Press.

Henry, S. F., Mello, D., Avery, M.-P., Parker, C., & Stafford, E. (2017). *Home Language Survey Data Quality Self-Assessment* (REL 2017–198). U.S. Department of Education, Institute of Education Sciences, National Center for Education Evaluation and Regional Assistance, Regional Educational Laboratory Northeast & Islands. http://ies.ed.gov/ncee/edlabs.

Herrera, S. G., Perez, D. R., & Escamilla, K. (2014). *Teaching reading to English language learners: Differentiated literacies* (2nd ed.). Pearson.

Himmel, J. (2012). *Language objectives: The key to effective content area instruction for English learners.* Colorín Colorado. https://www.colorincolorado.org/article/language-objectives-key-effective-content-area-instruction-english-learners

Hodge, S. (2023, August 29). *Open doors, open minds: 6 tips for effective peer coaching.* TESOL International Association. https://www.tesol.org/blog/posts/open-doors-open-minds-6-tips-for-effective-peer-coaching

Hoffman, D. M. (2009). Reflecting on social emotional learning: A critical perspective on trends in the United States. *Review of Educational Research, 79*(2), 553–556. https://doi.org/10.3102/0034654308325184

Honigsfeld, A., & Dove, M. (2019). *Collaborating for English learners: A foundational guide to integrated practices* (2nd ed.). Corwin Press.

Honigsfeld, A., & LaChance, J. (2023). *Collaboration and co-teaching for dual language learners.* Corwin Press.

Hoover, J. J., Baca, L. M., & Klinger, J. K. (Eds.). (2016). *Why do English learners struggle with reading? Distinguishing language acquisition from learning disabilities* (2nd ed.). Corwin Press.

Jagers, R. J., Rivas-Drake, D., & Williams, B. (2019). Transformative social and emotional learning (SEL): Toward SEL in service of educational equity and excellence. *Educational Psychologist, 54*(3), 162–184. https://doi.org/10.1080/00461520.2019.1623032

Jeon, E-Y., & Day, R. R. (2016). The effectiveness of ER on reading proficiency: A meta-analysis. *Reading in a Foreign Language, 28*(2), 246–265. https://files.eric.ed.gov/fulltext/EJ1117026.pdf

Kangas, S. E. N. (2021). "Is it language or disability?": An ableist and monolingual filter for English learners with disabilities. *TESOL Quarterly, 55*(3), 673–683. https://doi.org/10.1002/tesq.3029

Klinger, J. K., Almanza de Schonewise, E., de Onís, C., & Méndez Barletta, L. (2016). Misconceptions about the second language acquisition process. In J. J. Hoover, L. M. Baca, & J. K. Klinger (Eds.), *Why do English learners struggle with reading? Distinguishing language acquisition from learning disabilities* (pp. 57–81). Corwin Press.

Kohnert, K. (2013). *Language disorders in bilingual children and adults* (2nd ed.). Plural.

Krashen, S. (1985). *The input hypothesis: Issues and implications.* Longman.

Larrivee, B. (2000). Transforming teaching practice: Becoming the critical reflective teacher. *Reflective Practice, 1*(3), 293–307. http://ed253jcu.pbworks.com/w/page/f/Larrivee_B_2000CriticallyReflectiveTeacher.pdf

Lau, W. S., & Shea, M. (2022). Empowering English learners in the classroom through culturally responsive social–emotional teaching practices. *Journal of Multilingual and Multicultural Development.* https://doi.org/10.1080/01434632.2022.2078337

Lave, J., & Wenger, E. (1991). *Situated learning: Legitimate peripheral participation.* Cambridge University Press.

Lawrence, M. (n.d.). *How to support the social and emotional health of middle/high school ELLs.* Colorín Colorado. https://www.colorincolorado.org/article/social-and-emotional-needs-middle-and-high-school-ells

Lee, Y., & Martin, K. I. (2020). The flipped classroom in ESL teacher education: An example from CALL. *Education and Information Technologies, 25*(4), 2605–2633. https://doi.org/10.1007/s10639-019-10082-6

Lesaux, N., Koda, K., Siegel, L., & Shanahan, T. (2006). Development of literacy. In D. August & T. Shanahan (Eds.), *Developing literacy in second-language learners: Report of the National Literacy Panel on Language-Minority Children and Youth* (pp. 75–122). Lawrence Erlbaum.

Levine, L. N., Lukens, L., & Smallwood, B. A. (2013). *The GO TO Strategies: Scaffolding options for teachers of English language learners, K–12.* Project EXCELL. https://www.tesol.org/media/sx0l4qnn/the-go-to-strategies-booklet_c2013_levine-lukens-smallwood.pdf

Levine, L. N., & McCloskey, M. (2013). *Teaching English language and content in mainstream classes: One class, many paths* (2nd ed.). Pearson.

Li, S., & Vuono, A. (2019). Twenty-five years of research on oral and written corrective feedback in *System. System, 84,* 93–109. https://doi.org/10.1016/j.system.2019.05.006

Lightbown, P., & Spada, N. (2014). *How languages are learned* (4th ed.). Oxford University Press.

Linville, H., & Whiting, J. (2020). Social justice through TESOL advocacy. *TESOL Journal, 11*(4), Article e553. https://doi.org/10.1002/tesj.553

Loop, E. (n.d.). *How to plan a family literacy night at school.* Classroom. https://classroom.synonym.com/elementary-activities-family-reading-night-6376975.html

López, F., Scanlan, M., & Gundrum, B. (2013). Preparing teachers of English language learners: Empirical evidence and policy implications. *Education Policy Analysis Archives, 21*(20). http://epaa.asu.edu/ojs/article/view/1132

Louie, B. Y., & Knuth, R. (2016). Home visit tips for ELLs. *Principal, 95*(4), 44. https://www.naesp.org/sites/default/files/LouieKnuth_MA16.pdf

Lynch, E. W. (2011). Developing cross-cultural competence. In E. W. Lynch & M. J. Hanson (Eds.), *Developing cross-cultural competence: A guide for working with children and their families* (4th ed., pp. 41–78). Brookes.

Lyster, R., Saito, K., & Sato, M. (2013). Oral corrective feedback in second language classrooms. *Language Teaching, 46*(1), 1–40. https://doi.org/10.1017/S0261444812000365

MacSwan, J. (2018). A multilingual perspective on translanguaging. *American Educational Research Journal, 54*(1), 167–201. https://doi.org/10.3102/0002831216683935

Maier, A., Adams, J., Burns, D., Kaul, M., Saunders, M., & Thompson, C. (2020). *Using performance assessments to support student learning: How district initiatives can make a difference* [Research brief]. Learning Policy Institute. https://learningpolicyinstitute.org/product/cpac-performance-assessments-support-student-learning-brief

Marian, V., & Shook, A. (2012). The cognitive benefits of being bilingual. *Cerebrum.* https://www.ncbi.nlm.nih.gov/pmc/articles/PMC3583091

Mariani, L. (1997). Teacher support and teacher challenge in promoting learner autonomy. *Perspectives, 23*(2), 5–19. http://www.learningpaths.org/papers/papersupport.htm

Martin-Beltran, M., & Peercy, M. M. (2014). Collaboration to teach English language learners: Opportunities for shared teacher learning. *Teachers and Teaching, 20*(6), 721–737. https://doi.org/10.1080/13540602.2014.885704

Mayer, R. E. (1992). Cognition and instruction: Their historic meeting within educational psychology. *Journal of Educational Psychology, 84,* 405–412. https://doi.org/10.1037/0022-0663.84.4.405

Menken, K. (2010). No Child Left Behind and English language learners: The challenges and consequences of high-stakes testing. *Theory Into Practice, 49,* 121–128.

Michaels, S., O'Connor, M. C., Williams Hall, M., & Resnick, L. B. (2013). *Accountable Talk® sourcebook: For classroom conversation that works.* https://nsiexchange.org/wp-content/uploads/2019/02/AT-SOURCEBOOK2016-1-23-19.pdf

Minn, S. (2022). AI-assisted knowledge assessment techniques for adaptive learning environments. *Computers and Education: Artificial Intelligence, 3*, Article 100050. https://doi.org/10.1016/j.caeai.2022.100050

Mohamed, N. (2021, September 22). *3 ways to harness the power of translanguaging.* TESOL International Association. https://www.tesol.org/blog/posts/3-ways-to-harness-the-power-of-translanguaging/

Mohamed, N. (2023, February 14). *Helping students to recognise and respond to social injustice: Suggested strategies and resources.* TESOL International Association. https://www.tesol.org/blog/posts/helping-students-to-recognise-and-respond-to-social-injustice-suggested-strategies-and-resources/

Muir, C., & Dörnyei, Z. (2013). Directed motivational currents: Using vision to create effective motivational pathways. *Studies in Second Language Learning and Teaching, 3*(3), 357–375. https://doi.org/10.14746/ssllt.2013.3.3.3

Nadzrah, A. B., Latif, H., & Yaacob, A. (2017). Fusion of technology with language learning: Blog community. *3L: The Southeast Asian Journal of English Language Studies, 23*(4), 200–211. http://doi.org/10.17576/3L-2017-2304-15

Nagy, W. E., & Scott, J. A. (2000). Vocabulary processes. In M. Kamil, P. Mosenthal, P. D. Pearson, & R. Barr (Eds.), *Handbook of reading research* (Vol. 3, pp. 269–284). Lawrence Erlbaum.

Nakanishi, T. (2015). A meta-analysis of extensive reading research. *TESOL Quarterly, 49*(1), 6–37. https://doi.org/10.1002/tesq.157

Nassaji, H., & Kartchava, E. (Eds.). (2017). *Corrective feedback in second language teaching and learning: Research, theory, applications, implications.* Routledge.

Nation, I. S. P., & Webb, S. (2011). *Researching and analyzing vocabulary.* Heinle.

National Academies of Sciences, Engineering, and Medicine. (2017). *Promoting the educational success of children and youth learning English: Promising futures.* National Academies Press. https://doi.org/10.17226/24677

National Board for Professional Teaching Standards. (2016). *English as a new language.* https://www.nbpts.org/wp-content/uploads/2017/07/ECYA-ENL.pdf

National Center for Education Statistics. (2021). *Digest 2021, Table 209.48: National Teacher and Principal Survey (NTPS), "Public School Teacher Data File" 2020–21.* U.S. Department of Education, National Center for Education Statistics.

National Center for Education Statistics. (2022). *Digest 2022, Table 204.27: EDFacts file 141, Data Group 678.* U.S. Department of Education, National Center for Education Statistics.

National Education Association. (2015). *All in! How educators can advocate for English language learners.* https://www.nea.org/sites/default/files/2020-07/ALL%20IN_%20NEA%20ELL_AdvocacyGuide2015_v7.pdf

National Institute of Child Health and Human Development. (2000). *Report of the National Reading Panel. Teaching children to read: An evidence-based assessment of the scientific research literature on reading and its implications for reading instruction: Reports of the subgroups* (NIH Publication No. 00-4754). U.S. Government Printing Office. https://www.nichd.nih.gov/publications/pubs/nrp/smallbook

New York State Education Department. (n.d.). *Culturally responsive-sustaining education framework.* https://www.nysed.gov/sites/default/files/programs/crs/culturally-responsive-sustaining-education-framework.pdf

Nieto, S., & Bode, P. (2021). *Affirming diversity: The sociopolitical context of multicultural education* (7th ed.). Pearson.

No Child Left Behind Act of 2001. Pub. L. No. 107-110 § 115, Stat. 1425 (2002). https://www.govinfo.gov/content/pkg/PLAW-107publ110/pdf/PLAW-107publ110.pdf

Norton, B. (2013). *Identity and language learning.* Multilingual Matters.

Nutta, J. W., Strebel, C., Mokhtari, K., Mihai, F. M., & Crevecoeur-Bryant, E. (2014). *Educating English learners: What every classroom teacher needs to know.* Harvard Education Press.

Patel, M., Solly, M., & Copeland, S. (2023). *The future of English: Global perspectives.* British Council.

Paterson, K. (2021). *Using home language as a resource in the classroom: A guide for teachers of English learners.* TESOL Press.

Pavlenko, A., & Norton, B. (2007). Imagined communities, identity, and English language teaching. In J. Cummins & C. Davidson (Eds.), *International handbook of English language teaching* (pp. 669–680). Springer.

Pawan, F., Daley, S., Kou, X., & Bonk, C. (2022). *Engaging online language learners: A practical guide.* TESOL Press.

Pentón Herrera, L. J. (2020). Social-emotional learning in TESOL: What, why, and how. *Journal of English Learner Education, 10*(1), 1–16. https://stars.library.ucf.edu/jele/vol10/iss1/1

Pentón Herrera, L., & Martinez-Alba, G. (2021). *Social-emotional learning in the English language classroom.* TESOL Press.

Pier, L., Christian, M., Tymeson, H., & Meyer, R. H. (2021, June). *COVID-19 impacts on student learning: Evidence from interim assessments in California.* Policy Analysis for California Education. https://edpolicyinca.org/publications/covid-19-impacts-student-learning

Protacio, M. S., & Jang, B. G. (2016). ESL teachers' perceptions about English learners' reading motivation. *Literacy Research: Theory, Method, and Practice, 65*(1), 166–181. https://doi.org/10.1177/2381336916661532

Rhinehart, L. V., Bailey, A. L., & Haager, D. (2022). Long-term English learners: Untangling language acquisition and learning disabilities. *Contemporary School Psychology.* https://doi.org/10.1007/s40688-022-00420-w

Rimm-Kaufman, S. (2021). *SEL from the start: Building skills in K–5.* W. W. Norton.

Rutgers, D., & Evans, M. (2017). Bilingual education and L3 learning: Metalinguistic advantage or not? *International Journal of Bilingual Education and Bilingualism, 20*(7), 788–806. http://dx.doi.org/10.1080/13670050.2015.1103698

Sanderson, G. (2004). Existentialism, globalisation and the cultural other. *International Education Journal, 4*(4), 1–20. https://files.eric.ed.gov/fulltext/EJ903804.pdf

Sankey, M. (2020). Putting the pedagogic horse in front of the technology cart. *Journal of Distance Education in China, 5*, 46–53. https://michaelsankey.com/2020/05/22/putting-the-pedagogic-horse-in-front-of-the-technology-cart/

Sato, M., & Ballinger, S. (2016). Understanding peer interaction: Research synthesis and directions. In M. Sato & S. Ballinger (Eds.), *Peer interaction and second language learning: Pedagogical potential and research agenda* (pp. 1–30). John Benjamins. https://doi.org/10.1075/lllt.45

Schmitt, N., Jiang, X., & Grabe, W. (2011). The percentage of words known in a text and reading comprehension. *Modern Language Journal, 95*(1), 26–43. https://doi.org/10.1111/j.1540-4781.2011.01146.x

Seddon, J. (2015). School counselor support for the academic, career, personal, and social needs of ELL students. *Culminating Projects in Community Psychology, Counseling and Family Therapy, 8.* St. Cloud State University. https://repository.stcloudstate.edu/cpcf_etds/8

Seilstad, B., & Kim, S. (2020). "Colibrí" 'hummingbird' as translanguaging metaphor. In Z. Tian, L. Aghai, P. Sayer, & J. L. Schissel (Eds.), *Envisioning TESOL through a translanguaging lens* (pp. 253–273). Springer.

Short, D., & Echevarría, J. (2016). *Developing academic language with the SIOP Model.* Pearson.

Short, D., & Fitzsimmons, S. (2007). *Double the work: Challenges and solutions to acquiring language and academic literacy for adolescent English language learners.* Alliance for Excellent Education.

Short, D., Vogt, M. E., & Echevarría, J. (2017). *The SIOP Model for administrators* (2nd ed.). Pearson.

Short, D. J., & Mendoza, G. M. (2020, May). Using the 6 principles to support language learning in times of crisis. *TESOL Connections.* https://tcnewsletter.s3.amazonaws.com/newsmanager.commpartners.com/tesolc/issues/2020-05-01/4.html

Singh, K., & Bhasin, A. (2023). *Smiling chalk.* Blue Rose.

Smith, R., Snow, P., Serry, T., & Hammond, L. (2021). The role of background knowledge in reading comprehension: A critical review. *Reading Psychology, 42*(3), 214–240. https://doi.org/10.1080/02702711.2021.1888348

Sprenger, M. (2020). *Social-emotional learning and the brain: Strategies to help your students thrive.* Association for Supervision and Curriculum Development.

Staehr Fenner, D. (n.d.). *TESOL report: The changing role of the ESL teacher.* Colorín Colorado. http://www.colorincolorado.org/blog/tesol-report-changing-role-esl-teacher

Staehr Fenner, D. (2014). *Advocating for English learners: A guide for educators.* Corwin Press.

Staehr Fenner, D. (2016). *The preparation of the ESL educator in the era of college- and career-readiness standards: A summary of the TESOL International Association convening February 2016.* TESOL International Association.

Staehr Fenner, D., & Snyder, S. (2017). *Unlocking English learners' potential: Strategies for making content accessible.* Corwin Press.

Stembridge, A. (2020). *Culturally responsive education in the classroom: An equity framework for pedagogy.* Routledge.

Sutton, E., & Lawson, L. (2023, June 25–28). *Links between social-emotional learning and academic outcomes across three school districts* [Paper presentation]. ISTE Conference, Philadelphia, PA, United States.

Taylor, M. (1987). *The gold Cadillac*. Penguin-Putnam.

Teachers of English to Speakers of Other Languages, Inc. (1997). ESL standards for pre-k–12 students. TESOL.

TESOL International Association. (2006). *PreK–12 English language proficiency standards: An augmentation of the World-Class Instructional Design and Assessment (WIDA) Consortium English language proficiency standards.*

TESOL International Association. (2018a). *The action agenda for the future of the TESOL profession.*

TESOL International Association. (2018b). *Community and family toolkit: Engaging the families of English learners in classrooms, schools, and communities.* TESOL Press. https://www.tesol.org/media/424amu1n/tesol-community-and-family-toolkit.pdf

TESOL International Association. (2019). *Standards for initial TESOL Pre-K–12 teacher preparation programs.* TESOL Press. https://www.tesol.org/media/v33fewo0/2018-tesol-teacher-prep-standards-final.pdf

TESOL International Association. (2023). *TESOL guide to using Microsoft Learning Accelerators with multilingual learners of English: Literacy edition.* TESOL Press.

TextProject. (n.d.). *Core vocabulary word zones.* https://textproject.org/teachers/vocabulary-instruction/core-vocabulary-word-zones

Tomlinson, C. A. (2014). *The differentiated classroom: Responding to the needs of all learners* (2nd ed.). Association for Supervision and Curriculum Development.

Toppel, K., Hyunh, T., & Salva, C. (2021). *DIY PD: A guide to self-directed learning for educators of multilingual learners.* Seidlitz Education.

Turkan, S., Bicknell, J., & Croft, A. (2012). *Effective practices for developing the literacy skills of English language learners in the English language arts classroom* (Research Report ETS RR-12-03). Educational Testing Service. http://files.eric.ed.gov/fulltext/EJ1109828.pdf

U.S. Department of Education. (2011). *MEMO: OSEP memo 11-07 response to intervention (RTI) (January 21, 2011).* https://sites.ed.gov/idea/idea-files/osep-memo-11-07-response-to-intervention-rti-memo/

U.S. Department of Education. (2022, April 8). *Office of Special Education Programs fast facts: Students with disabilities who are English learners (ELs) served under IDEA Part B.* https://sites.ed.gov/idea/osep-fast-facts-students-with-disabilities-english-learners

U.S. Department of Education, National Center for Education Statistics. (n.d.) *The nation's report card.* https://www.nationsreportcard.gov/about.aspx

U.S. Department of Education, Office for Civil Rights & U.S. Department of Justice, Civil Rights Division. (2014). *Information on the rights of all children to enroll in school: Questions and answers for states, school districts and parents.* https://www2.ed.gov/about/offices/list/ocr/docs/qa-201405.pdf

U.S. Department of Education, Office for Civil Rights & U.S. Department of Justice, Civil Rights Division. (2015a, January 7). Dear colleague letter: English learner students and limited English proficient parents. http://www2.ed.gov/about/offices/list/ocr/letters/colleague-el-201501.pdf

U.S. Department of Education, Office for Civil Rights & U.S. Department of Justice, Civil Rights Division. (2015b). *Information for limited English proficient (LEP) parents and guardians and for schools and school districts that communicate with them.* https://www2.ed.gov/about/offices/list/ocr/docs/dcl-factsheet-lep-parents-201501.pdf

U.S. Department of Education, Office of Educational Technology. (2022). *Advancing digital equity for all: Community-based recommendations for developing effective digital equity plans to close the digital divide and enable technology-empowered learning.* https://tech.ed.gov/advancing-digital-equity-for-all

U.S. Department of Education, Office of English Language Acquisition. (2017). *English learner toolkit for state and local education agencies (SEAs and LEAs)* (2nd rev. ed.). http://www2.ed.gov/about/offices/list/oela/english-learner-toolkit/index.html

U.S. Department of Education, Office of English Language Acquisition. (2023a). *English learner family toolkit.* https://ncela.ed.gov/educator-support/toolkits/family-toolkit

U.S. Department of Education, Office of English Language Acquisition. (2023b). *High school graduation rates for English learners.* https://ncela.ed.gov/sites/default/files/2023-06/ELGradRates-FS-20230602-508.pdf

Valdés, G., Kibler, A., & Walqui, A. (2014). *Changes in the expertise of ESL professionals: Knowledge and action in an era of new standards.* TESOL. https://www.tesol.org/media/y5mj4cdr/changes-in-standards-professional-paper-26-march-2014.pdf

Visible Learning. (n.d.). *Hattie ranking: 252 influences and effect sizes related to student achievement.* https://visible-learning.org/hattie-ranking-influences-effect-sizes-learning-achievement

Vogt, M. E., & Echevarría, J. (2022). *99 ideas and activities for teaching English learners with the SIOP Model* (2nd ed.). Pearson.

Weingarten, R. (2013). Comparative graphematics. In S. R. Borgwaldt & T. Joyce (Eds.), *Typology of writing systems* (pp. 13–39). John Benjamins.

WIDA. (2004). WIDA *English language proficiency standards, 2004 edition, preKindergarten through grade 12.* Board of Regents of the University of Wisconsin System

WIDA. (2007). WIDA *English language proficiency standards, 2007 edition, preKindergarten through grade 12.* Board of Regents of the University of Wisconsin System.

WIDA. (2014, May). *Collaborative learning for English language learners* [Research brief]. University of Wisconsin-Madison. https://wida.wisc.edu/sites/default/files/resource/Brief-CollaborativeLearningforELLs.pdf

WIDA. (2020). *Can do descriptors.* University of Wisconsin-Madison. https://wida.wisc.edu/teach/can-do/descriptors

Williams, C. (2021). *A new federal equity agenda for dual language learners and English learners.* Century Foundation.

Williams, M., Mercer, S., & Ryan, S. (2015). *Exploring psychology in language learning and teaching.* Oxford University Press.

Zacharian, D. (2023). *Transforming schools for multilingual learners: A comprehensive guide for educators* (2nd ed.). Corwin Press.

Zimmerman, B. J., & Schunk, D. H. (2012). An essential dimension of self-regulated learning. In D. H. Schunk & B. J. Zimmerman (Eds.), *Motivation and self-regulated learning: Theory, research, and applications* (pp. 1–30). Routledge.

Zong, J., & Batalova, J. (2015, July 8). The limited English proficient population in the United States. *Migration Information Source.* https://www.migrationpolicy.org/article/limited-english-proficient-population-united-states

Zwiers, J. (2014). *Building academic language: Grades 5–12* (2nd ed.). Jossey-Bass.

Zwiers, J. (2019). *Next steps with academic conversations: New ideas for improving learning through classroom talk.* Stenhouse.